KENNY MCCALL was bo
devoted husband and father
been an engineer since he
follower of Dundee United.

JOHN ROBB was born in Dundee in 1972 and has trained and
worked as a printer since he left school. He is a passionate
follower of the other club in the city, Dundee FC. He is a
devoted husband and father of twin boys.

KENNY McCALL AND JOHN ROBB

AFTER THE MATCH
THE GAME
BEGINS

THE TRUE STORY OF
THE DUNDEE UTILITY

JOHN BLAKE

Published by John Blake Publishing Ltd,
3 Bramber Court, 2 Bramber Road,
London W14 9PB, England

www.johnblakepublishing.co.uk

First published in hardback in 2008
Published in paperback in 2010

ISBN: 978 1 84454 898 9

British Library Cataloguing-in-Publication Data:

A catalogue record for this book is available from the British Library.

Design by www.envydesign.co.uk

Printed in Great Britain by CPI Bookmarque, Croydon CR0 4TD

1 3 5 7 9 10 8 6 4 2

Papers used by John Blake Publishing are natural, recyclable products made from wood
grown in sustainable forests. The manufacturing processes conform to the
environmental regulations of the country of origin.

Every attempt has been made to contact the relevant copyright-holders, but some were
unobtainable. We would be grateful if the appropriate people could contact us.

DEDICATION

This book is dedicated to our wonderful patient wives and beautiful children, Kenny's two girls and John's twin boys. Also, to all the boys who stood side-by-side with us and became mates for life, especially Steve, Tony, Ryan, G, Stu, Matt, Sean, Grahame McK and all the rest. You know who you are. A massive thanks to Monteil for help with a lot of the more recent stories. Thanks also to Mike and Big Steve for helping with the book. Many thanks to Tommy from the SCF for the photos. Finally, a massive thank you to everyone at Blake, especially Michelle.

In memory of those who've passed away. RIP lads.

CONTENTS

PART 2 – A NEW DAWN

PART 3 – TAKING IT ABROAD AND INTO THE MILLENNIUM

INTRODUCTION

Turn around, pull the door shut and I'm off down the stairs. Sort the scarf, zip up the jacket and away we go. I'm bouncing along the road now, the butterflies are going and this is it, this is the start of the buzz. This to me is the start of the day, not knowing what lies ahead. I picture thousands of doors up and down the country slamming shut around the same time, feeling the same as me. I wonder what today will bring.

What is exciting about walking along the road? I hear you ask. Well, for you who don't know what I'm talking about, I'll try to explain. For those who do know – this is our story.

I know what you're thinking: 'Not another book about football hooligans. How many stories are there to tell about "unbeatable" firms?' But, after reading some 40 books on this much talked-about and misunderstood subject, myself and my good friend John have decided to tell our story.

What's different about our story? Well, the story we want to tell is of our strange and wonderful city and its two football teams. This is the true story of the ups and downs, highs and lows – and, most of all, the laughs and the adventures – of the Dundee Utility thugs.

I don't believe that anyone who has written a book on this subject has captured what 95% of the people involved are all about. Every book has been written from the viewpoint of a top man – the 'general', or someone who has been in and out of prison all his adult life. The tabloids always like to tell how soccer hooligans come from all walks of life, that they are bankers, office workers and tradesmen and don't just come from poor backgrounds. But we are from a working-class background and that's the story we are going to tell, that of the normal lads who've never been to prison and have no intention of going there either! We're lads who have held down the same jobs since we left school and are now in our thirties. On the face of it, we are normal blokes – it's just that our Saturday 'addiction' means that we're willing to put all of that in jeopardy. This story might seem especially weird when we talk about how Dundee's two sets of fans hate each other for 90 minutes each derby day, but are happy to stand side-by-side and take on the world whenever we face any other teams.

To our friends down south who think the 'disease' of football violence only really happens there, we will tell of our countless battles with both halves of the Old Firm who, if memory serves, have in almost every pre-season friendly or testimonial that they've been invited to in the last 40 years taken over and demolished every town and city in England that they've visited. Just think, this small city of ours has to welcome this lovely bunch at least eight times a year and take them on!

There are recollections of countless battles with our greatest rivals, including the Aberdeen Soccer Casuals (ASC) and the two halves of Edinburgh – Heart of Midlothian's CSF and Hibernian's CCS, who for a while were one of the most feared

INTRODUCTION

mobs in Europe. Then there are our near neighbours from Perth, St Johnstone (MBS, the Mainline Baby Squad) and the rest, who no doubt will crop up in the book.

This is also the story of how the third generation of Saturday lads entered the millennium, hoping to emulate – if not better – their predecessors in the 1980s and 1990s, only for it to end in tears with more than 20 lads being jailed after the 2005 cup final, and all for nothing more than what has happened at every ground up and down the country for the past 30 years. The police crackdown that day involved the imprisonment of lads on just their first offence. Amazingly, they even threatened to arrest actor Danny Dyer and his film crew, who were in Dundee to film to make the documentary *Real Football Factories*.

But, above all, this is the story of how two became one. This is the story of the Utility.

Kenny McCall

PART 1

THE FIRST
GENERATION

CHAPTER 1

EARLY DAYS

The story begins with me, Kenny McCall, the older of two boys born in Dundee in 1971. Dundee is Scotland's fourth largest city, with a population of around 150,000. It also has two football teams: Dundee FC, founded in 1893, and Dundee United FC, set up as Dundee Hibernian by Irish immigrants in 1909 which became United in 1923. Their grounds, just 100 yards apart, are the closest stadia in the UK.

I soon developed a passion for football as there wasn't much else to do in the early 1970s except play and watch football. My father would, like a lot of men in the Dundee area, go to watch both city clubs on alternate Saturdays. However, he soon developed a preference for the smaller of the two clubs, United. In those days, Dundee FC regularly drew crowds of up to 40,000 at Dens Park, while United only managed 6–10,000 at Tannadice.

Dundee were the only team to have collected any silverware, with a Scottish Cup win in the early 1900s,

3

two League Cup wins in the 1950s and a League Championship in 1961/62, followed by a run to the semi-finals of the European Cup, where they lost out to Italian giants AC Milan, and countless years above United in the league. Why my father chose to support United was typical. He's a man who is quiet, hard but fair and who never likes to be a follower of men, preferring to do his own thing most of the time. He's happy to go against the grain. However, the success United were about to enjoy in the next 20 years would eventually make going to Tannadice and round the country following United more of a pleasure than it ever had been in the past – and perhaps, sometimes, more of a heartbreak as well.

I can remember him coming home from a match around 1975, I think it was against Kilmarnock, and I'm sure they had won 2–1 because I can recall seeing the score on the TV round-up. I grilled him about the game: 'How was it? Who scored? How big was the crowd?' But I soon got to thinking that I should ask him to take me to a game, and before long I was going along to my beloved Tannadice on a regular basis.

My first memory of those early matches was that all the fans stood together – there was no segregation then. If it rained, most of the fans from both sides would crowd together under the shed, which, apart from the old stand, was the only part of the ground under cover.

I remember going to a pre-season friendly against Aston Villa, which I think must have been part of the deal that took Andy Gray from United to Villa. The weather was terrible, with almost the entire crowd of 6,500 crammed under the shed to get out of the rain. Most of the games my father took me to were against smaller clubs, because

I think he thought the Old Firm games would be too much of an ordeal for me. He didn't want me facing thousands of pissed-up fans as they rampaged through Dundee, terrorising the locals. But, since I lived so close to Tannadice and Dens, I got to watch them anyway from behind the safety of my living-room curtains.

I was fascinated and scared shitless by them at the same time. My window looked out on to the street where all the fans walked to the grounds. It was also the road where the cars and buses would park on match day and I would sit there and count all the vehicles going past. Most of the time, especially if it was the Old Firm, there would be well over 100 buses. The thing that always annoyed and scared me about the visiting Old Firm fans was the way that they would always get off these buses clutching their cheap bottles of Buckfast wine and start to intimidate the locals. Buckfast was and still is the drink of choice among that bunch of filthy cunts! They'd get out and start pissing on people's doors and cars and generally wander around doing whatever they liked. Then, they'd take over the ground and start singing all their sectarian nonsense, which still hasn't changed. To top it all off, they'd usually go on and win the game and then piss off back home leaving the place looking as though a tornado had just blown through!

On my way to school of a Monday morning, which took me down the street that separates Dens from Tannadice, we would be amazed at the mess around the ground after a game. There would quite literally be hundreds of wine bottles and empty beer tins strewn across the streets. The playground at the back of Tannadice looked as though it had hosted a New Year's Eve party.

AFTER THE MATCH, THE GAME BEGINS

The challenge on and off the park was about to change, though, as around the corner at United, manager Jim McLean had installed a youth policy that was about to pay off at home and abroad. At the same time, a certain Alex Ferguson was about to take charge at Aberdeen. The days of the Old Firm's dominance were about to come to an end.

United reached their first major cup final in 1974. Just getting there was a major achievement in itself for a club of United's size. It proved too tough a test in the end. The mighty Celtic were too strong for them and ran out comfortable 3–0 winners. I wasn't at that final, being only three, but as the decade progressed I turned into a fully fledged football fanatic. By the end of the 1970s, I was about to sample my first trip to the National Stadium. It was to be the first of many trips to Hampden – the vast majority of which have always turned out to be a pain in the arse. To say that United haven't had the best of times there is something of an understatement. I must have been there 25 times and I think I've seen United win twice, but more on that later.

CHAPTER 2

FIRST TRIP TO HAMPDEN

It was 1979 and I'd been a regular at Tannadice for a couple of years when my father took me to my first away match. United had been developing into one of the best teams in the country, with Jim McLean's youth policy just starting to pay off. Instead of just surviving in the Premier League, United and Aberdeen were starting to challenge the Old Firm for the league title on a regular basis. This also coincided with Dundee's fortunes going in completely the opposite direction. In 1976, relegation to the First Division was tasted by Dundee for the first time in many years and the footballing balance of power in the city began to shift.

The occasion for my first away match was the League Cup semi-final, against Hamilton Accies, at Dunfermline's East End Park. We travelled to the game in my father's car with my dad's friend and my uncle. When we got to East End Park, we weren't sure what end to go into. There was no segregation then anyway, plus we knew Hamilton were not likely to have much support with them, so we decided to go in the first end we came to. When we got in, I was surprised to see how different the ground was to Tannadice. The other thing that struck me was that we had gone in the wrong end! We could have walked round to the United end but we decided to stay put. The game was as one-sided as expected and United ran out 6–2 winners. All I could think about afterwards was the final. I harassed the old man into taking me all the way home. Eventually, giving in to my demands, he promised to take me to the final at Hampden against Aberdeen.

The big day wasn't long in coming round and the same four of us set off for the National Stadium, plus my grandad, who also squeezed in to the old man's Ford Cortina. When we got there, I was amazed at the size of the ground but a little disappointed at the rundown condition of the old place. I was expecting a state-of-the-art stadium, but in all honesty it was just a gigantic shit hole. In those days, the League Cup, being the least important competition, was done and dusted as quickly as possible and the final was played in November or December.

The weather was miserable and it had been chucking it down all day. The rain had been that bad, especially back home, that the game between Dundee and Celtic at Dens was called off at the last minute. As the final kicked off, the 8,000 or so United fans were housed in the corner of the north terracing, the traditional Celtic end. The larger Aberdeen support was in the old covered Rangers end.

The game was a bit of a non-event, ending up a 0–0 draw, but there was a bit of excitement during the game and I had my first glimpse, close hand, of a bit of football violence.

EARLY DAYS

A lot of Celtic fans, that had been on their way to Dundee when they were told of their game being called off, came to the final instead and ended up in our end. Before long, the two sets of fans were battling high up in the Hampden slopes. I'm not sure what kicked it off, but I remember the old man grabbing hold of me and telling me to watch myself, as I was only eight years old. I remember being totally engrossed in watching the fighting that was going on above me, high up in the massive terracing. I was hooked. As the glass bottles of wine were hurled back and forth (the ban on alcohol didn't come into effect in Scotland until the following year, after the Hampden riot between the Old Firm), the Old Bill eventually arrived to separate the two mobs. I remember them at least eight-handed, struggling to get this giant of a United fan through the gate in the fence and out on to the track. He wasn't going without a fight and it must have taken at least five minutes to get him out. I'll bet he got a few digs from Glasgow's finest on the way to the station.

That was more or less the end of the fun, in what had been a pretty eventful first trip to the National Stadium, even though the game itself was a no-score bore. So, it was home to Dundee – to find out that the replay was to be played on the Wednesday night at Dens, the home of our bitter rivals. Rather than ask both sets of fans to travel down to Glasgow again, Dens was settled on as a 'neutral' location for the replay. That was fine by me. When Wednesday came, it was just a five-minute walk down to Dens Park instead of a two-hour drive to Glasgow.

When we got to the ground the atmosphere was electric and the place was packed out with fans decked out in tangerine and black as we entered the Provie Road End.

AFTER THE MATCH, THE GAME BEGINS

The replay itself was completely different from the first match as we took the game to Aberdeen. Two goals from veteran striker Willie Pettigrew and one from my hero, Paul Sturrock, sent the United fans into ecstasy. Finally, after 70 years, we'd won our first major trophy – and we did it at the home of our greatest rivals.

CHAPTER 3

THE NEW FIRM

This was to be the start of a great period for United, as cup semi-finals, finals and European football were to become par for the course as we played against – and beat – the best at home and abroad for the next decade or so.

The following season we reached the League Cup Final again, against Dundee. This time, the SFA made the sensible decision to change the final from the National Stadium in Glasgow to Dens. We were happy not to have to travel to Glasgow. Plus, we had a great record at Dens.

The atmosphere in the city was electric in the weeks leading up to the final, with everyone having an opinion on what was going to happen. When the big day finally arrived, we made the five-minute journey by foot down to Dens to take our place in the queue at the Provie Road End. We got in the requisite 30 minutes before kick-off, just in time to see the players warming up (these days you can't drag me out of the boozer until about five to three).

When the teams ran out you just got the feeling that

AFTER THE MATCH, THE GAME BEGINS

United were going to win. At the time, Dundee weren't any great shakes and United were turning into a formidable team. United drew first blood through our striker, Davie Dodds. Doddsy wasn't the greatest of players, but he knew where the back of the net was and he had the uncanny knack of popping up in the right place, time after time. He was also one ugly fucker. He got teased by every set of opposition fans in the country, who used to sing: 'Davie Dodds, the elephant man!' But this only made it sweeter when he popped up in the box to put you one-up, especially in a cup final against your bitter rivals. The second half continued in the same vein, with my hero Paul Sturrock weighing in with a brace as we won the cup 3–0. The celebrations went on for days and the bragging rights at school were ours for quite some time.

In the same season, we also got to the Scottish Cup Final, to be played at the end of the season against the mighty Rangers at Hampden. Again, we travelled down to Glasgow in the old man's car to see if we could do the cup double and, most importantly, to win the cup for the first time. The match was a poor affair, only bursting into life in the final minute, when Rangers were given their usual dodgy decision when things aren't going their way and were awarded a penalty. However, it was us who were celebrating when Hamish McAlpine saved Ian Redford's penalty with his legs and the game ended up a 0–0 draw. The replay was set for the Wednesday, again at Hampden. I didn't go to the match, which ended up a disaster for United as Davie Cooper inspired Rangers to easily beat us 4–1.

United were starting to shock a few big names in Europe about this time, taking some notable scalps such as PSV

Eindhoven, Monaco, Borussia Mönchengladbach and Werder Bremen. We reached two UEFA Cup quarter-finals before being knocked out of each in disappointing circumstances.

The end of 1981 saw us reach our third League Cup Final in a row, this time against Rangers at Hampden. I went again with the old man and his friends and, once more, we took our places in the uncovered end of the National Stadium. This time, United took the lead just after half-time, through Ralph Milne. In the second half an absolute screamer from Paul Sturrock was incredibly ruled out for offside. It was the latest instalment in a long line of piss-poor refereeing decisions against United, especially where the Old Firm was concerned. Sturrock turned his marker inside out and unleashed a 30-yard stunner into the top corner, only for the linesman to flag against United defender John Holt, who'd strayed into an offside position. The linesman said Holt was interfering with play, but the keeper would have never got near it anyway. Rangers seemed to get a lift from the decision and scored twice in the last 15 minutes to deny United a third straight win. It was a long and unhappy journey back to Dundee in the old man's car.

1982/83 was to see the greatest achievement in United's history. A great run at the end of the season took us to Dens Park for the final match, with United only needing to win to ensure the league title would come to Tannadice for the first time in our history. The ground was chock-a-block. With Celtic and Aberdeen still in with a chance of lifting the title it was sure to be a nervy afternoon. United took an early lead through an incredible goal by Ralph Milne, when he picked up the ball at the centre circle, waltzed past a couple of tackles, looked up and chipped Dundee's keeper Colin Kelly from 35 yards. They then doubled their lead through Eamonn Bannon, when he blasted home the rebound after missing a penalty. It was absolute bedlam in the United end. Being only 12, I struggled to stay by my old man's side. In typical United fashion, they had to give us a bit of a sweater when Dundee pulled one back in the second half, but United held on to win the match and lift the league title. I remember at the end of the game that the United players came back out to salute the waiting fans and my old man turned to me with a tear in his eye and said, 'That's it son, I'll no' be coming back. I've seen it all now.' Twenty-two years later, he's still got his season ticket!

It was an incredible achievement for a small club. It will probably never happen again, in an environment like today's where the richer clubs dictate who wins what.

So, it was on to season 1983/84 and everything in my life was starting to change. United were to start the season as defending champions and would play in the European Cup. They had a great run in the competition, reaching the semi-final where they were knocked out by Italian giants Roma. We took the first leg 2–0 at Tannadice, but lost 3–0 over there to go out 3–2 on aggregate. If we'd won we would have gone through to play Liverpool in the final. When you think of where United are today and consider how we nearly played Liverpool in the European Cup Final, it doesn't bear thinking about!

CHAPTER 4

ALL CHANGE

At this time I made the big step up from primary to secondary school. This was where I'd meet a lot of mates who would influence the next part of my life. I'd noticed a shift on the streets and the terraces, where fashions were changing from the old skinhead and suedehead look, with Fred Perry shirts, sta-press trousers and Doc Marten boots, into the 'casual' look. Suddenly, everyone was wearing bleached jeans, white trainers and Pringle and Lyle and Scott jumpers. I don't think I'd ever seen anybody wear white trainers before. Little did I know, but this new look was to change my life forever.

I'd always been fascinated as much by what was going on off the pitch as on it. Living so close to Dens and Tannadice, the away fans would always pass my house or park outside. I remember every time Rangers or Celtic played. More often than not, they'd outnumber the home support. The only thing I could imagine on a par in England was back in the 1970s, when Manchester

United's Red Army would descend on towns and cities. For most English clubs, though, they'd only have to endure Manchester United once a season, unless they drew them in the cup as well. We had the Old Firm at least eight times a year. Eight to ten thousand Buckfast-fuelled Glaswegians, eight times a year, is enough to strike fear into any city.

Funnily enough, the supporters that struck me at the time as the craziest were Hearts. They seemed to have a lot of skinheads and always looked up for a carry on. Around 1979, my father and his mates had moved round from the traditional United covered end behind the goal, which is known as the Shed, to stand on the north terrace, which had been done up with the £400,000 that United had received from the sale of Ray Stewart to West Ham.

It had a new roof put on and there were two fences about 10 yards apart to segregate the supporters. I personally think this had a bad effect on the fans, as it had been a quiet area of the ground before. As soon as they split the terrace it seemed to encourage all sorts of mischief. Coins, golf balls, bottles and even darts would be chucked back and forth during most big games – and I ended up sitting on the wall at the bottom of the terrace watching the trouble rather than the match most of the time. My old man was forever telling me to watch the game. I think he didn't want me being influenced by what was going on up at the fence, but I was already hooked.

The first casual I got to know was a kid called Wayne and his mate Ronnie. Wayne was the lad of my best friend Steve's sister. One night about late 1983, I was at Steve's house after school listening to records when Wayne and Ronnie popped up to see Steve's sister. They came into

Steve's room to have a blether with the two of us. In walks Ronnie first, thinking he's the dog's bollocks, dressed in a red cagoule and bleached jeans with the soon-to-be compulsory frayed bottoms and a pair of white Puma G Villas. Me and Steve looked at one another and then burst out laughing.

'What the fuck are you wearing?' we both said at the same time, thinking we were the business with our Fred Perry T-shirts and sta-press trousers.

'This is what everyone in England's been wearing and the Aberdeen casuals are wearing,' he said.

We'd heard of the casuals, and in particular the Aberdeen casuals, but had never given it much thought. We didn't realise it at the time, but within a few months we, along with many other young lads, would be completely hooked by this new fashion. Every now and then, I look back on this day and smile to myself. If only we knew!

The Fred Perrys and sta-press trousers were ditched soon after our encounter with Ronnie and Wayne. It became apparent pretty quickly that the casual look was the way ahead. Steve was always a step ahead of everyone else and, with some fashion tips from Wayne, was soon kitted out in the best gear: Kappa cagoules, Fila tracksuits, Lois bleached jeans and Diadora Venice trainers were the order of the day. I had to make do with an Adidas cagoule, Sergio Tacchini polo shirt (the white one with dark-blue shoulders, as worn by John McEnroe), bleached Lee jeans and a pair of Adidas player trainers.

CHAPTER 5

HAVING A BROWSE

The first time I had seen a group of casuals in Dundee was at a derby match at Dens, between Dundee and United in season 1983/84. I remember standing behind the goal at the TC Keay end with some mates from school. We were all watching the main stand more than the match itself. Sitting in the seats were Wayne, Ronnie and around 20 of the first casuals in the city, trying, as you did at the time, to show off their supposed wealth.

The casuals adopted the city centre as their stomping ground, away from the housing schemes and the gang culture. This to me was the start of the casuals in Dundee. All they really cared about was what they looked like. It didn't matter if they followed one team or the other and they were happy to sit together on derby day and pose like pop stars.

Also, because the two grounds are only 100 yards apart, there are no real United or Dundee areas in the city. In Dundee, your next-door neighbour, your best mate and, quite a lot of the time, other members of your family, could support one team or the other. It didn't matter to other fans, so fighting one another didn't even come into the equation. As far as I recall, there has been the odd punch-up after a derby, but nothing to write home about – just the usual arguments about the game or between a couple of people with a grudge. I'm led to believe that in the 1960s there was a bit of rivalry between the two, with the Dens' 'Derry' and the Shed's 'Shimmy' boys having a pop at one another. But, in my time, there's 90 minutes of hatred during the match and that's about it. After the game there'll be a few disagreements about the match itself, usually over a few beers.

Being only 13 at the time, we were far too young to take things to the next step. We could see the violence on the terraces but couldn't yet join in. The first game we went to for a proper nosey was the mighty Aberdeen. Now, unless you've been in a coma for the last 25 years, you'll know Aberdeen at that time were a formidable team on and off the park, conquering all before them on the domestic front and abroad. They topped it off by winning the European Cup Winners Cup, beating the mighty Real Madrid in the final. Off the park, the Aberdeen Soccer Casuals (ASC) were headline news every other week, with reports of up to 1,000 of them causing havoc at every ground they visited. They were becoming legendary and every team in Scotland was trying to follow suit.

After the Aberdeen match, which was at Tannadice, Steve and I decided to tag along on the fringes to see what would happen. We'd been clued up from Wayne that every Dundee casual was more or less representing the city and not one club or the other. This suited me and Steve, especially as I was United and he was Dundee and we went to each team's games together. We brought up the rear of around 100 Dundee boys, mostly scarfers and skinheads, but with around 40–50 casuals. They made a beeline after the game to have a pop at the famous ASC, charging down the Dens Road into what looked like hundreds of Aberdeen. The Old Bill quickly stepped in before it went right off, but with the lights flashing, sirens blaring and bodies running everywhere it was pandemonium. The sheer excitement was unbelievable. Even though Steve and I weren't really involved we were pumped up and we had to keep our wits about us at all times.

Next day at school, as you can imagine, the stories we told about it were exaggerated out of all proportion. We went from being mere observers, to being almost at the front line, to by the end of the day having almost exchanged blows with some of the legendary Aberdeen A-Team. Our school friends listened with disbelief as we told of hundreds of casuals going toe-to-toe with each other.

The new craze was spreading like wildfire. Everybody wanted to be a casual and part of the Dundee Soccer Crew, shortly to be renamed the Dundee Utility Thugs. I went to a few more games as a mere spectator that season, but by January 1985 I made my proper debut as a crew member.

CHAPTER 6

THE DEBUT

A few of us from school started knocking around in Stobswell, or 'Stobie', as we call it, and we were beginning to gather into our own little mob. The Stobie Elite was almost all casuals, which was rare among the schemes in the town. Other areas, like Menzieshill, Pole Park and Whitfield, have also laid claim to being the housing schemes where the casuals took off in Dundee, but we believed if nothing else that we were at least the best-dressed mob. Stobie is one of the smallest housing schemes in Dundee – and not one of the most notorious – but nevertheless we formed a close-knit gang of around 30.

There were around 10 of us who were 14 at the time, with 10 15-year-olds and another 10 who were 16. Around 15 of us had arranged to venture into the city centre before a Dundee United v Celtic Wednesday-night match on a cold January night. I remember all that day the butterflies were doing me in. I couldn't concentrate at school for thinking of the night ahead. At about 5:00 pm, I left the house to make my way to Steve's and then down to Stobie to meet up with the rest of the lads: Andy T, Andy C, Mike B and Sass, the brothers Mike and Sandy B, Mudie, Big Brian G, Russell, Dave M and Big Forbsy. We had a laugh walking into town, but I was also wondering what the fuck I was getting myself into. We soon bumped into another small group of Dundee lads and teamed up with them. I didn't know any of the boys at the time, but I've since become lifelong friends with them.

About eight of the lads went for a browse and the rest of us parked up just across from what was to become our meeting place for the next 10 years – Boots in the city centre. As we stood there, I went into a bit of a dream, thinking to myself: 'I wonder what's going to happen from here to the match?' I soon got my answer, when one of my mates shouted: 'Fucking leg it!' I looked straight ahead and walking towards me were about 20 Celtic, most carrying glass bottles. My mates had already taken to their heels and I soon followed at a speed I didn't think I was capable of. Bottles and glass whizzed past me as I ran. When I caught up with my mates they were at a pub on Castle Street, from which spilled out about 40 older Dundee lads. Steve's brother-in-law Wayne and the rest of his mates were there and they asked what had happened. Steve told him the story and then asked what had happened to me. I told him that I had been daydreaming and hadn't noticed him legging it. 'We shouted to run but you never took us on,' he said. 'You're lucky you never got your life taken, you big daft cunt!'

As if my heart wasn't pounding enough, everybody then

made their way up to meet the football special that they knew was bringing in the Celtic fans. We got there and saw about 500 Celtic, 90% of them scarfers walking towards us. A roar went up of 'Come on, Dundee, come on, Dundee', and I thought, 'Fucking hell, we're away to get a serious tanking here.' But there was a huge police escort with them and they didn't make any attempt to get at us. But even though there were loads of Old Bill, we still made a charge at them. The Old Bill, followed by Celtic, came back at us and we backed off and made our way up to the game.

When we got to the turnstiles, the same Celtic casuals who'd tried to bottle us earlier – boosted by another 10 or so – made a show outside the ground. They were soon scattered by our superior numbers and the Old Bill, and we finally got in to see the match. For the life of me, I can't remember the score that day. I just couldn't concentrate on the match. Afterwards, we made our way down Dens Road, about 75-strong, hoping to bump into the Celtic coming down Arklay Street.

The roar soon went up and we charged into them, only for the Old Bill to arrive very quickly with truncheons out and not taking any prisoners. I was grabbed by a copper and I thought, 'Shite, I'm going to get lifted in my first match.' When I looked at the copper who was holding me, I saw that it was the son of one of my old man's mates. I don't know if he recognised me, but he let go of me and threw me across the road, where I was able to get away.

The rest of the walk into the town was a non-event, but I lay in my bed that night, awake for hours and thinking about the night's events: What a buzz! What would have happened if I hadn't snapped out of my dream in time before the match? I could have been done right in. 'Am I cut out for this?' I thought. 'Nah, forget about all that, this was the biz! I canna wait until next week!'

CHAPTER 7

SECTION B

The next match we all got together for was a midweek cup game at Dens against First Division Airdrie. Going to Dundee games was never a problem for me, even though I was a staunch United fan. Like I've already said, I've never had a problem going to Dens.

I met up with the boys – the usual faces – and we went into town before the game to see if anything was going on. The nerves weren't there this time. Even though we'd heard Airdrie had a mob called Section B, we thought that they couldn't be as bad as Celtic. Could they?

There wasn't anything happening in the town, so we got the bus up to the match. When we got off at Dens we agreed to go into the stand enclosure. This was a sort of neutral area, but was mostly used by away fans. The traditional ends at Dens for the home fans were Provie Road and the South Enclosure, also called the Derry (which has nothing to do with Northern Ireland or anything sectarian). We went in brave, not expecting much resistance, and had a nose around the few hundred Airdrie fans. Nothing much seemed to be going on, but about 10 minutes into the match we saw something happening behind us. A double-decker bus had arrived at the back of the main stand and unloaded what can only be described as a mob that wouldn't have looked out of place in that film *The Warriors*. Seventy lads, consisting of skinheads, mods, punks, bikers, casuals, you name it, came piling into the stand enclosure chanting: 'Section, Section B, Section B, rules OK.' With that, they unfurled this fuck-off skull-and-crossbones flag with 'Section B' written across it.

We all looked at one another. Fucking hell, what do we do now? 'Not so brave now lads,' I thought to myself. A few of them came over and stood beside us. We just knew it was going to go off. You've got to remember that the average age of our little mob was about 15 – and that the rest of the Utility were in the home end. We were like a suicide squad. A few words and looks were exchanged between the two groups and then ... bang! Stevie hooked this big biker and it went off. A few blows were exchanged before the Old Bill were in rapid, separating the two of us.

We realised that we'd have to get out before the end of the game or get murdered. So, one by one, we sneaked out the back in the second half in true *Escape To Victory* style. I was one of the last to go and by the time I got out, with only five minutes left, a few of the earlier 'escapees' had gone round to the home end to rustle up a mob.

By now, there was a good 80 Dundee outside the enclosure. When the final whistle went, everybody was up for it. Out came the Section B and we went right into them. There was no backing off from either side until the Old Bill arrived en masse to split up the two groups. We tried to have another pop before they went but were pushed back by the Old Bill.

We had a great laugh afterwards, swapping stories about what had happened. Plus, we'd learned a valuable lesson that day – never underestimate a smaller team.

CHAPTER 8

BATTLE OF BRITAIN

United were to do well in Europe again that season and progressed past the first couple of rounds, only to be paired with Manchester United.

The first leg was at Old Trafford and 5,000 United made the trip. I was only 14 at the time, so I had to stay at home and listen on the radio and then wait for the highlights on the box later.

It unfolded into a classic. For an hour of the match, Man U were all over us and it was only the heroics of veteran goalkeeper Hamish McAlpine, including a penalty save from Gordon Strachan, that kept the score reasonable. In response to goals from Gordon Strachan and Brian Robson, we pulled one back via our skipper Paul Hegarty to keep things respectable. Meanwhile, McAlpine still managed to keep them out, making numerous stops against Jesper Olsen in particular. Then, the magical moment came – what is to this day my favourite goal scored by a United player.

AFTER THE MATCH, THE GAME BEGINS

We were camped in our own half, as Man U looked to kill the game and score a third. Suddenly, we broke out of our box and, following about half a dozen swift passes, knocked the ball out wide right to Stuart Beedie. He curled a cracker of a ball across the edge of the box, just past the outstretched leg of Mike Duxbury, where it was met by Paul Sturrock, shirt hanging out, socks at ankles, who scampered through to rifle a shot past the despairing dive of Gary Bailey.

Sturrock took off behind the goal to take the adulation of the travelling support. The end of the ground was a swaying mass of 5,000 delirious Arabs. In those days, not many teams took that many hardcore supporters up to the so-called Theatre of Dreams, so for us to do it and pull the game back to 2–2 was something that could bring a tear to a glass eye. Unsurprisingly, the talk of the town for the next fortnight was the return leg at Tannadice.

As it turned out, the next game ended in disappointment for us. Man U won 3–2 on the night to take the tie 5–4 on aggregate. There was no trouble after the game either. A couple of thousand Man U came up and were housed in the Stand Enclosure and half of the Arklay Street end behind the goal. Steve and myself went down to their end after the game for a nose but nothing much was going down. One thing we did notice was how differently our lads and theirs were dressed. We were still in sportswear – Tacchini, Fila and so on – while they were wearing tweed jackets, jumbo cords and running trainers. We thought that this was weird, but it soon caught on. Fashions changed on a monthly basis in those days.

CHAPTER 9

A STEP TOO FAR

Another match that springs to mind towards the end of my first season as a football casual involves one of the most horrific beatings ever seen in Dundee. It was so bad that it almost forced me to give up my new 'hobby' before I'd even really got started.

Celtic were playing Dundee at Dens and myself and Steve went along for the last 15 minutes. This was something we'd often do, especially at Dens with me being a United fan. If we didn't sneak in (sometimes we paid), they'd sometimes open the gates 15 or 20 minutes from the end in case anyone wanted to leave early. But this allowed the traffic to run both ways and it meant that we could just walk in.

When we got into the ground you could have cut the atmosphere with a knife. Everyone, including normal scarfers, told us that there had been loads of battles both before and during the game. There was an older guy standing beside us with blood running down his cheek from a cut in his head. He told us how he and a few of his mates had been done in by a bus-load of Celtic pissed up on Buckfast.

As soon as the final whistle went, we made our way out of Dens and down the Provost Road towards the town centre via Hilltown. 'Hulltoon', as it's known to the locals, is a quiet steep road leading into town. It's always been known as a blade area and not too welcoming to strangers. It's also got lots of side roads running off it and is really handy for staging ambushes. If you get it right and work your way behind a rival mob, it can be almost impossible for them to stand their ground.

As we headed down the hill, which was so steep that it was hard not to break into a trot, we kept ourselves together in case it came on top. We knew the pissed-up Celtic masses were up for a carry on and we wanted to be ready. They were developing a now legendary hatred for the casuals of other teams, so we knew we were a particular target.

When we got to the bottom of the hill and walked into Reform Street in the town centre we knew something was up. We got close to our corner, by Boots, and saw what looked like a few Celtic casuals running off. We broke into a jog, heading towards where they had come from. We were met by a wall of Old Bill and it was clear that it had gone off already and that something bad had happened. As we looked around, we saw a load of distressed-looking shoppers being interviewed by the Old Bill.

It turned out that 20 or so Celtic casuals had managed to walk through the city centre undetected and tooled up to the eyeballs. They were all armed with plastic bags filled with half bricks, to make it look as though they were carrying something legitimate. They found a small mob of young Dundee and ran at them and backed them off. At the same time, Paul D, a casual from Whitfield who had not been at the game and who was not involved in anything after the match, came walking out of Littlewoods on his own and was set upon by the Celtic.

They attacked him from the side and from behind, hitting him on the head with the bags containing the bricks. The fucking cowards then jumped on his head when he was flat out, in full view of hundreds of Saturday-afternoon shoppers. The attack left Paul with a fractured skull and in a coma for months, while a couple of the Celtic lads ended up doing a few years for the attack.

CHAPTER 10

BECOMING ONE OF THE LADS

Towards the end of the 1984/85 season, myself and the rest of the Stobie boys were getting to know a lot of the other lads our age from other areas of Dundee. The first few lads that made the effort to get to know me are still good friends of mine to this day – Big Steve and Tony D from Lochee, Sammy and Wilson from the town, John R from Menzieshill, Deano, Cusy, EO and Martin fae Pentland, Big Fobo, plus Tubby and Jimbo from Whitfield. Then there was Andy D and Andy R, Mattie and John and Stu from Ardler, Dode Web and the lads from Douglas, Grahame Mck and Cooney from the Hulltoon and Benzo from the Perth Road. These were the lads I first spoke to and who became my mates back at the start. Most of them, to this day, are still some of the best mates I ever had.

We became known as the Alliance Under Fives, 'Under Fives' being the nickname given to the lads under 18 and too young to get into pubs – not that it stopped anyone from drinking and going to the boozer before a game though. The Alliance Under Fives was so named, according to one of my best mates Mattie, after the boys had spent an evening in the doorway of the Alliance and Leicester building society in the town centre while sheltering from the rain. I wasn't there, but Mattie says that he was the one who came up with the name, so who am I to deny him the honour? Anyway, the young lads still use the name today.

For me and the lads, the 1985/86 season couldn't come quick enough – it was all that we spoke about during the summer. Little did we know that it, and the following season, would in my opinion become the two best and most dramatic seasons in my lifetime, on and off the park.

It was a time when the Old Firm's dominance was crumbling. For the best part of 100 years, Celtic and Rangers had dominated everything to do with Scottish football. But in the mid-1980s, even though they would remain the two biggest clubs by some distance, they no longer completely dictated things.

With United winning the league in 1983, Aberdeen in 1984 and 1985, then Aberdeen winning the European Cup Winners Cup in 1983 and United getting to the European Cup semi-final in 1983/84, it was obvious that the Old Firm's iron grip on Scottish football was loosening. Add to this the fact that Hearts were also becoming a main force and it was clear that things were changing.

Meanwhile, the casual scene was growing outside of the influence of Rangers and Celtic. It was pioneered by Aberdeen, followed by Motherwell, and then picked up by Dundee, Hibs and Hearts. Within the casual movement itself, fashions came and went. At first it was all golf wear, such as Pringle and Lyle and Scott, then moved on to the more sporty Fila, Tacchini, Ellesse and Cerrutti, before turning into the 'dressing down' look of Pop 84 tweed jackets, Barbours, deerstalker hats, Burberry and Aquascutum scarves and Daks. One minute bleached jeans were in, the next they were out, replaced by jumbo cords and stonewashed jeans such as FUs and Pop 84.

The tennis-player look had now been replaced by the gamekeeper! Another label on the way up was Next. It's hard to imagine now, but this was the year that the first Next opened in Dundee. It was rare stuff in those days, with hooded jackets costing around £50–£80 and jumpers £40. A nice shirt would set you back £25–£40. This was a lot of money in those days and I can't believe that if you walk into a branch of Next now the prices are about the same today as then.

The first home game of the season would see me and Steve go walkabout on our own. We wanted to see the Aberdeen mob for ourselves and we didn't have to wait long because we bumped straight into the Aberdeen A Team. This was the nickname given to the top boys of Aberdeen, the founders of the casual movement in Scotland. About 20 of them had travelled down to Dundee in a van and they all piled out of it at exactly the same time as Steve and I walked past. I'd love to see a picture of our faces at that moment. We must have looked as though we'd seen a ghost. A change of underpants was definitely the order of the day!

We put our heads down and kept walking. They gave us a couple of looks but didn't say anything. To be honest, a top gang of hooligans in their twenties probably weren't interested in a couple of 15-year-olds. But we didn't know that at the time. We got round the corner and I said to Steve, 'They shat themselves!'

He replied, 'I know, we would have taken them!'

We burst out laughing and didn't stop all the way to the ground.

The game itself passed without much incident. The police had Dundee sewn up, but Aberdeen were untouchable that day. They had the biggest mob of casuals I've seen in Dundee in my life. There must have been between 700 and 800 in the ground for a game which ended in a 1–1 draw. It was a statement that the champions Aberdeen were still the top boys in the country – but they were to get a run for their money up and down the county for the rest of the season.

In the media, football hooligans were big news. The riot at the Luton–Millwall game was still fresh in the memory, while there had also been a TV documentary, *Hooligan*, which followed West Ham's legendary Inter City Firm (ICF).

If I had a pound for every time I've watched that documentary over the last 20 years, especially in 1985 and 1986, I wouldn't need to write this book. The look, the quotes and the walk – they were all studied by budding firms up and down the land. I'm sure I even spoke with a cockney accent for a while, it was that bad!

CHAPTER 11

TAKING ON THE BIG BOYS

Another game at the time that proved we were becoming a force was at Dens, when Dundee were hosts to Aberdeen and the mighty ASC.

As was to become the norm in a fixture involving the ASC, the turnout was much bigger than usual as everyone wanted to take part against the founders of the casual movement. Around 150 lads were dotted around the city square, eagerly waiting on the shout to say they had arrived. After a while, a rumour went round that a huge Aberdeen firm had been met off the train by the Old Bill and had been escorted up to the ground. A bunch of our lads went into the match while another group of us went off to a mate's house to listen to the game on the radio. As usual, 20 minutes before the end of the game we made our way to Dens, hoping to get in for free when they opened the gates.

Just as we turned the corner of the Provie Road a few Dundee lads who had already sneaked into the Aberdeen end suddenly came running towards us. They'd gone into the Aberdeen stand on a bit of a suicide mission and, after exchanging a few punches, beat a hasty retreat. A couple of hundred pissed-off ASC followed them out, as did a load of our boys in the ground who had seen what was going on. The result was that we were caught in the middle of two angry mobs heading towards each other. The police had been caught completely unawares and were nowhere to be seen.

I picked up a traffic cone and let the first of the ASC that came at me have it. Within seconds there were more than 400 lads on the street. Aberdeen seemed surprised at the ferocity of the Utility and we got them on the back foot. After a brief battle, the cops regained control and sent both mobs on their way, although we tried in vain to have another pop at them before they boarded the train north. Although it had been short, it was nevertheless the first time we'd taken on the mighty Aberdeen.

Another game I remember where we had a good result was when Rangers came to Dens. As we got up to the ground the area behind the Derry end was absolutely crawling with fans from both sides. It was hard to make out who was who, but at a guess I'd say there were about 120 of us, including a lot of the older lads, and there seemed to be a quiet determination about everybody. As we turned the corner and walked up the Provost Road, which is as steep as Hulltoon, we saw hundreds of Rangers fans standing around and drinking the customary bottles of wine. There looked like a fair contingent of the Rangers ICF among them.

The roar went up and, led by Davie M, God rest his

soul, we fanned out across the road and charged at them. I couldn't believe what I was seeing. There was complete panic among the Rangers lads and they started to leg it up the road. I looked left and right and saw my mates getting wired right into them. Just as we had them on the back foot, and before they had a chance to regroup and use the huge advantage of running down the very steep road, the Old Bill came screaming round the corner and it was off back down the road and out of sight. Job done.

We were fucking buzzing after that. Some of the lads went into the ground and about six of us had a toe-to-toe with about 10 Rangers on Canning Street, with Tam B right at the front of our small mob and swinging a brush that he'd picked up at the side of the road. As they tried to save face, we backed them off down the pavement and bolted again as the cops came up the street towards us. We went up to a mate's house during the game and I don't think any of us stopped for breath in the next hour and a half as the stories of who did who and who hooked who went on and on.

In my opinion, that was the day when I knew little old Dundee could mix it with the big boys. I couldn't help but think of the days when I'd been a kid, peeking out of the window at the marauding invaders from the west – and here I was now, having it with them on our own patch.

We made our way to the game with 15 minutes to go. After the final whistle it was back down the Provost Road and on to Dens Road, with about 150 lads. Everyone was still buzzing from before the game. The plan was to go straight into them as soon as they appeared. We got to the bottom of North Isla Street and saw them, but this time they were mob handed and out for revenge. The two mobs went straight into each other, but after a brief skirmish the local constabulary appeared en masse to spoil the fun.

Later that evening, around 8:00 pm, about 10 went to the town centre to see if anything was still going down. As soon as we got there it went off, with about 50 Under Fives and 15 or so men out on a smoker.

What kicked it off was something that I would see 100 times over the years, where grown men would walk through the town saying things like: 'There's the casuals. They're all a load off wee shites.' Next thing, it would be straw hats and trumpets. One of the men got caught and got a severe kicking from the 'wee shites'. It resulted in a few guys getting nicked and massive fines being handed out.

We headed back up the road to Stobie, avoiding a weekend spent in Bell Street nick, and there ended a particularly eventful day.

After this, the only thing that I hadn't yet experienced was an away day. I missed what was supposed to be a big one at Tynecastle, to take on the Hearts and their firm. It was my old man's birthday and I'd arranged to go to Tannadice with him to see United play Hibs. It turns out I never missed much. Around 130 Dundee made the trip, but, apart from a carry on with the Old Bill as they got out of the train station, and a couple of arrests, the Hearts casuals never showed face.

At the United match with the old man I couldn't concentrate on the game. I kept thinking about what was happening at Edinburgh. I noticed a lot of Hibs CCS at the game, looking a bit bemused at the lack of Dundee lads and obviously not realising that everyone was in Edinburgh. After the game I couldn't get the tea down the hatch quick enough. As soon as possible, I headed into town to meet the lads off the train. As I made my way down Crighton Street I noticed about 10 lads standing on the corner. As I got closer, I realised that they were the Hibs casuals I'd seen in the match. I put my head down and crossed the road, thinking to myself, 'What the fuck are they still doing here? They're going to get smashed as the train is due in five minutes.'

I got to the station, having successfully avoided getting any stick from the Hibs boys, to find that when the train came in none of the boys was on it. Puzzled, I headed back to the city centre, taking a different route this time to avoid our friends from the capital. On the way, I bumped into a couple of older lads who I know by sight. 'Any idea what time everybody's due back from Tynecastle?' I asked them.

They told me that they'd left the match at half-time. It was shite and they wanted to get back to Dundee to meet the Hibs. As they walked away, they shouted, 'Watch out for the Hibs, young ane. Some of them are still about.'

Right enough they were. A couple of minutes later the same two older lads came sprinting round a corner at me, with the Hibs hot on their heels. 'Fucking leg it,' one of them shouted.

I crashed straight through the flower beds outside Littlewoods, just in time to miss an umbrella whizzing past my head. 'Come on, Dundee, CCS,' the Hibs shouted.

I thought I was a goner and my legs went into overdrive. I ran down Castle Street and into this door which I thought was a boozer. I went up the stairs and the barman shouted at me, 'Come on, son, over 18 only.'

I was sweating by now, and thought to myself, 'I can't

45

go back out on to the street.' I didn't make a fuss, but just told the guy, 'Nae bother, mate,' and pretended to leave. Instead, I went and sat on the stairs.

After 10 or 15 minutes, I ventured outside and it was all clear, so I headed back to Stobie to see my mates. I thought, 'Fuck me, I'll get stick for not going to Edinburgh and I've still ended up in more bother than any of the cunts that did go!'

If I'd have known the lads were back home by five, I wouldn't have bothered going into town. And they say that mobile phones have ruined football violence!

After missing that first away day, I made a vow to myself that I wouldn't miss another. I wouldn't have long to wait until the next one – when we went up to see Aberdeen and the ASC. Well, if you're going to learn to swim, you might as well jump in the deep end.

CHAPTER 12

THE 5:15 TRAIN

22 March 1986. D Day. The mood among the lads was one of total excitement. Everyone was buzzing at the thought of going to Aberdeen and taking on the ASC. Dundee FC were the visitors to the Granite City, which meant a trip away for me to watch the dark blues. As mentioned earlier, being part of the Utility meant following both clubs. This was a necessity if you wanted to remain a respected member of the firm.

Most of the older lads were Dundee fans, due to the fact that they were brought up at a time when the only team in the city with any history was the dark blues. But during the 1980s Dundee FC lived in the shadow of United for once. A whole generation of lads like me swore allegiance to the tangerine half of the city, while great friends like Steve and my co-author John suffered as their team went backwards fast. Off the park, though, our firm was always at its best when Dundee played, because as well as us younger lads from United it meant that we also had the older more experienced Dundee FC boys.

To make sure we were properly organised, a Utility fact sheet was drawn up and handed out. It told everyone where and when to meet and even what to wear. Steve was even questioned by the Old Bill when he handed the sheets out at school – a story that was reported on the front page of the local paper.

Me and Steve were up in town by 9:00 am, buying some new gear for the trip. I got myself a new shirt and a green summer jacket from Next. Bright colours were in that summer. We took our new purchases back to Steve's to get changed and then went down to Stobie to meet the mates.

Around 10 of us from Stobie went down to the town, where we were met by Sid and Mackie. They were grinning like Cheshire cats. 'Are you all going to Aberdeen?' they asked.

'Definitely,' we replied.

'Well, when we get off the train in Aberdeen, stick these on,' they said and handed each of us a surgical mask.

We burst out laughing and stuck them in our pockets. 'It's going to be one of those days,' I thought to myself.

We boarded the train about 140-strong and set off for the Granite City. The mood was one of nervous excitement. The closer we got to Aberdeen the more the butterflies kicked in, especially when I walked through a carriage full of all the older heads: Ned, the general, Wayne, Ronnie, Dek G and others. I overheard one of them say that when they got off the train they would leg it from the Under Fives and go and do their own thing. This suggestion was probably shot down in flames, but it didn't make me feel any better. I didn't say anything about it when I got back to where my mates were standing. Instead, I looked out the window, only to see painted in white letters on a wall: 'TURN BACK OR DIE. ASC!' 'Maybe this isn't such a good idea after all,' I thought.

When the train pulled in we were up on our feet and out on to the platform in no time, everybody raring to go. 'This is it, mate,' I said to Steve and he just smiled back.

Soon, the Utility battle cry of 'E I O, E I O, E I O, E I O' went up. It echoed around the railway station as we headed towards the exit. As we burst through the doors, we were attacked by a lone Aberdeen casual. I couldn't believe my eyes when I saw this kamikaze lad in a black Lacoste cardy run out of a doorway and aim a flying kick into our boys. A few of the lads started getting wired right into him, but then the Old Bill appeared and started dishing out the heavy treatment. Two of the Dundee older lads got nicked and the lone attacker just brushed himself down and walked away. 'What the fuck's it going to be like when we bump into a few hundred of them?' I thought.

We were given a huge police escort and marched off towards the ground. We passed a boozer with a load of Aberdeen outside, but we couldn't get at each other. As we headed away one of the coppers turned and said, 'I canna be bothered with this. I think they should just put the Aberdeen casuals and the Dundee casuals in a big field and let you sort it out!' We were pissing ourselves laughing and it broke the tension a bit.

We got to the ground and a few Aberdeen were walking about and trying to mingle in. A few small skirmishes broke out, nothing heavy. One lad who walked past was asked by Tony D from Lochee if he was Aberdeen. He denied it, but Tony gave him a cracker of a right hook anyway and burst his nose all over the place. When we got into the ground, we saw the guy that Tony punched in the home end, so it turns out he was bullshitting all along.

Just after half-time, the word went around that everybody was going. We went out and headed towards the Aberdeen end. When we got there it looked as though there were about 500 of them piling down in our direction. 'Fuck, here we go,' I thought. But the fun was spoiled by the Old Bill. They arrived before Aberdeen got out and we were held in a park for a while before they marched us back to the station. All the Aberdeen could muster was a few token charges at us. It was never going to happen as the Old Bill were on top and won the day.

The Old Bill loaded us on to the 5:15 pm InterCity train home and by the time we got to Stonehaven we were all larking about. At first, there was a bit of toy fighting between the United fans and Dundee fans. A few plastic cups and empty beer cans were lobbed around. And then it all went off. Seats were ripped out and a window got put in. Tables and then a toilet seat soon went sailing through the hole where the window used to be. Chairs were set on fire and the emergency cord got pulled about a dozen times. In no time all three carriages were completely and utterly devastated. Not one window was left intact, which meant that the rest of the journey home was a cold one. Every train station from Montrose on was lined with dozens of coppers with Alsatians preventing anyone getting off. As we got to Arbroath, a few Arbroath lads who ran with us tried to get off but were put back on the train.

THE 5:15 TRAIN

As we pulled into Dundee we couldn't believe the amount of coppers on the platform. There must have been 75 and about a dozen dogs. We were told to sit where we were and a few photographers from local newspapers and the police came on and took a few snaps of the wrecked train. A few well-known lads got pulled from the Old Bill as soon as we got off. They let us out one carriage at a time and lined everyone up in a circle, taking our names and addresses and getting photographs of everyone. In the end, about half a dozen lads got massive fines for the vandalism.

Welcome to the world of the away day.

CHAPTER 13

BACK TO EARTH WITH A BUMP

Even though our firm was growing by the week and getting a few good results, we were about to be knocked off our stride. Late on in the 1985/86 season Hibs came up to Dens Park – and they took with them the Capital City Service. These boys were just about to take Aberdeen's title as the top dogs in the country for the rest of the 1980s.

We met in the city centre and the mood was pretty good. Around 150 lads were dotted around the city square. The older lads were as usual holed up in the Executive Bar, which is further along the town. Around 2:00 pm a roar went up: 'They're here, they're here.' We headed off to meet them and ran into them as they came up from the station. They just marched right into us and, for about a minute, it went off big style with about 250–300 lads going toe-to-toe in the street.

I don't know if it's because we didn't back them off with the initial charge, but they started getting the better of the fight. Once the lads at the front started to back off, the domino effect kicked in and soon everyone was backing off. It's hard to stand when everyone else is running and what looks like panic is setting in. We beat a retreat and then regrouped at the top of Reform Street. The Hibs followed on but were stopped by the Old Bill about halfway up Reform Street and escorted back down through the town. They never made another attempt to get at us. They didn't need to. It was a serious result to them. In fact, it's probably the best result any team has ever had in Dundee in 25 years.

Everyone was shouting at one another. The boys that were usually right at the front – Millar, Tony D and the twins from Fintry – were giving it to everyone with both barrels, and quite rightly so. If there is any excuse (and it's only a small one), it's that 95% of our firm there that day were Under Fives. When you've got 150 of the best mob in the country coming at you, it takes a lot of nerve to stand against them.

And it wasn't long before our nerve was to be tested again. As we got to Dens Road Primary School, we turned up the small path at the side of it and saw the Hibs coming up North Isla Street without their escort. Once again, everyone was at one another to stand and make up for what had happened in the city centre. They came charging up the road and we went right into them. There were fights breaking out all over the road and I remember seeing Big Forbsy from Stobie right at the front and getting stuck into the Hibs front line.

I don't know if what happened in the town had a psychological effect on us, but panic set in again when they never backed off and everyone turned and ran. A few of the harder lads tried to stand and fight back, but they just got overwhelmed. The Old Bill arrived again and broke things up. Hardly anyone said a word during the match as we all felt the same. If truth be told, most of us were glad to just get the day over with. It was a sharp reminder that we were far from unbeatable. Hibs had an Indian sign over us for the next few years and I believe it all stemmed from that day. We were to get our revenge soon, but it didn't last long.

CHAPTER 14

AN UNFORGETTABLE END

That season St Mirren came down to Tannadice. For a laugh, about 10 of us decided to embark on a suicide mission and take on St Mirren's brilliantly named LSD – the Love Street Division. We'd heard they were a firm of sorts but weren't up to much. With this in mind, we thought we'd go solo against them.

We reckoned that they would probably come in by bus, so we headed off to the place where the buses and coaches parked up on match day. Sure enough, about 2:30 pm a few coaches turned up together and off the last of them about 15–20 LSD got off. They must have been about five years older than us, but we were right into them as soon as the got off. As we took them by surprise, another 10 or so Dundee Under Fives led by Steve T from Lochee appeared and also fired right into them.

There was panic in the St Mirren ranks at this ambush and they legged it off to the ground. We went after them, only to be met by a load of coppers, who arrested one of the Dundee lads. In the meantime, the LSD, realising how young we were, tried to make amends by coming back at us. The Old Bill forced them back and shoved them into the ground. We were cock-a-hoop. Handshakes and back-slaps were dished out all the way down into the town and we couldn't wait to tell the older lads about our surprise attack.

And so it was on to the last game of an eventful first full season for me as a soccer casual. And what a game it was. What was to unfold next was probably the most dramatic end to a season in Scottish football history.

With a handful of games to go, Dundee United, Aberdeen, Celtic and Hearts were all in with a more than realistic chance of winning the title. With Hearts having the far better end to the season, they were in pole position with only one game to go. All that was required was a single point away from home – at Dens Park. On top of that, even if they lost, Celtic would have to win their game about 4–0 because of Hearts' superior goal difference.

Dundee went into the game with something to play for, as they were still in with a chance of qualifying for Europe if other results went their way. Because Hearts hadn't won anything for years and years, Dundee braced itself for a maroon invasion. As we made our way into the centre of town, the place was alive with lads. At a rough estimate, there must have been 200–300 Under Fives spread out around the city centre, sitting about in the glorious sunshine. There were also hundreds of Hearts fans walking around, getting ready to celebrate finally winning the title.

Even though the mood was tense in the city centre there was no violence. At around 2:00 pm we headed up to the ground, a huge firm of Under Fives. I wish I'd had a camera that day. It must have been something to see: 250–300 casuals, all dressed up, with hardly any of us over 18, marching in the glorious sunshine up that steep road to the ground.

At the ground itself a few small battles were breaking out here and there, but nothing special. Then our attention was taken by a firm of 150, walking up the Provost Road towards us and singing, 'We hate football and we hate football, we hate football and we hate football, we hate football and we hate football, 'cause we are the soccer casuals!' We made our way towards them, but soon put the breaks on when we realised it was a firm of Dundee older lads who'd spilled out of a nearby boozer.

As everyone went into the ground a few of us decided to wander off and have a nose about. Me and three mates broke away from the rest of the lads and made our way along Sandeman Street and back up to Dens to see if anything was going down. As we turned back into Tannadice Street we bumped into around 300–400 Hearts fans who'd arrived late for the match.

With odds like that against us all we could do was merge into them and keep quiet. We exchanged a few nervous smiles, but luckily the Hearts fans were too pissed and too wrapped up in thinking about winning the Championship to bother about us.

As we got near to Dens we all got a bit braver and started singing along to the famous Hearts song, 'H, E, A – R, T, S'. I was just about wetting myself. I looked over at Dek W and saw that he was taking things that bit too far. He had his arm wrapped around this Hearts fan and was singing at the top of his voice. 'Typical Dek,' I thought, 'fucking daft as a brush!' As soon as we got through the turnstiles and into the ground, the four of us jumped out of the crowd and ran across the grass towards the home end.

A few of the Hearts lads saw what was happening and about a dozen of them tried to break after us. 'Cheeky Dundee bastards,' one of them shouted as we pissed ourselves laughing. After a bit of the old pavement dancing, the coppers arrived and the Hearts boys realised that the gates were about to close so they backed off and went in to see the game. The Dundee coppers in their usual polite manner told us to piss off, so we headed up to Steve's house, which was two minutes from the ground, to listen to the match on the radio.

When the half-time results came through, it was not looking good for Hearts. Celtic were winning 4–0 and it was 0–0 at Dens. Hearts only needed a point, but at 0–0 things could easily go against them.

With 20 minutes of the game remaining we left Steve's and headed up to the ground. We got there to find dozens of Hearts fans locked out and hanging around outside. As we passed them a couple of punches were thrown – but then what happened next was quite bizarre.

As we were giving it the big come on, with outstretched arms, a huge roar went up from the ground. We all stopped in our tracks and ran to see what had happened. Deano from Pentland greeted us as we walked into the ground with that big grin of his. 'Albert Kidd's just scored. It's 1–0 the Dees.' Albert Kidd had come on as a sub and had scored with virtually his first touch. Suddenly, the Hearts fans could see their dream fast disappearing.

At this point I remembered that earlier in the year we'd planned to get the final match of the season stopped with five minutes to go by staging a pitch invasion. But what was happening out there now was even better than that. We were on the verge of ruining Hearts' season. With five minutes to go there was still time for Hearts to take the title if they equalised. At that point, word came through that Celtic had gone 5–0 up. Then, as if on cue, Albert Kidd played a one-two, darted into the box and stroked the ball past the keeper. 'Oh ya fucker, this is mental!' I thought.

Suddenly, it all went off around the ground. There was fighting in the corner of the Derry and behind the goal, while Hearts and Dundee fans ran on to the pitch, with coppers and stewards in hot pursuit. Order was resumed just in time for the final whistle to go, ending the Hearts dream. The title went back to Glasgow and from that day to this has never left the city.

Thousands of Hearts spilled on to the pitch to console their fallen heroes. The sight of grown men lying on the pitch in tears is something that will live with most of the fans who saw it for the rest of their lives.

Around 400 of us made our way out of the ground, buzzing with what had just happened. As soon as we spilled on to the street, it came on top. Men of all ages, regardless of whether or not fighting at football was their thing, were now taking out their frustration on anything or anyone they came across.

We crossed Dens Road and faced them. Fuck me, there must have been over a thousand easy. Scarfers, casuals, old men, the lot! And it went off big time, all the way to the top of the Hulltoon. To this day, I've never seen fighting like it. The police completely lost control as the two sides went at it hammer and tongs.

AFTER THE MATCH, THE GAME BEGINS

Bodies went down as bottles and bricks lit up the sky. It was a complete war zone. People were screaming at one another to stand as lads were being pulled into each side by snatch squads. Because of the sheer numbers of people involved, it took the police ages to restore any sort of order using dozens of dogs and vans.

The walk into the town after that wasn't exactly peaceful, but compared to what had happened in those last 10 minutes it was a lot more under control. There were a few charges at one another, resulting in a few arrests, but as they walked down the hill we just concentrated on getting into the town and on to level ground.

Once around the Wellgate and into the Albert Square, there was a last charge from them. We stood our ground and, after a few punches, they were taken down another street by the Old Bill. A few more small skirmishes broke out over the next hour or so, with late arrivals from the ground, but nothing on the scale of what had happened earlier. After that, we made our way up to Stobie to what we thought was the end of an unforgettable day and season.

We headed to the local park and sat in the sun and had a couple of tins of beer. We then decided to have a walk back into town to see if anything was still going on. On arrival, a couple of lads from Douglas who were heading in the opposite direction told us: 'Better keep your wits about you, lads, it's been kicking off all night.'

It turned out that hundreds of Hearts' 'normal' scarfers, who hadn't left the ground until well after the final whistle, had gone into town to look for anybody to take out their frustration on.

As the six of us approached the city centre and passed

the Boots corner, my old mate John Les from Ardler came towards us. 'Come on, come on,' he said, 'we're getting done in round the back of Littlewoods, gee's a hand'.

We got there to find around 10 young Dundee lads having it with these older Hearts men. We ran into them and they backed off, but just as we did this a pub full of Hearts emptied and another 20–30 of them piled straight into us. A few punches were thrown quickly, but as the majority of Hearts approached the 15 or so of us turned and legged it. The six of us from Stobie stuck together. As we ran through the town centre, I looked behind me to see about 15 Hearts giving chase and looking as if they wanted to tear me to pieces. 'Fuck me,' I thought, 'they're about 50 years old. Are they not tired yet?' When we got to Boots I was fucked and couldn't run any more. 'That's it, I'm a goner,' I thought. 'I'm going to have to turn and face the music.' I looked at Steve and I could tell that he was thinking the same.

Then, just as we crossed the bottom of Reform Street into Samuels Corner, a brown Ford Escort CID van came screeching around the corner. Steve and I looked at each other. I don't think either of us had ever been so glad to see the Old Bill. I don't know if the Hearts scarfers knew they were coppers, but, as soon as the Old Bill jumped out and tried to get them to stop, the Hearts lads just piled into them and kicked them all over the road. Steve and I burst out laughing and I shouted to him, 'Let's get to fuck out of here before we're next!'

We ran along to the bottom of Princes Street, where we met up with the other lads.

So ended a dramatic season that will live with me forever.

CHAPTER

THE CASUAL PEEK

CHAPTER 15

THE CASUAL PEAK

Was the 1986/87 season going to be as good as the last one? That's what we all wanted to know. Well, it turned out to be bigger and better!

Whoever drew up the fixture list must have been a closet hooligan, because the first visitors to Tannadice were Aberdeen. We got to town early for that one, and there were at least 250 Under Fives spread out over the city centre, sitting around in the blazing sunshine. It looked as though every face from every scheme was out that day to welcome our friends from the north.

After a few false sightings of the ASC, we heard some singing coming from the direction of Crighton Street. We went to see who it was and found that it wasn't the ASC at all but about 50 of our friends from the Arbroath Soccer Society, who had come up to join the party. They told us that they'd heard Aberdeen had already arrived and were a couple of hundred strong. They also said that the police were trying to sneak them to the game via the docks, so we headed off to try to catch them before they reached the ground. Unfortunately, the Old Bill were on to us. When we got to where the ASC were, the police were there in force too and kept us at arm's length.

We were taken straight to the ground and the new season got under way with a swing. The 90 minutes we spent up at the 'seggie' fence, singing and bouncing up and down, passed in a flash. At the end, we'd beaten our northern neighbours 2–1. But that was not enough. It was only now that the season started. For the Utility, after the match is when the game begins!

We went down on to Dens Road, 300-strong by now and looking for the famous ASC. We got halfway down the street and caught a glimpse of them being escorted away. We broke into a trot, which soon became a sprint away from the Old Bill, who we could see had lost control. We went along a side street and came out to meet them. It was on. We were just yards apart. There were around 500 lads on Lyon Street and it went off.

In fights like these it's almost impossible to keep your wits about you. There are so many bodies jumping around that I just start windmilling into anyone that gets in my way. Suddenly, the familiar sound of the Old Bill rang out and most of the lads split apart. The Old Bill didn't fuck about and at least half a dozen vans screeched to a halt in the centre of the two mobs and we both split.

I was now dodging meat wagons instead of punches. Someone grabbed me by the neck of my Classic Nouveau T-shirt. 'Bastard,' I thought, 'nicked first game.' But much to my relief the copper threw me back into the mob. One of my mates, Andy, did get lifted though. A few weeks later he appeared in court. I was called as a witness and we'd planned our story to say that we were just walking along and got caught in the middle of it all. However, just before I took the stand, the prosecution produced a Utility calling card that Andy had in his wallet and that was that – guilty as charged.

With the new season, fashions were changing as well. We were moving on from labels like Burberry, Aquascutum and Next. Now, new Italian labels such as Pop 84, Matinique, Fiorucci and Radio were in demand. As there were no decent shops in Dundee at the time, we arranged a shopping trip to Valentino's in Perth. This was the closest town to Dundee, about 20 miles away. Its team, St Johnstone, played in the lower leagues during the 1980s so we never had much opportunity to take on our near neighbours. With a population of only around 40,000–50,000, Perth could pull over 100 lads on a good day – and in my opinion they were the equal of any 100 lads in the country. You'd hear of teams getting results in Perth, but only through sheer weight of numbers.

Stories of Dundee lads coming under fire on shopping trips to Perth had done the rounds, so myself, Dek, Mike and Andy from Stobie planned our visit with SAS-style precision. We left Dundee early in order to get there for about 9:30 am, hoping the streets would be empty. That way, we could get there, grab the latest fashions and then get back to Dundee. We found Valentino's easily enough and the owner, Henry, was as helpful as could be. He greeted us looking like he'd just got out of bed. 'All right, lads,' he said, 'through from Dundee, are we? Just give me a shout if you need a hand.' With that, he wandered back upstairs.

My immediate thought was: 'How does he know we're from Dundee?' I also noticed that the guy behind the till was acting strangely. I put it all down to paranoia and got back to browsing, finding myself a new Fiorucci sweatshirt and pair of jeans from my new favourite label, Pop 84. Once we had all paid up, we left and made our way to the station. As we walked out, a lad walked in and brushed past me without looking back. 'Is it just me or is something going down? I said to the lads.

'Nah,' they replied, 'it's your imagination, Kenny, let's get back to Dundee.'

The train pulled up just as we arrived at the station. 'Perfect timing,' I thought. 'Mission accomplished.' We got on and sat down, but at that moment I saw the lad from the shop walk on to the platform. 'That's that guy who bumped into me at Valentino's,' I told one of my mates.

'Are you sure?' he replied.

Just as I was beginning to doubt myself, another six lads walked towards the train. This was it. We stood up and braced ourselves for the inevitable.

'Come on then, Dundee', they shout.

As soon as we answer, 'Come on the train then, you Perth pricks,' they do just that – with another 10 of them appearing from both ends of the carriage. It quickly got out of hand and we were swinging punches in all directions. More than our own safety, we were worried about the gear we'd just bought. Just as it looked as though we were fucked, the whistle went and the train started to pull out. We exchanged a few last blows before the Perth lads jumped off and we fell back into our seats still just about in one piece – and still holding our bags.

We all burst out laughing, but all the way home I couldn't help wondering if we had been set up. 'Oh, well,' I thought, 'I won't be going back there in a hurry. They must have anti-Dundee-lad sensors as you walk out of the train station!'

When the train pulled into Dundee Station, I was glad to see the old place for a change. As soon as we got off, we were met by Benzo. Now, Benzo is a great lad and he's as game as they come, but he's an awful story-teller. Any time you'd bump into him it would be: '300 Aberdeen just off the train' or '250 Rangers just walked through the town.' Most of the time he would be wrong. I put it down to him getting carried away, rather than downright lies, but he'd have you on your toes anyway. So, the first thing he said this time is: '300 Rangers are on their way to Aberdeen.'

We laughed. 'Good one, Benzo,' we told him, followed by: 'What the fuck are you doing standing on the platform anyway?'

'Just having a nose,' he said.

Just as he finished speaking, a train pulled up and I couldn't believe what I was seeing. It must have been packed with about 400–500 lads, 300 of them casuals. Their Union Jacks told me they were Rangers. They were banging on the windows and looking as though they were up for it big time. We stared at one another and we all knew that we were fucked. The closest door out of the place was 50 yards up the platform. We just stood there, ready to accept our fate ... only for the train to speed up again without letting anyone off and continue on its way north to Aberdeen.

The five of us let out the breath that we'd been holding

in for the past two minutes and then Benzo said, 'I knew it was a football special all along and not a service train! That's how it never stopped.'

I asked him is that why his face went as white as a ghost's as well. We got out of there after that, all of us hoping that someone would soon open up a decent clothes shop in Dundee so that we wouldn't have to go on any more suicide missions.

A few games into the new season, Celtic were due up to Tannadice. The town centre was buzzing as usual, with a couple of hundred Under Fives dotted about in their usual haunts. Our spot was usually outside H Samuel, at the bottom corner of Reform Street. Nothing much was going down, so myself, Steve, Mike and our new, much younger recruit from Stobie, Tony, decided to go for a wander up to the ground. Tony would go on to become one of my best friends, more like a brother to me, but at that stage he needed a lot of looking after as he was only 12 years old

After a casual stroll up the Hulltoon, we began to make our way back down when we saw a mob of about 150 in the distance coming towards us. We jumped behind a wall and waited to see who it was. When it became apparent that it was Dundee we jumped out and joined them in the walk up to the ground. 'What the fuck were you lot up to?' one of the lads in the firm said.

I told him, 'We were away to ambush your mob until we realised it was Dundee.'

He looked at me as though I was off my head until he realised that I was taking the piss and we both laughed and headed off towards the ground.

Down Main Street and across Dens Road, we decided to head up a small path at the side of Dens Road Primary School. The path was only wide enough to take two or three bodies at a time – and it was as we were going through it that Celtic decided to attack. Only the few at the front could fight, while the rest of us were necked in tight and couldn't get out as stones and cans of beer rained down on us. Lads were taking hits left, right and centre, and bodies were falling all over the place. I was more concerned about young Tony than anything else, although he seemed to be enjoying the whole episode and had that mad grin of his on his face the whole time.

A charge was made by the lads at the front, led by Fergie, who'd by now lost one of his shoes. That wasn't all he'd lost – he was going crazy and led the lads at the front right into the Celtic mob, backing them off. This gave us the breather we needed and we burst out on to the road and scattered them everywhere. You could see that most of the Dundee were hellbent on revenge. We didn't give up the chase easily and a few arrests were made of over-eager lads looking for payback.

We were then escorted to the ground by the Old Bill, but we were dying for another go at them.

After an exciting 2–2 draw we got it together and made our way to the away end, to be met with more opposition from their fans. Small battles broke out all the way into town, but the Old Bill had it under control. We hung around the town until after 6:00 pm, when all the shoppers had gone home. All that was left was around 20 of us dotted about the centre. Myself, Steve and Mike were standing outside H Samuel. As we blethered away about the day's events, Mike pointed up Reform Street to half a dozen Celtic coming towards us. At the front was this greasy-looking cunt with a Hugo Boss sweatshirt on, grinning from ear to ear. He had his hand up the front of his top, implying that he had something up it. Not taking any chances, we moved into the middle of the road and got ready for the off. I was aware that 15 or so other Dundee had moved towards them, so now it was just a case of brace yourself for what was up the jumper. As they got nearer, his hand came down and it looked like a half bottle of whiskey or vodka. I got an even closer look at it as it flew past my head. As soon as it passed we were right into them. After a couple of punches, it was obvious that the only thing they wanted to do was get out of there as soon as possible – which is exactly what they did.

Steve turned to me and said, 'Fucking Glasgow pricks, can they no' fight without weapons? That nearly took your head off, Kenny!'

'It wasn't that close was it?' I replied.

'Are you joking? I seen your hair move!' he laughed and we headed for home.

CHAPTER 16

AWAY DAYS

A couple of weeks passed and not much action. As there was no one of note home or away to get excited about, we decided to go somewhere for a laugh. 'Let's pick a game in the lower leagues,' Mike suggested. So, after scanning through the fixture list, Mike said, 'What about Raith Rovers v Stenhousemuir?'

'What?' we all replied.

'Come on, it'll be a laugh. Kirkcaldy is only about half an hour down the road,' he said, at which we all laughed and then agreed. Raith Rovers v Stenhousemuir it was then.

About 10 of us met up in Stobie at about midday on the Saturday and made our way to the train station. As we were walking through the town, a few lads that were hanging about asked where we were off to. 'Kirkcaldy, for Raith Rovers v Stenhousemuir, fancy it?' I replied.

'What the fuck are you going there for?' Big Steve asked.

'For a laugh, nothing's happening here today,' I told him.

AFTER THE MATCH, THE GAME BEGINS

After a brief discussion, we were joined by another 10 lads who followed us down to the station.

Once on the train, a couple of cans were cracked open and one of the lads from the town asked whose idea the trip was. 'Better ask Mike, it was his bright idea,' I said, to which Mike replied, 'It'll be a laugh! Trust me.'

With that, we settled down for the rest of the journey. We piled off the train at Kirkcaldy, not really knowing where we were going. We just headed towards the town centre and gave it the big Dundee Utility song, much to the surprise of the town's Saturday-afternoon shoppers. Kirkcaldy is a small sleepy town, about the size of Perth, in the Kingdom of Fife, about half an hour from Dundee. It is home to Raith Rovers Football Club. We walked through the centre and down towards the seafront, where we were met by a meat wagon. 'That's us fucked now,' said Steve, to which I replied, 'Just act dumb, mate, and say we're going to the game.'

'Where are you boys off to, then?' asked the sergeant.

'Just looking for the football ground, officer, we seem to be lost?' I replied innocently.

'It's right along to the end of the road. Turn right up the hill and you can't miss it, lads. And watch out for the troublemakers!'

The 20 of us were by now holding one another up, pissing ourselves laughing. 'If only the Old Bill were like that in Dundee,' Big Steve remarked and we made our way to the ground following the directions given to us by the ever-friendly copper.

It was only 1:30 pm when we got to the ground and it was as dead as a dodo. We headed for the away end, where someone said, 'Check this out.' We went over to a big steel gate which looked as though it was there for letting the fans out at the end of the match. 'Gee's a hand,' Mike shouted, and we pulled at the gate and it opened far enough to let us in.

So, it was 1:30 pm in the afternoon, Raith Rovers v Stenhousemuir, and the only 20 lads in the ground were the Alliance Under Fives. A couple of players walked out on to the pitch for a pre-match warm-up, and we all started to shout and sing 'Stenhousemuir, Stenhousemuir, Stenhousemuir,' much to our amusement. A couple of coppers saw us and got on to the walkie-talkies. We clocked them and knew that our days in the ground were numbered. 'How did you lads get in here?' Mr Officer asked.

'We paid in,' we replied.

'Did you now? Funny that, because the turnstiles aren't open yet. Now, fucking beat it before we nick the lot of you,' he told us, and we were frog-marched out of the ground and sent on our way back down the hill.

As we contemplated what to do for the rest of the day, a couple of the lads went on ahead and stopped outside the doors of this boozer at the bottom of the hill. They had a look in and shouted back to the rest of us, 'Come on, they're in here.'

Without waiting for us to arrive, they kicked in the pub's glass door – with my mate Andy cutting his leg in the process – and the pub quickly emptied. A few punches were thrown before what can only be described as a six-foot-tall female boxer came charging out of the place armed with a screwdriver. 'Fucking hell, look at her!' someone shouted, and we all leaped out of the way to avoid the long-haired beast! Cue the sirens and the flashing lights of our friends the police and we were all off in different directions. Steve and I headed down a road on our own, but I looked back to see Big Fobo from Whitfield getting chased up the hill by the bird with the screwdriver. 'Look at that big fanny!' I said to Steve.

'Which one?' he replied and the two of us turned and ran off, pissing ourselves laughing.

We got back to the station, where everyone eventually arrived in twos and threes. After a quick head count, when the train pulled in we found that we were all there and we headed back to Dundee. On arrival, we ran up Crighton Street towards where a few lads were standing. They didn't recognise us at first and thought we were another team. Once they recognised us, someone asked, 'What the fuck are you lot up to?'

We told them that we'd just got back from Raith Rovers v Stenhousemuir in Kirkcaldy.

'What? It's only 3:00 pm,' came the baffled response.

'You'd never believe me if I told you,' I said. 'I'll tell you later!'

After that, another away day was arranged, with the next port of call Paisley, home of St Mirren.

St Mirren weren't reckoned to be up to much. In fact, the main reason we chose to go there was that British Rail was running a promotion in Scotland that weekend offering adults the chance to go anywhere for a fiver – and for any under 16s with them to travel for a pound. Talk about waving a red rag in front of a bull. I bet every police force up and down the country cringed when they heard the news. Funnily enough, they've never done it since.

Anyway, as Dundee FC were away to St Mirren that afternoon, we had no choice. Paisley it was. The usual arrangements were made and eight of us met at the usual spot in Stobie at midday and walked into town to catch the train to Glasgow at 1:00 pm. When we got into the town centre we bumped into Big McMahon, who agreed to take five of us 'kids' with him for a fiver. McMahon was always flush – even though it was only a fiver, he thought he was being a Flash Harry by paying the adult fare, even though he was only a year older than us. He was a good lad, though, and was from the same area as us, so we agreed and went down and got our tickets with him. A quick head count told me that we'd over 100 lads already and the train wasn't even due for another 20 minutes. Ten minutes later, someone shouted, 'Here's the Aberdeen.' Confused as to what was going on, we all piled through on to the other platform. 'Fucking hell, check the size of that mob!' Steve said to me. It turned out that Aberdeen had also taken advantage of the cheap away day offer as well and had what looked like 300–400 on the train, which, if I remember, was heading to Glasgow. We tried to have a go with them and even got the train doors open, but we were held back by the Old Bill. Aberdeen were giving it the big ASC shout, with light bulbs and various other objects flying through the windows towards us. The incident passed and the train pulled out of the station to us giving them the wanker sign. It had all been a bit of a laugh, but there could have been some real fun and games if they'd got off the train.

Around 150 of us boarded the train to Glasgow, where we were due to change for Paisley. This meant leaving at Queen Street Station and walking through the centre of Glasgow to Central Station. The walk through Glasgow always adds to the spice, as the friendly locals usually crawl out from under their stones to have a pop at us. The mood on the train as always was excitement. It's never one of fear. When you are in a mob of more than 100 lads it just gives you the biggest buzz ever. It might come on top when you get off, but it's something you never think about. On this trip it was all about the coming together of all of Dundee's housing schemes with none of them fighting against one another. It really was a great time. Tins of lager were getting cracked open, and the usual dodging of ticket inspectors was in full flow, with lads hiding under seats, in the toilets and passing tickets around to each other.

When we got to Glasgow Queen Street everyone was practically bursting to get out of the train. We piled on to the platform, ready for action and on guard, as always. It's something you get used to doing, especially in Glasgow, as you never know who might be around. Could be Rangers or Celtic sniffing around, or any other team passing through on the way to somewhere else. You just never know. Like the tube network in London, it's a football hooligan's paradise.

We spilled out on to the street and over to George Square, where we were met by the Old Bill and escorted to Central Station. We picked up the pace to keep the police on their toes, singing all the while: 'Utility National Front, Utility National Front.' I'm not sure where the National Front thing came from. To be honest, 99% of us didn't believe in it or mean it. On a lighter note, we then sang, 'We all live in a casual housing scheme,' to the tune of the Beatles' 'Yellow Submarine'.

I was in my element. For most of the lads, Aberdeen is

the big deal; for others it's our neighbours Perth. Some lads want to take on the CCS of Hibs, but for me it's Glasgow. It probably stems from those days as a child when I was scared to look out of the window at the wine-fuelled invasion outside. So, for me, this was our time as we marched down the middle of the street on a busy Saturday afternoon, with people moving out of the way. Rangers? Celtic? No mean city? Come on, let's have it!

Halfway to Central I saw that we had visitors. A couple of dozen lads, possibly Rangers, were tailing us and trying it on. A big guy with glasses seemed to be leading them, trying to get us to walk down this alleyway and away from the Old Bill. We waited until we got to a corner, where the Old Bill were distracted in trying to stop the traffic, and that gave us the signal to charge into them. The Rangers lads scattered and Mr Glasses was left on his own by his not-so-loyal mates. He tried it on, but he had no chance.

We got into Central and were put on a tube to Paisley. Fifteen minutes later we were there. Off the tube and into the street, we made a break from the Old Bill and ran into a small mob of the LSD. We charged at them and they backed off, but we were soon pushed back by the Old Bill. Our ever-eager boys in blue made around 10 arrests, all Dundee, and then we were marched to the ground. The LSD followed on, led by a tall thin lad, who I recognised from our incident in Dundee earlier in the year. But they'd no chance on this occasion as we outnumbered them too much and the police presence was too strong.

We got to the ground and the older lads went into a boozer at the back of the away end. I wasn't that interested in watching Dundee, but the lads were, so I went into the ground with them.

Half-time came and went and I was losing the will to live. Dundee were four down, thanks to a Frank McGarvey hat-trick, and most of the lads who were in the ground were starting to leave. I said to the mates, 'Come on, are we getting out of here?' The lads agreed and we decided to go for a browse around the ground. As we got to the home end behind the goal, we saw about four or five St Mirren lads hanging around outside the big exit gates, which were now open. We stopped and ducked back behind the wall and decided what to do next. 'Come on, let's get into them and they'll not know whether or not the full mob is coming around the corner,' said Joe. 'If we make enough noise, they'll think we're at the front of the full mob.'

So we got ready and charged around the corner at them. They chucked a couple of bottles at us and legged it. We got a bit carried away and ran into the back of the home end where they'd disappeared into the crowd. We decided to back out at that point, before our kamikaze mission got out of hand. As we ran along the back of the main stand we could hear the noise of people trying to get out of the home end to take on the intruders. If only they knew there had only been five of us.

We walked towards the away end, where the Dundee mob were out on the street and being escorted back to the station. A few of the lads saw us and thought that we were St Mirren. They began to head towards us, but stopped when they recognised who we were. Unfortunately, the coppers did think that we were St Mirren and they tried to send us back up the road. 'Where do you think you lads are going?' said the copper.

'We're from Dundee,' I replied, as if butter wouldn't melt in my mouth. 'We got lost coming out of the ground and we've just been chased by casuals.'

The copper almost swallowed this and shoved us back into the escort, telling me, 'Any more shite from you and you'll be spending the weekend in the cells with the rest of your mates.'

After a quick tube ride we were back on the streets of Glasgow, heading for Queen Street. Once again we were shadowed by Glasses and his Rangers mob, but they didn't try anything on. At Queen Street we were kept in a pen for almost 45 minutes, much to our annoyance. The rumour was that Aberdeen were on the platform, but there was no sign of them. Eventually, they let us on the train home, minus about a dozen lads who had to spend the weekend in Paisley and were due to appear in court on the Monday.

The journey home was a scream. They put a couple of police in each carriage – and one of ours was a female copper. She got the 'Oi, Helga, what do they feed you on?' treatment each time she turned her back on us. But she got the last laugh towards the end of the journey when she and her sidekick marched up to the eight of us from Stobie and bellowed in our faces, 'Think you're fucking smart, do you? Well, you lot are staying on the train when it stops in Dundee and then you're coming back to Paisley with the 10 of us and you'll spend the weekend in the jail.'

As she marched back to her post, her little mate scuttling along behind her, we all began to argue among ourselves, blaming each other for what had just happened. 'This is your fault, you cheeky cunt,' said one.

'You had to take it too far,' said another.

AFTER THE MATCH, THE GAME BEGINS

'You're taking the blame, you cunts. I'm on bail and I'm not going to jail for this pish,' said Joe.

With that, we all slumped back in our seats for the rest of the journey, thoroughly pissed off. The only other bit of excitement on the journey back was the usual warm welcome as we went through Perth. The train was pelted with stones and one of them went in and showered one of the lads with glass.

As the train rolled into Dundee, I decided to try to make a break for it. But at that moment Helga came marching back down the aisle and I slumped back in my seat. 'You're all in luck,' she told us, 'we've changed our minds, so get off the train and get to fuck.'

Before she had time to change her mind we were off the train and halfway out of the station – pausing just to give her a wave as we left.

In the town centre we all agreed that we'd go to Edinburgh to see United play Hearts the next Saturday. We'd got the away bug – but the next week that was all about to change.

The following Saturday arrived and I headed into town early for a spot of shopping in preparation for the visit to Tynecastle. I picked up a Pop 84 hooded flying jacket that I'd had my eye on for a while. It was a shiny black ski jacket, with a detachable hood and a fur-lined collar and green lining. When I tried it on I thought that I looked the dog's bollocks. With my new gear on, I set off for Stobie to pick up the mates, and the eight of us headed into town. All the mates complimented me on the new coat, which added a spring to my step, but as soon as we got into the town centre the first thing I saw was one of the older faces, Mike H, wearing exactly the same coat as me – much to the amusement of the boys. But, rather than get upset about it, I actually felt quite chuffed that one of the older lads had good taste like me.

We'd been tipped off by one of the older lads to buy our train tickets from a travel agent instead of in the station, as the train station had been told to report large numbers of lads travelling together. As we arrived on the platform a quick head count revealed that there was around 60–70 Under Fives there. Just before the train arrived, around 45 older lads appeared. I heard one of them say, 'Too many young lads going, let's give it a miss,' and they turned around and walked out.

Pissed off at this, one of the younger lads said, 'Fuck them, let's go anyway.'

So we did. There were 68 of us in total. In today's terms, this doesn't sound too bad, but in those days, when superfirms were the norm, anything less than 100 was like a suicide mission – especially when the average age of our firm was 16 or 17. Even though it was only Hearts, we settled down for the rest of the journey and decided to make the most of it.

As we approached Edinburgh Haymarket, the butterflies started to kick in. As soon as the train pulled in and the doors opened, it was all systems go. We burst out of the place and straight into about a dozen CSF outside the station. We scattered them and set off down the Gorgie Road, thinking we were the bee's knees, giving it the big: 'Scotland's, Scotland's number one'. 'Who needs the older lads anyway?' we thought.

Around halfway to the ground, a couple of local buses passed by with about a dozen Hearts lads in the back of each. Insults were exchanged and then the buses continued up the road and out of sight. After this, we saw around 30 Hearts lads tailing us in the distance. I began to think that something was up, especially when I also noticed another 100 or so Hearts about 50 yards away and heading towards us. Add to that a load of scarfers, another 50-strong mob coming at us from the right, and the lads from the buses, all heading for us, and it was clear that we were in trouble. A few more Hearts late arrivals meant that our 68 was now faced with about 200 of their lot. We decided that the only thing we could do was head straight for them and try to break through.

As we slammed into them, I took big hits left, right and centre. I was rapidly running out of breath and swinging wildly at them. It was real head down and every man for himself stuff. Every five yards was like running into a brick wall – and when I did eventually get a bit of momentum going, one of my great friends, Big Welshie, fucking shoulder-charged me out of the way and sent me careering into an ice-cream advertisement.

Suddenly, my life flashed before me as I got booted all over the pavement. I tried to get up but my jacket – my new jacket – had gone over my head and I couldn't see where I was. Finally, the kicking stopped for a second and I got to my feet and headed off again. At least, that was the plan. As I tried to move I found that some cunt had hold of my hair and wouldn't let go. I took a few swats at him and he eventually let go. By this time, we were at the away end and the Hearts had fucked off. What I saw was like a scene from a war movie, with all the walking wounded gathered at the turnstiles. I was hurting like hell, thinking, 'Some cunt must have a handful of my hair. Oh well, everyone says I needed it cut anyway.' Still, I was glad of the new coat that day, as it covered my face when I was down on the deck.

Big Welshie appeared and laughed. 'You all right?'

'Fantastic, mate,' I said. 'Cheers for the shoulder charge, you big dick,' and we both laughed.

Inside the ground, one of the lads came over and said, 'Only half of us are in the ground, the other 30 have pissed off.' Fucking great. What do we do now? 'I think we should give it 20 and then do one,' he said.

This sounded like a good idea to me. At the same time, I heard some lads from Douglas saying, 'Did you see the big lad in the Pop 84 jacket going down? He looked as though he'll have a sore one.'

'That was me,' I shouted over at them. 'I'm all right, but where did they all come from?'

We agreed that the lads we headed outside the station must have gone off and rustled up a firm – and that, for them, it was payback for what had happened at Dens on the last game of the season.

A lad I'd never met before came up to me and asked, 'You all right, mate? I picked you up off the deck back there. I saw you were down and were getting a bit of a leathering, so I got in about them and picked you up by the hood. The name's Nacky.'

I thanked him and introduced myself, and from there we've gone on to become firm friends.

After giving the game 20 minutes, we headed off, only to be met by the Old Bill as we left. 'Right, over here,' shouted this bearded plain-clothes copper. 'Right, the first three, on you go,' he said and then sent us up the Gorgie Road in groups of three, of which me, Steve and big fucking 'Jonah Lomu' Welshie were the last. The rest of the lads were almost out of sight when we were let go, but we soon caught them up as we didn't fancy walking through the town on our own. We all made it to the station in one piece, but as we waited there for the rest of the lads the Hearts made an appearance. We charged out of the station and indulged in a little boxing before the police arrived and forced us back up on to the platform.

The other lads eventually appeared and we got on the train to go home. The mood was very quiet to start with but after a while and a couple of tins we forgot about the day and we started to have a laugh. When the train arrived at Kirkcaldy, we noticed a few lads hanging around the station, so we got off the carriage and took out our frustrations on them, scattering them everywhere.

We got off in Dundee, disappointed at the day's result but not too downbeat. At least we'd made the effort, which was more than could be said for the older lads. It was something that would stand us in good stead for the future. Our confidence was dented but was far from destroyed.

CHAPTER 17

SUPER FIRM

The next big game was Rangers at Tannadice on a Wednesday night. For that one, we took the five-minute walk along to the ground from Stobie, rather than go into the town and have a browse around the ground.

I love the midweek games, especially on a dark winter's night with the floodlights on. You have to be on your toes, as you never know who's walking about. On this night, we walked around to the back of the Shed, the traditional home end behind the goal. It has a grass play park at the back of it and that was where we hung around and waited to see if anyone would appear. We were standing around in twos and threes, contemplating the night ahead, when a few Rangers came charging around the corner, led by this big lad in a white ski jacket, shouting, 'Come on Rangers! Chelsea National Front!' He had a London accent and he was signalling as if he had some huge mob behind him. Thinking that we were about to be overrun by a Rangers and Chelsea crew, we backed off a bit into the park to give ourselves a better chance to see what was coming. It quickly became apparent that we'd fallen for the same trick that we pulled at Paisley. What made it even worse was that our London friend wasn't a cockney. He was from St Andrews! When we realised that we'd been had, we charged into them and Mr Chelsea and his mates ran off.

We then spotted Tony D running down Tannadice Street on his own, giving it to us big time for backing off at the start. When I told him that it was all right for him, that he could see how many of them there really were, he calmed down and came into the ground with us. Typical Tony. He'd probably have charged head-first into them anyway, regardless how many of them came around the corner. Tony in my opinion has been the gamest lad in Dundee in the Utility's 20-odd-year history.

Inside, we headed for what is called the 'seggie' and the steepest terracing I've ever stood on. The atmosphere was electric as the teams came out and it looked like a full house. The thing that struck me right away was that we had with us at the game probably the biggest mob at the ground that I'd ever seen. The lad standing beside me told me that the Lochee had over 100 lads on their own, and had even been given their own police escort from their housing estate. One hundred lads from just one scheme! 'Fuck me,' I thought, 'there must be some firm out tonight.'

As the game got under way, the usual coins and stones were hurled, but this time there were bangers and fireworks, too. After all, it wasn't that long after Bonfire Night. Just before half-time, Benny pulled this big fuck-off rocket from his coat and asked me for a light. 'Where did you get that fucking thing? The fucking marines?' I asked him.

He laughed and said, 'Just light the end and watch this.'

I lit the touch paper and he waited a second and threw it over the fence. I swear, the explosion was like nothing I'd ever heard. With the end being under a roof, it sounded like a bomb going off. Just seeing all the Huns shit themselves and dive for cover was worth the admission money alone.

The game ended and we hit the street. Because of the fence at the back of the seggie across Sandeman Street, we were forced to go around the back of the Shed and down North Isla Street and Dens Road. I couldn't believe my eyes when I saw that we'd broken away from the normal supporters and that it was just us casuals marching down Dens Road. Steve tugged at my jacket and said, 'Come on, let's get a move on and get nearer the front.'

When we took a proper look, we saw that we were as close to the front as we were to the back. I would put the size of the firm that night at about 600, easily the best mob we've ever had.

The police had completely lost control by this stage and everyone broke into a jog and ran off in search of the Rangers ICF. Unfortunately, we didn't find any takers, apart from at the bottom of Dens Road where we bumped into a mob of Rangers lads from Fife and who disappeared the way they came as soon as they saw us. I don't blame them. We were unbeatable that night. Anyone who's been in a firm that size will know what I'm talking about when I say unbeatable. As soon as you see that you're in a firm that big, you just know that you're untouchable, no matter what. It was a pity that we didn't come up against a big

AFTER THE MATCH, THE GAME BEGINS

Rangers, Aberdeen or Hibs firm that Wednesday night. There really would have been fireworks.

When we got into town, a huge police presence stopped us at the top of Commercial Street and some sort of order was restored. We were then marched into the centre, past the Fife Rangers mob that was boxed in by the Old Bill. They looked as though they'd seen a ghost.

CHAPTER 18

IN AND OUT

We were on a roll now and next up was another away trip to Glasgow, to visit the mighty Celtic. As per usual, we met in Stobie and then headed off to town.

We got to the station a bit late, but as we arrived I was shocked at the size of the mob that we had. After the huge show against Rangers, all we could muster for this one was about 65. 'Fucking 65?' said Big Fobo from Whitfield. 'We'll get murdered through there. If not by their firm, but from 40,000 scarfers who, remember, all hate casuals with a passion.'

'Thanks for filling me full of confidence, you big dick,' I laughed, and we all let out a sort of nervous giggle and stared out of the windows and wondered what we'd let ourselves in for.

First stop was at Perth, where Tony D was wrestled off the train by the transport police, meaning that we were one of our finest down already. Turns out Tony was banned from British Rail trains for wrecking their carriages. 'Fucking great, that's us even more fucked now, is it?' said Fobo, to which we all turned at once and shouted, 'Will you shut your puss!' This broke the tension a bit and we burst out laughing.

Next up was Stirling, home to a big contingent of Celtic fans, a lot of whom boarded the train. The atmosphere was getting moody. They knew who we were and what we were up to, but nothing happened. On arrival in Glasgow's Queen Street we got off the train, short on numbers but not in determination. Our firm was, for a change, mostly older lads, with around 25 Under Fives. We were met on the platform by a few Celtic who, safely protected by the Old Bill, gave it a bit of mouth but soon started to back track as we walked towards them. Before we got too close, we were pushed in the opposite direction and out of the side door by the Old Bill's welcoming committee.

We were then given an escort through Glasgow city centre, towards Parkhead, followed all the way by a bunch of Celtic casuals at all sides of our small-but-together firm. This was a whole new ball game to us. Usually the Old Bill, like in Dundee, Aberdeen and Edinburgh, tried to keep everyone well segregated and attempted to get you to the ground as quickly as possible. But this time, the Glasgow police seemed happy to let the Celtic mob follow us, almost setting us up for a fall. This only helped to bond us closer together as it made us feel that everyone was against us – Celtic, the police, the lot. The only way I can describe it is to say that we were like caged tigers, being poked and prodded from all sides.

After getting through the town, we came to the long road up to Parkhead. We got to a junction where the meat wagons following us had to turn away and this was our signal to move. One of the older lads shouted, 'Come on, Dundee, this is it. Fucking stick together and let's do it.'

We turned to the 40 or so Celtic in front of us and ran at them. They scattered after just a few blows and we turned as one and went into the 25 or so that had been following behind us. We had the bit between our teeth at this point and we were baiting any cunt who came close: 'Come on, you weegie bastards, let's have it! Dundee Utility, ya bass!'

The Old Bill came screaming back down the road and restored order. You could tell that they were pissed off to have let things slip – especially as it was us who had done the damage.

As we got off on our way again we could see that the Celtic mob across the way from us was getting bigger by the minute. Strangely, it included a few Perth lads who we recognised from our trips up the road. What they were doing with Celtic is anybody's guess. I suppose some people will do anything to have a pop at us.

Parkhead was in sight now. The Celtic firm was about 100 by this time and, for some reason, the Old Bill disappeared again and it was game on. We pulled together again and split across the road. After a brief stand and a few punches, we scattered their full mob. The sight of 14-year-old Terry from Ardler chasing a bearded Celtic casual brought a smile to my face as we completed the rout and chased them off in different directions.

The Old Bill appeared again. This time, they were not so lenient and half a dozen Dundee lads were hauled off, which took our numbers down to 60. I'm sure the Old Bill had fucked off, thinking that we'd get a hiding, only to return and find out that 'their lads' were doing the Glasgow half marathon.

The Old Bill, thoroughly pissed off, asked us what we wanted to do next. Some of the lads said that they wanted to go on to the game, but the general feeling was that if we went to the match we'd have about 40,000 Celtic after our blood. One of the older lads stood up and said, 'If we turn back now and get to fuck, it's job done. We've done the damage. Why risk it with over 40,000 coming for us?'

In the end, the police made the decision for us, as they turned us round and marched us back to the train station.

We found that we only had five minutes to get the next train, and with the one after that not due for another 90 minutes we all broke into a sprint and charged towards Queen Street. Nevertheless, we still found time to have a pop at a small group of lads outside the station, who quickly disappeared at the sight of 60 sprinting Utility coming straight at them. Luckily, we made it to the train, raided the buffet and settled down to crack open a few cans. In and out, job done, and home before half-time! Nice meeting you, Glasgow!

CHAPTER 19

REVENGE

The next big game was Hibs at home. Could we get the monkey off our back? Better yet, could we get revenge for the mauling at the previous match? We were about to find out.

A few of us took the walk into town, which was always a nervy affair when the CCS of Hibernian were in town. Most clubs would get off the train at about the same time. If they came by bus, we'd try to entertain them up at the grounds, but Hibs were a different kettle of fish. They'd arrive early in the morning or late at night, or even pull the emergency cord on the train as they approached Dundee and get off beforehand to try to take us by surprise. They did it all. The only thing they never tried to do was parachute out of the sky – and I wouldn't put it past them thinking about that as well.

One afternoon, we were even standing in the city square when this young lad appeared and stood right in the middle of us. He couldn't have been any older than 13. We all looked at him, wondering who the fuck he was, and he just laughed and clapped his hands and shouted, 'Come on, Dundee, let's disco!'

At this, a mob of Hibs came charging around the corner and straight into our confused mob.

Back in the town centre on match day, we were not our usual bubbly selves, as we knew that they could appear at any moment. As for our lot, we were dismayed to see that there was hardly anyone about. 'What the fuck are we gonna do now?' I asked.

'Let's have a look about and if no one appears in the next 10 minutes let's head up to the ground,' said Steve.

We picked up about another 10 lads, to add to our 20, and walked up to the ground. We got to Alexander Street, which runs from the Hulltoon to Dens Road, and which is home to four huge tower blocks which run from one end of the road to the other. The end one at the Dens Road side is a great vantage point for watching to see if any mobs are coming up from town. We stopped there and looked on to Dens Road and waited to see if anyone appeared. A couple of police cars went past but they couldn't see us in our vantage point.

Fifteen minutes passed and one of the lads alerted us to the fact that a firm was walking our way. We eventually saw that it was Dundee and we ran off to meet it, which brought our numbers up to around 120. Also, it was 120 of our top boys. It was the Utility. We were about the youngest there and it looked as though we'd joined a crew that was off on some pre-arranged mission. Hardly anyone spoke as we headed off up the back streets. In fact, we seemed to be heading away from the ground as we walked on with a purpose. We took a left up Main

Street and across the road past the Dundee FC supporters' club. Then, we went down by the GJ's pub and up the Provost Road behind Dundee's ground. We couldn't believe our luck, as our silent firm had not as yet attracted the attention of a single copper. We were on our own. By this time we were the top of the 'Provie' and then took a right along the Clepington Road, towards the Ambassador boozer. Suddenly, it all made sense: this was where the Hibs had been known to drink in the past.

We broke into a trot and Steve tugged at my sleeve and said, 'Come on, let's get to the front. I'm not missing this.'

We weaved through bodies and headed towards the front rows. We could see the pub and it was clear by now that it was about to go right off. Around 80 Hibs had been standing around drinking outside the pub and as they saw us the bottles came raining down in our direction. It was game on and we went through them like a train, scattering bodies everywhere.

There was one well-known Hibs lad up against a car taking a fair tanking. Someone shouted, 'Stab him!', but he managed to squirm away, taking hits in every direction as he went. Just as he was about to get away, he ran into Big Tambo, who rugby tackled him to the floor and ripped the coat off his back. Never one to miss a trick is Big Tambo!

We were all swinging punches at any Hibs that we saw. Just as the last of them made his getaway, we heard the familiar sound of the police sirens, so we set off down Hindmarsh Street and towards Tannadice.

As we approached the ground, around another 40 Dundee appeared, to be greeted with hugs and grinning faces. We were buzzing now like we'd never buzzed before. We swapped stories with the unfortunate lads who'd missed out. Revenge had been sweet and was about to get sweeter.

We got into the ground and made our way straight to the seggie fence. We started giving it to the Hibs, knowing that they'd be hurting like fuck and wanting revenge after the game.

On the pitch, Eamonn Bannon scored in United's 1–0 win, to top off an excellent day so far. Even better, once the whistle went we were straight out of the ground and ready for round two.

We were 300-strong as we walked down the dark Arklay Street with a spring in our step. As we got close to the corner of Tannadice Street, we saw them coming, a good 150–200 of them, and it went off right away. We were spread right across the road and everyone was in, with no one budging an inch. This was the Hibs mob, and us at our finest, and we were going at it hammer and tongs. I remember one of the older lads, DD, right in the middle and with his hood up, screaming, 'Come on, Dundee this is it.'

The sirens sounded and the Old Bill arrived, pushing us up the hill slightly with the help of their four-legged friends. We went along a side road and down Clepington Street, which runs parallel to Arklay Street. We tried to make a run at them, but were pushed back again by the Old Bill, so we headed off down another side street where, to our surprise, we caught the police napping and went right into the full Hibs mob. After a brief stand, they turned and ran. The by-now super-pissed-off Old Bill pushed us up, bringing an end to the festivities.

We walked the rest of the way into town, but the Hibs

were in front of us and were taken straight down to the train station and sent back to Edinburgh to mull over what had just happened. As for us, we headed back up to Stobie after a mass back-slapping exercise and went along to Baxter Park, where we drank a carry-out and had a sing-song late into the night. It had been one of the best days of my life.

I sat back and thought, 'Have we finally shaken the monkey off our backs? Knowing the CCS, they'll come back harder the next time, but we'll enjoy it just now regardless.' Lads have said for 25 years that Dundee weren't up to much in the 1980s, but I can tell you that when we were good we were very good!

A couple of weeks later, it was Celtic again at home. In the mid-1980s, we had a lot of small violent clashes with the CSC, whom we didn't rate as much as Rangers, Hibs or Aberdeen. It was probably down to the fact that the likes of Aberdeen were seen as high-profile by the police, who concentrated a lot of their efforts into keeping them down. Celtic, on the other hand, were a different kettle of fish. They never brought big firms with them and came to games in small mobs and by various different means. We had countless battles with them involving just 20 or 30 people in total, usually during the game. It was harder with the likes of Aberdeen, with an almost guaranteed 200-plus coming off the train. These sorts of confrontations were always easier to police.

Back at the Celtic game, we walked around the town in wintry conditions, the same 20 of us as the week before, and walked up to the ground and hung around at our new vantage point of the multi-storey block at the end of

AFTER THE MATCH, THE GAME BEGINS

Alexander Street. As we waited for anyone to come by, the weather turned bad and it started to snow heavily. Within seconds, our firm of hardened hooligans turned into a bunch of little boys as a spontaneous snowball fight broke out. I don't know what another firm would have thought had they seen us, but we had a right laugh.

Just as we were really having some fun, Andy L shouted, 'Someone coming.'

We dropped arms and looked out to see about 50 CSC on their way up to Tannadice, followed by a similar-sized group of Dundee, separated from each other by the Old Bill. The weather had put paid to any big mobs turning out but, as ever, some people can't resist their Saturday fix, come what may.

Knowing we'd no chance of any action because of the Old Bill, we headed up through a side street and tried to catch them at the top of Tannadice. Past the United supporters' club, down Main Street, up past Radio Tay and … bang! We timed it perfectly, but the Celtic caught us a bit on the hop. The Old Bill had taken them up Tannadice Street and then left them in order to make sure that the Dundee mob didn't follow on. Free of the police, the Celtic ran up to the turnstiles to go round Gussie Park in order to get back at the Dundee. Instead, they ran straight into us.

Thinking we'd pulled a fly move, we didn't know they were coming and thought they were still a couple of minutes away. When they came screaming around the corner at us, we weren't quite ready. Suddenly, it was right on top and we were taking a few blows. One of my mates, Dek, slipped in the snow and took a bit of a kicking. His brand-new red and white Poco Loco ski jacket was covered in footprints and ripped down the sleeve. This seemed to bother him more than his fast-developing black eye (we've all been there, where we're more worried about damaging our new gear than we are about broken bones).

As it had all gone off right outside the ground, things were soon broken up by the police. We didn't bother going to the game and spent the next hour or so at a mate's house just up from the grounds. We left with 25 minutes to go and made our way back to the game. As soon as we got to Provie Road, we got into a battle with half a dozen Celtic scarfers. Any other scarfers on the planet are a no-no, but the Celtic are fair game. This happens all the time with them, where they either don't even go into the game or get themselves thrown out in order to go walkabout in other towns and cities and abuse people. We weren't having any of them and, after a few words, it was on.

I picked up a traffic cone, a big heavy fucker, and bounced it off the prick at the front who was giving it the most lip. Down he went and we were all over them like a rash. A cop car came up the Provie and we calmly walked away before we got picked up. They tried to come for us again, but the Old Bill drove in front of them and we walked away laughing. The self-proclaimed 'Best Supporters in the World', my fucking arse. Foul-mouthed drunken wankers.

As we approached the game, there were only a couple of minutes to go. The Dundee firm was walking behind the Shed end and we blended in for the walk ahead. Past radio Tay and down Dens Road we went, and as we got to the bottom of Arklay Street they appeared. They had a huge

AFTER THE MATCH, THE GAME BEGINS

police escort with them, so only a token attempt was made to get at one another. For my trouble, all I nearly got was a bite in the arse from a police dog. As the Old Bill clearly had things under control we decided it was game over for the day – so it was heads down and hoods up as we made our way home in the arctic conditions.

CHAPTER 20

ALL ABOARD

The Scottish Cup started up in the New Year and we were drawn away to near neighbours Brechin City. It's a small place about 30 miles north of Dundee, with a population of about 20,000. It was rumoured that they had a small but game firm of around 50, but that they also had a bit of an alliance with Aberdeen.

On match day, a double-decker was ordered to leave from North Lindsay Street in the centre of town and around 10 of us from Stobie turned up to make the trip. When we got to town, I was surprised to see that almost 100 lads had squeezed on to the two-tiered bus. After nipping to the off licence to stock up on beers for the trip, we climbed on board as well.

There were no hangers-on for this trip. Every good lad from every housing scheme was there, plus a lot of the older boys as well. Just as we were about to pull away, someone noticed that Davie M and Billy P hadn't turned up yet. We yelled at the driver to stop and wait for them, which some of the older boys weren't keen to do for too long as it might have attracted the attention of the Old Bill. As we waited, a few lads told a story of how they'd heard that Dave and Billy had had a bit of bother with some bouncers in a boozer in the city centre. They'd heard that Dave had got a bad one, smashed in the face with a crowbar and then put through the window of the pub.

'Surely if that's true he'll no' be here today,' said one of the Fintry lads.

'Fuck knows. But you know what Dave and Billy are like. They'll not want to miss anything,' came the reply.

Then, right on cue, the two of them got on the bus to a round of applause. When we saw Dave's face, it was clear that the stories had been true. To this day, I've never seen two black eyes like it. His face was a total mess. 'Fucking hell, Dave, I canna believe you're getting on the bus like that,' said one of the lads.

Dave just turned with that great big grin of his and said, 'How not? What's the matter, like?'

The whole bus was in uproar and the lad said to him, 'You're off your fucking nut Dave!'

We settled down after that and listened to the story of what had happened to Dave.

The journey to Brechin is a short one and we were there in half an hour. The bus parked around the corner from the tiny high street and we piled off and hit the streets. As much as I hate the way the Old Firm come to towns and cities like mine and completely take over, I must admit that I got a huge kick out of spilling on to the streets of Brechin with the lads and doing whatever we pleased.

The older lads and a few younger ones headed for the nearest boozer, while a group of us went off for a nose around town. Within minutes, the pub doors burst open and our lads and a bunch of locals crashed out into the street, where a short but fierce battle took place. The Old Bill were on the scene right away and we were held back while they got the fighting under control. It turned out that a small group of Dundee had got into a battle with some of the locals over a game of pool. Big Steve took a sore one when one of the locals broke a cue over his head, which was followed by the inevitable battle. Covered in blood, Big Steve was taken away in an ambulance to sort out his head wound.

Around half a dozen of us walked away from the Old Bill and up an alleyway, where this Brechin casual was trying to lure us up the road with all the usual nonsense. When we got around the corner there was another 10 of them, so we charged into them and after a few punches they were off. Led by Tony D, we seemed to chase them for miles. We finally reached this park, where a trap had been laid for us and there were about 25 of them waiting. This same group had already done four Utility lads that day, so without a moment's hesitation we crossed the road, ran into the park and went straight into them. Even though we were outnumbered and took a few hits, every one of us ran right through them. Because we'd caught them by surprise they started to panic and they turned and ran. I couldn't believe my eyes. Here was just six of us chasing 30 of them – and four of us were only 16.

We stopped going after them and turned back into the park. Tony put an arm around Steve, who'd had his brand-new Naf Naf jumper torn off his back, and put his other arm around me. Grinning from ear to ear, he said,

'Fucking brilliant, lads. That's made up for that carry on with the Rangers.'

That's true, we agreed, but added, 'By the way, we never ran from the Rangers, Tony. It was only a tactical retreat.'

We all laughed at that and made our way to the ground. If we had been playing Hibs or Aberdeen, would six of us have run into that park to take on 30 of them? I doubt it. I believe that 95% of what we did was psychological – but it felt good anyway!

We never went to the game, which ended up being a battle for United anyway. They always seemed to struggle against the smaller teams, but they got the result that mattered, which was a 1–0 win, and moved on to the next round. As we made our way to the ground for the final whistle, we met a similar-sized squad of lads from Dundee who'd been doing the same as us during the game, which was walking about and taking in the scenery. They told us that the police had ordered our driver to move the bus to outside the ground, alongside the buses and cars of the 'normal' supporters. When we got to the ground, the final whistle had just gone and the crowd was coming out. As we got on the bus, I could see United's ordinary fans looking our way. They were intrigued and disgusted to see our coach surrounded by 20 coppers. This started to rub some of our boys up the wrong way and things began to get a bit heated as lads tried to get off the bus to confront the scarfers. Typically, the coppers went in heavy-handed to put our lads back on the bus.

As the scarfers' buses pulled away, with much head shaking on their part, the Old Bill got out the loud-hailer and told us to calm down and that we'd got five minutes to leave, otherwise it was the weekend in the cells for all of us. This did the trick and we prepared to set off – only for the United team coach to roll by. We caught sight of United's legendarily fiery manager, Jim McLean, and the chant of 'Jim McLean, baldy-headed cunt' went up. This even had the players laughing, as they'd probably had it tight from our hard-to-please gaffer.

As we were finally ready to go, Joe F and John T appeared to a great round of applause, as did Big Steve, who'd left the hospital with a few stitches in his head after the battle at the boozer earlier. Joe was sporting a cracker of a black eye, as him and John had had it off with another group of lads. With Joe's eye, Steve's bandaged head and Davie's smashed-up face, it looked as though the bus has been in a fucking car crash.

It just goes to prove that fun can be had anywhere if there are enough of you – even in Brechin!

This story is dedicated to the memory of three of the lads there that day: Davie, Billy and John. RIP, lads. You'll never be forgotten.

CHAPTER 21

A CCS WAKE-UP CALL

After Brechin, a few weeks passed without any further action until it was time for the CCS of Hibs to visit Dens. I have to laugh at the accusations of some lads from other teams who claim that we didn't travel back then. We were too busy trying to defend our own turf for one thing. When you think that we had the Old Firm here at least eight times a season, it's clear that there was plenty of action to be had back then without having to venture too far from home.

Even though we'd got a great result the last time the CCS came to Dundee, there was still a nervousness around the city leading up to the match. I can only put this down to everyone knowing that they were up for revenge in a big way.

I was up early on the Saturday and was out the door at 10:30 am and off to Steve's. Even that meant that I was on my toes, as my walk passed the pub that Hibs usually drank in when they were in Dundee. 'Surely they wouldn't be here at this time in the morning,' I told myself. 'You're just paranoid.' When I got to Steve's I told him that I thought the Hibs might be in town early so we should get cracking.

He shook his head. 'Are you joking, Kenny?' he said. 'It's only just after 10:30 am. They'll never be here at this time in the morning, but we'll head in town now if you want.'

So the two of us set off and walked down Arklay Street towards the town.

We got about halfway down Arklay Street when I said to Steve, 'Who the fuck is that coming up the road?'

'What are you talking about?' he replied. 'There's no one there, it's just your imagination.'

We got a bit closer and I was convinced that a firm was walking up the road. 'That's the Hibs, mate, I'm telling you,' I said to Steve.

As we were both feeling edgy, instead of carrying on walking, we jumped on a bus into town, much to Steve's annoyance. However, I had the last laugh when we immediately passed about 150 Hibs marching up Arklay Street. We looked at each other and burst out laughing. 'Fuck, that was close,' I said to my now-relieved friend.

'I canna believe they're here this early. We'll have to tell everybody as soon as we get into town,' he replied.

Of course, once we got to the city centre there was hardly anyone there, as it was still too early. There were only a couple of lads and it was clear they'd also seen our rivals from the capital. 'They've already been through the town' said one of them, Sammy. 'There was no one here. I was walking about on my own waiting for everyone to appear, when a mob of around 150 just walked past and I about shit myself!'

I told them that we'd seen them on Arklay Street.

'They must be on their way up to the Ambassador,' said Big Steve.

I thought back to how I'd walked past that pub on my own earlier. It was my lucky day that I'd not bumped into 150 CCS hell bent on revenge following their last visit. Maybe I wasn't so paranoid after all.

The few of us began the walk up to Dens. We spoke about how the Hibs always come up with something to throw their rivals off the scent and how we should have anticipated them doing something like this. As we approached the top of the hill, about 20 older lads appeared and didn't look happy at all. Most walked past without even acknowledging us, but a couple stopped and spoke. 'The Hibs are already here,' said Sammy excitedly.

'Tell me about it,' said Ricky. 'We just got ran to fuck outside the Ambassador.'

Steve asked what had happened and Ricky told us, 'Around 70 of us, all older boys, walked up to the Ambassador with no Old Bill in sight and they came pouring out. Instead of hitting them as they started coming out, we waited for them all to get out, as we were confident with the firm we had that we would take them. We didn't think there would be as many as there was at this time of day. Just at that, a supporters' bus pulled up and they decided to join in the fun as well. We just panicked and after the first few punches we got done. We'll have to try and make up for it after the game.' He then told us to stay away from the pub, as the Old Bill were now all over it, and that his firm was off to another pub to hold court and plan a response.

We just looked at one another and didn't know what to

do. After a few minutes, we decided to go up to a mate's house to listen to the scores on the radio and then head to the game for the last 20 minutes. So, with 20 minutes to go, we arrived at the ground just in time for them to open the gates. Perfect timing, as usual. Inside, it was clear that we had a big and hungry firm of 250-plus. As soon as the final whistle went we piled out and tried to get straight into them. Of course, the boys in blue were there and held us back, forcing us off down the road. I believe that if we'd made it through we would have routed them, but it was not to be.

Our determined mob had become agitated now as we were marched by the Old Bill down the Provie and up towards the top of the Hulltoon. It was dark, eerie and pissing with rain and we thought that we'd missed the chance to exact some sort of revenge. As we walked down the Hulltoon the atmosphere became more and more intense. It's such a steep road at the top that if you gain a spot up there and stay there you are almost unbeatable. The further down you go the steeper it gets – and the more open you are to attack. With this in mind, we were trying to stop at the high ground but were being pushed down by the Old Bill. About halfway down, as we were getting nervous and wondering where the CCS were, a roar went up: 'COME ON!'

They appeared from nowhere and attacked us from the rear. They couldn't have timed it better if they'd tried. The lads at the back moved forwards out of surprise, setting off a domino effect right to the bottom of the hill. It was pandemonium, with lads falling over and getting trampled everywhere. In the meantime, the lads at the back were getting swamped as they tried to stand. It was the most frightening moment I've ever had in 25 years of going to football. But this wasn't fear of Hibs. It was all about the situation. Imagine the scene where you are on the steepest road you know and it's dark, misty and pouring with rain, while all around you 450 lads are running down it at full pelt. As you can imagine, it was chaos.

We tried umpteen times to regroup and have a go back, but it was hopeless. They'd done it again. The masters of the fly move had pulled off the single biggest stunt ever seen in Dundee – and they'd timed it to perfection. It proved again that the CCS were, in the mid- to late 1980s, the team to beat, no doubt about it. No other team could come close to pulling the stunts that they did in this era.

CHAPTER 22

NO REST FOR THE WICKED

The games now started to come thick and fast as United especially were doing well on all fronts. They were high up in the league and in the quarter-finals of the Scottish Cup and the UEFA Cup. The buzz around the tangerine half of the city was all about the team we were up against next in the UEFA Cup – the mighty Barcelona, managed at the time by Terry Venables, and boasting the likes of Gary Lineker and Mark Hughes in the team.

Football violence was forgotten for the night as more than 21,000 people crammed into our tiny stadium. The atmosphere was electric, as it always was on European nights. To add to the sense of occasion, a couple of hundred Spanish fans were parked in the Arklay Street end.

As the game kicked off, the atmosphere reached fever pitch. Our small club really was playing the Catalan giants. A few minutes after the start the unthinkable happened. A cross-shot by winger Kevin Gallagher flew over the keeper's head from 25 yards and went straight into the top corner. The place went absolutely bonkers: Dundee United 1, Barcelona 0. It doesn't bear thinking about now, does it?

The rest of the first half was end-to-end, but it was still 1–0 after 45 minutes. Their only real chance so far had been a glaring miss by Gary Lineker, who missed a tap-in from five yards. Compared to the first half, the second half was pretty uneventful and United held on for a famous victory. Funnily enough, we'd played them in 1966 and won home and away, to become the first team in Britain to defeat the Spanish giants on home soil (and remain the only team to have done so). The big question now was: could we repeat that performance and progress to the semi-final?

In the meantime, we had Rangers coming to visit that Saturday in what seemed like a never-ending season. There seemed to be a match every couple of days in Dundee that season. The usual rumours were doing the rounds in the town – that they'd got off the train, that the Old Bill had put them on a double-decker bus up to the ground – so we walked up to Tannadice to wait and see. When we got there, the 20 or so of us Under Fives had a brief battle with a similar number of ICF, but the Old Bill quickly got things under control. In the ground and after the game it was clear that there was a poor turnout from both sides, which I can only put down on our part to a long and expensive season taking its toll. A couple of minor skirmishes afterwards were all that could be mustered and the whole thing eventually petered out without much having happened.

The following midweek, we took on lowly Forfar in the quarter-final of the Scottish Cup. Due to our friendship with our Angus neighbours, no plans were made. A comfortable 2–0 victory ensured our passage to the semis, where we were unbelievably paired with our next-door neighbours, Dundee.

The SFA, much to the disgust of almost everyone in the city, decided that Tynecastle, the home of Hearts in Edinburgh, would host the semi. This caused uproar. Both clubs felt that it was totally unnecessary to travel to the capital when we could have played the game at either Dens or Tannadice. We were as happy as Larry, though, as it meant that we were on for a day out in Edinburgh.

Talking of days out in the capital, there was a legendary trip to Edinburgh around this time. I didn't make it, but I have heard enough of what happened to be able to tell the story. Dundee had drawn Meadowbank Thistle in the cup, and they were based in the Commonwealth Stadium close to the Hibs ground. Meadowbank were by far the smallest club in Edinburgh (and they were eventually bought by a businessman who moved them to nearby Livingston), but our boys decided to go over there anyway, hoping that they'd get the chance in the process to put one over on Hearts or, more importantly, Hibs.

As they were the masters of surprise, it was hoped that we could pull a Hibs-style stunt over them. Two minibuses left Dundee for Meadowbank that Wednesday night and every lad that went was as game as they come. They made a show of going into the game but left soon after kick-off and went off into the town centre to look for the CCS. Any Hibs that appeared were chased up and down Princess Street, but the fun was open to all-comers. At one point, the lads got involved in a vicious fight with some bikers and ended up pole-axing one of them off his bike. The Old Bill arrived en masse and more than 20 Dundee were arrested and spent two weeks on remand in Edinburgh's tough Saughton jail. They were later banned from every ground in Scotland for the rest of the season. Only around half a dozen Dundee escaped the Old Bill that night and had to hitch it home. One lad, my good mate John, was caught by some Hibs and got his arm broken.

But this was just to be a dress-rehearsal for the big one, which was talked about for weeks beforehand, with the usual letters going round and a trip to Easter Road finally arranged.

But first, there was the small matter of the UEFA Cup quarter-final second leg against Barcelona. The game was shown live on the TV, so it was off to a mate's house to watch it. Surely this was going to be the end of the road, we thought. Surely we couldn't get a result in the Nou Camp. We all settled down to find out.

A disappointing crowd of around 40,000 turned out, which by Barcelona's standards was less than half their normal home gate. Stuck up in the clouds high above them were about 1,000 United fans. The Barcelona fans probably stayed away as they thought the game was a foregone conclusion. But our 1,000 travelling Arabs didn't agree. When you think that, with 100,000 season-ticket holders, Barcelona only took 300 to Tannadice, while our 1,000 represented one-sixth of our hardcore of 6,000, it puts things into perspective. A few older lads had also made the trip to Spain and dropped hundreds of Dundee Utility calling cards written in Spanish over the bemused Barcelona Ultras below them.

United defended well in the first half and tried to hit them on the break. But, with five minutes to go before half-time, the Catalans scored to level the tie 1–1 on aggregate.

NO REST FOR THE WICKED

Our mates of the dark-blue persuasion, who'd started off hoping we'd do well, now began to take the piss once it looked as though our dream was over. The second half continued in the same vein as the first, with Barcelona pressing and United trying to hit them on the break. With 10 minutes to go it was still 1–1 when the unthinkable happened. Paul Sturrock, who was having a great game out on the left wing, suckered a defender into making a foul on the edge of the box, and when Ian Redford curled over the free kick there was big John Clark to thunder a header in off the bar. 'Oh, ya fucker,' I shouted as the Arabs among us broke into a jig of delight. 'We're through! We're through!' I hollered deliriously.

'Calm down, Kenny,' I was told. 'It's not over yet.'

'They've got to score three now,' I reminded the boys, because of the away goals rule, and with that we were all off singing and dancing again.

With just a couple of minutes to go, Sturrock set off again and delivered a pin-point cross to the back post, where Ian Ferguson directed a header into the bottom corner. By this stage we were doing cartwheels across the floor of my mate's house. Even the blue noses were staring at the TV in disbelief. The final whistle went and it was all over: Dundee United 2 Barcelona 1 (3–1 on aggregate). We'd beaten the Spanish giants home and away – not once, but twice. When the draw was made for the semis we got the German side Borussia Mönchengladbach. The final was a real possibility.

Next up on the domestic front was the big one – Hibs away. We'd talked about this one and planned it for weeks and we knew that we'd have to be at full strength to take them on.

AFTER THE MATCH, THE GAME BEGINS

On the morning of the game we met in the usual spot. It was clear that the game was a big one, as the usual six or seven of us were now 20. We were greeted by the ever-excitable Dek, who claimed he'd been there for two hours because he couldn't sleep! We walked into town down Albert Street, where a lot of the buses from the housing schemes run, and nearly every bus was filled with lads. It was apparent that this was going to be a bigger than normal firm today. When we got to the centre of town the word was to go to our HQ at the time, the Executive Bar. When we got there, the numbers looked a little low, and there was about 100-plus of us. Joe came in and said what we were all thinking: 'This is pish. It looks like there is only 150 tops.'

I chipped in with: 'I wonder where the fuck every cunt else is then.'

With that, we drank up and headed out.

One of the boys, Andy, asked me if I could come with him and head down to the station by a back route, as his old man was drinking in a pub on Union Street with his mates and Andy didn't want him to see him. So we left and walked along and down the next street. When we came out at the Union Street, we were greeted with the sight of our firm in all its glory. It was three deep, from the station doors across the car park, over the dual carriageway and right to the top of Union Street and around the corner. We turned and started hugging one another and cackling like a couple of kids.

We hurried up and caught up with our mates who were crossing the dual carriageway. They were just as hyper as we were. Unfortunately, our secret get-together wasn't as undercover as we'd thought. Everybody in Dundee was talking about it – and so were our friends the police. When we tried to enter the station, a massive line of Old Bill were standing at the top of the stairs. They searched every last person before letting them down on to the platform. The amount of knives and coshes that were dropped on the floor and kicked away was frightening. When we finally boarded the train, a head count revealed around 350. It sounded a lot nicer to the ear than the 150 that we thought we had earlier.

When the train stopped in Edinburgh, I'd never seen anything like it. A lot of mobs up and down the country will have experienced that feeling when 300-plus lads pile off a train in another town. No scarves, just purely lads dressed head to toe in designer gear, some young and some old. There was no gang fighting, just everyone together for the same reason. You can take all the drugs you like, but I'll tell you that the rush that went through my body that day when I walked along that platform in Waverley Station in the capital was like nothing I've experienced in my life.

We burst out of the station doors and the huge police presence was only able to walk with us, rather than tell us where to go. We tried to make a run down one street, with flares going off and bouncing all over the place, but more coppers arrived and the rest of the walk became slightly more civilised. A few Hibs were spotted walking around on their own, as if they were keeping an eye on what was happening, but they never came near us. Whether or not they didn't know if we were coming, or didn't want to lose face, we'll never know.

Just as we entered the ground, another flare was fired up into the air, and then one went off at the Hibs end, much to the annoyance of the Old Bill and the 'normal' Dundee fans. Funnily enough, when we got into the ground a casual from Newcastle happened to be in the Dundee end and he was walking around trying to be wide by asking why Dundee and United ran together, unlike Hibs and Hearts, who fought every other day like cat and dog. One of the older lads gave him a swift boot up the arse and told him to do one and mind his own business, so he disappeared out of sight. Funny thing was, if they didn't know we were coming, why send in a scout to town to suss us out? Very strange.

With about 20 minutes to go we decided it was time to go. This didn't bother me at all – after watching United beat Barcelona, this didn't appeal much. Unfortunately, the walk back to the station was almost identical to the one going there. All we could do was try to escape from the Old Bill every other two minutes to look for the non-existent CCS.

So, we got back on the train home after a pretty uneventful day. But I still always remember that game with a smile on my face, as it's not every day a small city like ours takes 350 lads away from home and has one of the most feared and respected firms in Britain hiding at home to save face. The CCS said later that they had been in the north of England at a game and didn't know that we were coming. I'll let you make up your own mind on that one.

The next big game was the German giants Borussia Mönchengladbach at Tannadice in the semi-final, first leg, of the UEFA Cup. Again, like the Barcelona game, we all went as fans only. Another big crowd packed into Tannadice to get behind the team and to try to help get them become the first Scottish team to reach the UEFA Cup Final. A disappointing match saw United fail to break down a stubborn German rearguard and the game ended goalless. The Germans were cock-a-hoop, convinced that they'd done the job in Scotland. They bragged for the next fortnight that they'd roll United over 6–0 in Germany.

Three days later, we had another semi-final, against Dundee, in a game played at Tynecastle, the home of Hearts. The city had been buzzing for ages, as the match guaranteed that one of Dundee's teams would be in the end-of-season showpiece final. United were trying to make another final – and win the cup for the first time – and Dundee were trying to get to their first final in years. The wind-ups had begun in earnest and we all wanted our own team to win, but on top of that the casuals had their own agenda.

The majority of the Under Fives had arranged to go on the football specials that were laid on for the fans of both clubs. Me and Steve, on the other hand, through his brother-in-law, had heard that the older lads were travelling on an early service train in order to try to have a pop at either Hibs or Hearts. We were welcome to come along, he said, as long as we kept it to ourselves and didn't spoil it by inviting the whole town. We did as we were told and so just four of us, me, Steve, Garry and Big Alan, made our way down to the station to catch the 125 service at 9:30 am.

When we boarded the train, it was clear this was the Utility. There were over 100 lads – and we must have been the youngest, at 16 and 17. A few tins of beer were passed around and after a while the Dundee and United lads started winding one another up. I know this must seem strange to any lads from a city where there are two or more teams, but the only way I can explain it is that we were like a family. You'll argue about things until you're blue in the face, but you back each other up in a fight till the death. That was how it was that day. In fact, just as the banter was starting to get out of hand, the tannoy announced that we were approaching Edinburgh and we all suddenly remembered why we were there together in the first place.

A quick decision was made not to get off early at Haymarket but to carry on to Waverley Station, Edinburgh's main station. There were a few coppers around when we got off and they followed us up the bridge and on to the street. We were on the march by now and walked right along the middle of the famous Princess Street, but there were no takers. A few lads appeared but vanished just as quickly. We walked up to their usual hangout, the Wimpy, but again no one showed. We hung around for a minute to see if anyone would come, but one of the top lads reminded us that the longer we hung around the sooner the Old Bill would be on our case. It was decided that we would head off to a nearby pub.

A few pints later, we bounced across the road and into the local strippers' bar. There was only room for around 80, but somehow 120 of us squeezed in and waited for the nice lady to come out and entertain the troops. The manager kept telling us to calm down, only to be answered by a cry of 'UTILITY NATIONAL FRONT'. This was followed by the optics getting smashed as we proceeded to wreck the place. The manager ducked behind the bar and must have called for the police, as they soon arrived en masse.

The fun was over and we were escorted to the ground. When we got there, most of the lads with us, being brought up in the 1960s and 1970s, were Dundee, whereas I was United. I decided to stick with the lads in the Dundee end rather than go to the United section on my own.

We stood at the back, which was my decision, as I didn't want to be right in among the blue noses when the game kicked off. Around the 20-minute mark, a great turn and shot from United striker Ian Ferguson put us 1–0 up. I was smirking so much that my mates threatened to blow my cover. The goal stung Dundee into life and before long they'd equalised and then gone 2–1 up. There was absolute bedlam in the Dundee end, but I must have looked right out of place as I was the only one standing there looking pissed off. After half-time, things changed again. United levelled it at 2–2 and then, in what was an unbelievable game, went 3–2 up.

Suddenly, the Dundee end was down in the dumps and it was me trying to keep a lid on my excitement. After a nerve-shredding last couple of minutes, United held on to win the tie and go through to another cup final. I couldn't get out of the ground quick enough, feeling that I'd spent quite enough time with the 'enemy'.

We all walked up the Gorgie Road together and, apart from a few scarfers who were a bit heated with each other, there was no bother. We settled down in a pub in Hearts territory, across from Haymarket, and had few beers. A few of the lads came into the pub and said that they'd headed a few lads they believed to be Hearts, but apart from that it was pretty much another no-show from Edinburgh's big two. A lot's been said about Dundee at home in the 1980s, but there was hardly ever a game when a firm came to our city and never met with any opposition, especially on a big day like this one.

Me and Big Alan decided to bunk on the special and head home, as the older lads decided that they were getting the later train home to wait and see if Hibs showed face. The theory for us was that we'd get home early, but as we sat on the train swapping stories about the day's events with a few boys it suddenly ground to a halt. At first we thought someone had pulled the emergency cord, but a scarfer came through the carriage and told us that a United fan and a Dundee fan had started to argue about the match and one of them had got stabbed. So much for the peaceful rivalry! And they called us casuals hooligans!

After an hour waiting on an ambulance, with the train stopped in the middle of nowhere, the joke began to wear thin. If it wasn't for Shaggy and his daft wisecracks, I'm sure someone would have lost the plot. Another 15 minutes, the train started up and we got back to Dundee – an hour and a half late. Would you believe it, but the service train with all the older lads had already arrived. They told everyone that Hibs had appeared as they waited for the service train and the boys had done the business on them there and then. They'd also managed to squeeze in a set-to with the Old Bill before they got back as well.

Alan and I just laughed and walked away. 'Whose bright idea was it to get on the special then?' he said. 'How'd we manage to get home 90 minutes late and miss a fight with Hibs and the Old Bill!'

'At least we beat you blue-nosed cunts,' I replied and we both laughed and walked up the road.

The rest of the season was a non-event, hooligan-wise, but there were still some of the biggest games in United's history left to play. First up was the UEFA Cup semi against Borussia Mönchengladbach in Germany. A couple of thousand United fans made the trip, and a few older lads went too. Near the end of the first half, United scored their compulsory away goal, as a goalmouth scramble ended with Ian Ferguson heading home the opener, much against the run of play. The second half was a complete back-to-the-wall job as the cocky Germans pushed forward, realising they now had to score twice. They hit the post, the bar, had shots kicked of the line and, just as United looked as though they were going to cave in, we broke away right at the end with Kevin Gallagher. He looked as though he was going to shoot, but squared the ball to Ian Redford, who took a touch, rounded the keeper and calmly rolled the ball into the net. Cue absolute pandemonium in the United end. How I wished I was there. The whistle went and that was it – little old Dundee United were in the final of the UEFA Cup and were the first Scottish club to do so.

The first leg of the final itself was away against the Swedish team, Gothenburg. Thousands of Arabs made the trip, but due to lack of finances I had to make do with the TV. The game was played on a terrible pitch and ended up 1–0 to Gothenburg. After a long season, United looked jaded and, all things considered, it was a good result for us, apart from not getting our customary away goal.

After the final league game of the season, we just had the last two cup games to play – the Scottish Cup Final and the second leg of the UEFA Cup against Gothenburg. First up was St Mirren for the domestic trophy. Surely this time, we thought, we'd break the Hampden hoodoo and win the cup for the first time against the lowly saints. As was normal for us, but probably unusual for most other teams, we didn't take an organised mob to the final. As our firm was a mixture of United and Dundee, the blue noses didn't really want to be at the final to see us win. This was understandable, as us Tangerines would have felt the same way if the shoe had been on the other foot. Those who went to the final went not as casuals but as normal scarfers for the day.

A few of us got on the special train heading for Glasgow, where we met a few other lads and settled down with a few tins for the journey ahead. The trip seemed to pass in no time at all. As it was a football special the train by-passed the city centre and stopped at Mount Florida tube station, right outside the National Stadium. We got off and had a walk around the ground to kill time. We ran into small groups of LSD and some small but half-hearted battles went off outside the ground. To be honest, myself and probably the others didn't want to get lifted and miss the best chance we'd ever had of finally winning the Scottish Cup. Once in the ground, it was amazing to see the amount of part-time fans that, to me, always spoil these occasions.

United have a hardcore of around 6,000, St Mirren even less, but there were about 50,000 at the final. It looked good but it pissed me off. Where were these people week in, week out? As in the UEFA Cup Final first leg, we looked a bit jaded and struggled to break them down. Then, in the second half, Ian Ferguson knocked one in from close range and it was bedlam in the United end. It looked as though we were finally going to do it. But then one of my mates pointed to the linesman standing there with his flag up, ruling the goal out for offside. Almost immediately, St Mirren broke up the park and bulleted one in from the edge of the box and we lost the cup again, 1–0.

I didn't even bother looking for St Mirren after the whistle went. I just wanted to get out of there and get home. But when we arrived back at Dundee we found a load of Dundee lads waiting for us in order to take the piss and give us a slagging.

A few days later, on the Wednesday, we dragged ourselves to Tannadice for the small matter of the UEFA Cup Final, second leg. The big question was: could the players summon up one last effort, after an unbelievable season, and put behind them the disappointment of the previous Saturday's cup final defeat to St Mirren. Tannadice was absolutely full to the rafters. As the teams came out, me and a few of the lads found a space behind the goal usually reserved for away fans. The atmosphere cranked up a gear as we soon forgot Saturday's disappointment and got behind the team. After a few near-misses from United, the unthinkable happened and Gothenburg broke and scored to make it 2–0 on aggregate. It now meant United would have to score three. Into the second half, and big centre-half John Clark, now playing as a striker, turned on the edge of the box and rifled one into the bottom corner to make it 1–1 on the night. United huffed and puffed for the rest of the game, but couldn't find another gear. When the final whistle went, it brought down the curtain on a mega-disappointing end to the season – one that I'll never forget and will never see the like of again.

As we walked out of the ground, we contemplated the

trophy-less season that had just ended on the park – and we comforted ourselves that at least we'd had plenty fun off it!

CHAPTER 23

THE BEGINNING OF THE END

Season 1987/88 would see the beginning of the end of the first generation of the casual movement in Scotland. Graeme Souness, with a season under his belt at Glasgow Rangers, had begun to pull away from the rest. Alex Ferguson had left Aberdeen to become manager of Manchester United and Dundee United manager Jim McLean had begun to lose his grip. With Rangers threatening to dominate the league, it fell to Celtic to pick up the challenge, as United, Aberdeen and Hearts all began to go into decline.

Lads began to drop out of the casual scene and mobs fell to their lowest numbers for three years. In Dundee, this forced a new bunch of lads to reorganise themselves and resurrect the Alliance Under Fives. Most of the lads that I'd jumped about with had disappeared for their own reasons. Many, like myself, had started to settle down and were letting go of the football scene.

New young lads from Stobie, like in every other

housing scheme in Dundee, were coming through the ranks. They were forming into smaller but much more tightly knit – and violent – firms. From my area, there were lads like Tony and Ryan, to this day among my best ever friends. My co-author John, Terry and Scott from Ardler, Paul, Barry, Johnny, Gilky and Fraser from the town, Ian and Ronnie and others would form the backbone of the mob for years to come. This new young and violent firm, together with the hardcore of the original movement, would see Dundee not just compete with the rest in the 1990s but arguably become Scotland's number-one firm. Here's the first input from John about how he became a fan of the other club in the city and also how he, as with every other lad in Dundee, came together under the one firm. It is a tale of how his young firm came about, took on the mantle of what had gone before them and then eclipsed everything that had happened so far.

John's story, part one

I was born in Dundee in 1972, into a family that didn't have any sort of football background. I was the youngest of three children, having an older brother and sister. In 1980, my family moved to Dens Road, which was just a 10-minute walk from Dens Park, the home of Dundee Football Club. As a result of this move, my brother took up an interest in Dundee FC and started to attend their matches. I would go along with him, and being younger would rarely pay to go in. More often than not I'd just jump over the wall via the phone box in Dens Road, or simply ask someone to lift me over the turnstile. When my brother saw that I was seriously interested in Dundee, he bought me my first season ticket.

Unfortunately, the 1980s was probably the worst decade to start following Dundee FC, as our neighbours across the street were about to turn the tide on us. Seeing our rivals Dundee United win the league at Dens Park in 1983 was probably the worst day of my life – or at least it felt that way at the time. United's highs were Dundee's lows, and that state of affairs continued throughout most of the 1980s. To say I didn't like going to the derby games against United back then was an understatement. Nine times out of 10 they would hammer us.

My first encounter with football casuals was in the season of 1984/85. I was standing with my brother in the Derry watching Dundee play Motherwell when I saw a group of around 20 lads climb over the wall into the Dundee end. They were all wearing bleached jeans and different-coloured cagoules. At first I thought they were Dundee fans, until they ran up the steps and started fighting with the people in the Derry. I was totally shocked but also intrigued at what was unfolding in front of me. More and more Dundee fans got involved and eventually the Motherwell casuals were beaten back down the steps. Lucky for them, the steward at the bottom opened the gate to let them out of the ground. They turned quickly and fled up the Provie Road to escape the bricks that were being thrown over the wall by the Dundee. I joined in but was stopped when my brother briskly grabbed me by the neck in disapproval. This began to happen more and more often, with most weekends seeing the casuals fighting around the stadium. As I walked down Dens Road, I would see hundreds of lads running *past me, followed by a roar, and you just knew a fight had broken out around the corner.*

Around 1986, I started going to the football with my best mate Sean. We would wear all the designer gear (don't worry, Sean, I won't mention the perm you had at school), and would stand in the terraces with the rest of the lads. It would be Dundee FC one week, then United the next. We were now fully fledged casuals.

Living on Dens Road also meant that it was only a 10-minute walk into town. It was quite common to bump into away mobs walking up the Victoria Road from the town on their way to the match. I remember one occasion when my dad asked me to take back some films he had hired from the local video shop in the town. I walked down Dens Road and just as I turned the corner into Victoria Road I banged straight into the ASC, the feared Aberdeen Soccer Casuals. I kept my head down and walked past them. As I got to the end of their mob I caught the eye of a couple of cocky cunts. One said, 'What the fuck are you looking at?' and took a swing at me.

I had the carrier bag full of videos in my hand so I swung it at him and hit him in the face. The bag burst open, scattering the videos everywhere. I quickly ran down the street and they didn't chase after me, so I waited until they were gone before I went back to pick up the broken videos that were lying scattered all over the pavement. I couldn't believe it. I was going to get a right hiding from my old man if he found out. I picked up the pieces, put them into the bag and continued on my journey to the video shop. When I got there I put the bag of broken videos on the counter then swiftly walked out before anyone could notice. A couple of months later, my dad came into the house going absolutely mental, saying that he had been banned from the video shop and that he owed them loads of money. I sat there all quiet, wanting to tell him what happened, but I just couldn't bring myself to do it. So, if you are reading this, Dad, you will now know the real reason why you got banned. Sorry, 20 years too late!

Around 1988/89, I'd been going to the football with the Utility for a couple of years with Kenny and the rest of the lads, but I was in a minority of younger lads at the time. During the late 1980s, when the majority of the older lads not just in Dundee but all over the country were ducking out of football and into the rave scene, we began to get a firm of younger lads together. As had been done five years previously, we decided to form our own version of the Under Fives, as our firm of young lads was beginning to grow. Around this time, one of the clubs in the city centre put on an under-18s night on Fridays. It became really popular and even a lot of over 18s came in and stayed until they were turfed out. All the same faces went to the club each week, including a lot of the football lads, and it basically became a breeding ground for the rebirth of the Alliance Under Fives (AUF).

My first job was as an apprentice printer and this allowed me to make calling cards and leaflets for the AUF. These calling cards became very popular and were distributed around all the pubs and clubs in the city centre, and mainly in the club on a Friday night. The buzz around town had come back again and we were dying to test ourselves at a match.

After one of the Friday nights, when the club had finished, everybody marched along towards the city centre singing 'AUF, AUF'. We must have been nearly 80-strong. It was an incredible feeling that we'd drummed up that size of firm already.

Our first away trip was planned against Aberdeen, and they don't come any bigger than that. The Friday night before, in the club, there was a huge mob of us all singing about what we were going to do to the sheep-shagging bastards. Things were looking good, or so I thought.

The next day, I walked down into the city centre and was met by a couple of the lads. When I asked them where everyone was, they replied that they hadn't seen anyone. We took a walk down to the train station to see if anyone was about and when we got there I was amazed to see that only about 15 had turned up. Pathetic. Everybody that had arrived was raging about the no-show from all the lads that had promised to go the night before. It ended up that there were just 18 of us, but we decided to go to Aberdeen for a laugh anyway, even though we knew deep down it was fucking stupid and we would probably get our heads kicked in. None of us had been to Aberdeen before, but we knew exactly what they were capable of and that they had a massive mob in the 1980s.

I'd seen with my own eyes how Aberdeen had brought 200 casuals on a train to Dundee one time. Just as I was thinking to myself, 'What a mob', another train packed with 200 more arrived an hour later. I'd also heard the stories of how at home they could easily pull in 1,000 casuals, so heaven knows what the fuck 18 young casuals from Dundee thought they were going to do.

As the train pulled into Aberdeen, I was totally shitting it, but I also remember feeling really excited. It was the not knowing what was ahead that got the butterflies *going – and the not even knowing how to get to Pittodrie from the station!*

We somehow managed to get to the ground without any incident, much to the relief of me and the rest of the lads. Once inside Pittodrie, all the stories about their massive mob seemed to be true. Fuck knows how many casuals were sitting there, but it seemed like they had their own section of the ground to themselves.

After the match, our little mob of AUF mingled in with the crowd and made our way back to the train station. We were standing on the platform when two lads came over to us and asked us where we were from. We told them we were Dundee and that we had been in Aberdeen all day. They just gave us a funny look and walked away. A couple of minutes later, the two lads appeared again, but this time they were with around 20 older Aberdeen lads. One of the young Dundee lads took it upon himself to get a luggage trolley that was sitting on the platform and shouted to them to come ahead. He then charged right into the middle of the Aberdeen lads and the rest of us followed behind. The Aberdeen lads backed out of the station and into the car park. After a brief scuffle, we headed back into the station and on to the waiting train. We couldn't believe our little result! We'd gone to Aberdeen, half expecting to get our lot, but ended up walking back and forward to the ground and getting a result before we got home.

Once back in Dundee, the 18 of us walked back up to the Boots corner in the city centre. There were around 25 Under Fives standing there, all in their nice new trendy clothes and thinking they were the dog's bollocks. When asked why they hadn't travelled north to Aberdeen, they gave us the usual excuses that they'd missed the train or had to work. The bottom line was that they just couldn't be arsed. Either that or they were too scared to take on the ASC. A couple of these casual dressers got a smack and were told that if they wanted to hang around with us they would be there at every game we went to. After that trip north we made sure that there wouldn't be any hangers-on in our young firm and that the weak would be weeded out.

Being a member of the AUF will live with me forever. We were young casuals and we loved every minute of it. The AUF didn't really have a main boy, as we were all mates and classed each other all the same. There were boys that organised things, but as far as having a top boy that was about as far as it went. It didn't mean the lads that organised things were the hardest in the AUF. There were just too many nutters in our mob for that to happen.

One of the early ways we would arrange things with other young firms was through the calling cards we had made. These had the numbers of the phone boxes on the corner of Reform Street where we hung around. We got hundreds of these cards made and wherever we went we would take them with us and leave them – at train stations, service stations or in all the bars and pubs that we visited on our football trips. Soon, casuals from other towns were phoning us up and asking to speak to the AUF. No one had mobile phones at the time, so this method kept us in touch with every firm in the country. We didn't arrange specific meets with anybody; just knowing if the team that was coming to Dundee that Saturday was bringing a mob was good enough for us. We quickly became a very close-knit, organised and violent young firm, ready to take on anyone who was up for it.

THE BEGINNING OF THE END

We had quite a few battles during the next year or so, on the days that I could escape the clutches of the girlfriend. The first one that season came out of the blue, as a few of us were hanging around in the afternoon sun. We decided to go for a dander down to the train station, just to pass the time, when all of a sudden newly promoted Morton, who were the visitors to Dundee that day, came charging out of the train station around 30-handed. They ran right into the 15 or so of us who were still in a state of shock at what we were seeing.

A brief but very violent fight took place in the train station car park, where one of the mates was almost taken off his feet by the casuals' weapon of choice at the time, the golf umbrella. The Old Bill arrived and escorted the Morton off through the centre of town. We followed them right up to the ground, but the Old Bill never let them out of their sight. We were amazed at the cheek of them, to waltz through the town with only 30, but we weren't to know then that the days of the super mobs were at an end and that the era of the more compact mobs was coming in. Lads were going to places like Aberdeen 20-handed and getting results, where before we wouldn't have dreamed of going there with less than 100.

Another game that springs to mind that season came later in the year. Our old foes the Hibs were visitors to Dundee. This was the day that was mentioned earlier, when a young CCS lad appeared among us laughing and shouted, 'Come on, Dundee, let's disco!', at which they came piling around the corner into the centre and it went right off. This resulted in a few arrests, so we waited until after the game until we had another pop. A few of us tailed them into town, as they had an escort, and we kept close by, hoods up and heads down, until we were almost in the city square. I remember it was pouring down with rain, which made the atmosphere tense. You want to have your wits about you if it goes off suddenly and not be blinkered by a hood.

The further we got into town, the more lads tagged on and, as we turned the corner at Boots and under the old Overgate front entrance, it was game on. The Old Bill now had a look of panic, as around 50 Hibs and 50 Dundee were side-by-side under this crowded tunnel-like shopping centre. We got behind them and started to tease them, singing, 'Come on, Hibees, come on, Hibees.'

Just as the Old Bill were going mental at us and trying to calm the situation down, I noticed one of the Hibs lads shouting, 'Come on, Hibs let's do it.' They turned as one and got straight into us.

It went right off and everyone was scrapping like fuck. Because of the tight space it was hard to move. I was fighting with this big lad when a blow to the side of my head from another Hibs lad made me lose my balance and I fell into the doorway of C&A and took a few boots. One of these crunched my knee against the door, which hurt like hell, but I managed to get on to my feet and bundled my way through the shop doorway. There I was standing like a right plum in C&A, hobbling like fuck with all the shoppers staring at me and amazed at what was going on. I just smiled and walked away, pretending I'd had nothing to do with it all.

Just as I was about to get back into the fray, the Old Bill split up the two groups and hauled off a couple of lads for a weekend in the cells. Not wanting to join them, I about-turned back past the wide-eyed shoppers. I gave them a smile again and scarpered through to the back of the shop and into the lift.

I eventually got back into the centre and my leg was killing me. I sat down on a bench and one of my mates came over and asked if I was all right. I rolled up jeans to see that I'd got this fucking huge graze on my knee and it was swelling up like a balloon. We hobbled off up the road with me thinking, 'This casual game's not quite all over yet.'

The next day out was a trip to St Johnstone, as told by John.

John's story, part two

A trip to Perth to visit our old rivals St Johnstone was one I was really looking forward to. It was my first visit there as a casual and would possibly be the last game at the old Muirton Park, which would eventually be demolished to make way for a superstore. Not a bad result from their point of view. The old ground was a crumbling wreck, so at least they got a brand new 10,000-seat stadium out of it.

It was a place that had good associations for Dundee fans, as it was where we won the league back in 1962, the only time we've ever won it.

This game with St Johnstone was a pre-season friendly. Strangely, it was played on a Saturday night, which was a recipe for disaster in our eyes. Fuck knows what the authorities were thinking when they allowed a derby to be played on a Saturday night. It was just too good to be true.

Ten of us younger lads who were trying to get the AUF up and running again decided to get the train early on the Saturday morning. Eager to get through and see if there was going to be any early action, we couldn't wait to get there. We'd been told many a story of trips to Perth by the older lads. A visit to Valentino's, which we knew sold all the latest football clobber, was also on the agenda. Knowing the MBS would lie in wait around the arcades or bars close to Valentino's made the trip all the more interesting.

When the 10 of us arrived in Perth, we planned to head towards the closest off-licence to get a carry out. With all of us too young to get into the pubs, we planned to hit the nearest park and to sit in the sun, have a drink and wait on the older lads arriving.

There was a couple of Old Bill waiting on the platform at the train station, but they didn't even take a second look at us younger lads. Straight across the road from the station is the Station Hotel, which has a big beer garden with a tall hedge around it. As our small firm went past the gate that opened into it, I looked inside and saw that the beer garden was packed with MBS. The Perth lads had mobbed up big time for the game and were out early doors. One of the Perth lads spotted us walking past the gate and the shout went up: 'Dundee's here!' They all jumped out of their seats and came steaming out of the garden. There must have been about 100 of the cunts in there. We were on our toes and we had only been in Perth for two minutes! They soon realised that there was only a few of us, and we were just the young Dundee Under Fives. Some of them gave up the chase; but, Perth being Perth, most continued after us. They soon got fed up, though, and we made our way out of the city centre. I must admit that I for one didn't expect to see a Perth mob *that big. Especially at that time sitting directly across from the train station when it was an evening kick-off. But, with Dundee being their closest rivals they were obviously well up for it.*

It was now around 1:00 pm and with Dundee's main firm getting on a later train we had at least six hours to kill. The 10 of us must have walked at least two miles out of the city centre, where we eventually found a park where we could drink our carry out and just lie about in the sun. After a few beers, we started getting excited at the prospect of what could happen later when our main mob got off the train. With the Perth mob in the station hotel beer garden, I couldn't wait!

A few hours had now passed, so we decided to walk back into the city centre. Tanked up, we thought that we could take on the world. Its amazing what a few tins can do for your confidence. After our earlier encounter with the MBS, we decided to take another route to the train station as we knew they would be well and truly pissed by this time and that if they saw us again we might not be so lucky. We managed to get into the train station unnoticed. The 10 of us were now standing on the platform, waiting on the service train due any minute from Dundee and hopefully packed full of Utility.

As it entered into the train station and opened its doors, loads of Dundee fans got off – but no casuals. I thought to myself, 'What the fuck is going on? Where is our mob?' I saw a couple of lads that I knew and asked them where everybody was.

They said there were about 150–200 back in Dundee, but the Old Bill were searching everybody on the platform before they let anybody travel through. This meant that they would all have to get the next train. Great, at least we knew that they were coming. With the next train from Dundee due in half an hour, we decided to wait on the platform for it. Perth Station is quite small. It has a bridge over the two platforms and there is only one way in and one way out. There was no way we were going back out, so we decided to stay put.

Suddenly, we heard a shout echo round the station: 'MBS! MBS!' The Perth firm were now running across the bridge to where our small Under Fives mob was standing. We were well outnumbered but had nowhere to run. The only way we could get out of this was to run across the tracks and over a wall into some back gardens. We decided quickly: fuck it, let's do it.

We looked to make sure there were no trains coming and then jumped on to the tracks. The funny thing about it was that we were all pissing ourselves laughing. Whether or not it was the fact we were getting chased again by the MBS, or were close to getting flattened by the next train, I'm not sure. None of this was what I'd had in mind when I left Dundee!

The day was turning out to be a complete nightmare and we still had half an hour to wait until Dundee's main mob arrived in Perth. I couldn't wait. We were all sick to death at having to run from those Perth cunts. Thankfully, the Perth mob didn't follow us over the tracks, so we just waited down the street a bit for the next train to arrive. We stood under a railway bridge so that we could see when the train came in. Half an hour passed and there was still no sign of it. Then, up the street from where we were standing, two police vans pulled up.

The roar went up: 'UTILTY NATIONAL FRONT!

UTILITY NATIONAL FRONT!' This was music to our ears and was what we had been waiting all day to hear. We jumped about in the road, hugging each other with sheer excitement. It was weird seeing Dundee's mob coming out the station towards us, as I was always in it, but it was a fantastic sight I can tell you. Very impressive.

In no time at all it was kicking off down the street outside the station. I thought, 'We'll see how game the MBS are now.' The 10 of us ran up the road towards the rest of the lads, but the main firm of Dundee was being forced down towards us by the Old Bill, who were struggling to get control.

Thankfully, we were now in the heart of the Dundee Utility mob and ready for action. We were maybe a little too cocky getting the early train like that, but we were young and eager and you learn from your mistakes. We had to say fair play to the St Johnstone lads. They had waited in that hotel beer garden all day and were obviously really up for it, but this was a different ball game now. The MBS had run down a side street from the hotel to try and have a pop at Dundee again. There were at least 100 of them, easily the biggest Perth mob I had ever seen, and they charged down the street, straight at us. Without a moment's hesitation, we also steamed straight into them. With only a few cops standing between the two mobs they had no chance of preventing the inevitable, as we clashed head-on.

One of the older lads turned to me and handed me his golf brolly. With me only being a 16-year-old, he must have thought I needed a helping hand – and I was only too happy to oblige! Because the Perth stood their ground, it kicked right off. It was complete mayhem. We were now fighting with them all over the road. Some big MBS bastard came running straight towards me and before I had a chance to lift my hands he caught me a cracker in the face and I hit the ground.

The lad, a lot older than me, surprisingly had an English accent. I thought to myself, 'You English bastard.' Before he had the chance to get another hit in, I picked myself off the ground and smacked him straight in the face with the metal tip of the golf brolly. It cut the side of his face and he backed off, holding his cheek. More Old Bill eventually arrived and got it under control, so I quickly disposed of the brolly before they rounded us up and escorted us to the match.

I later saw the older Dundee lad who had handed me the brolly. He said he had seen me hit the lad with it and that I'd given him a right cracker. I told him the boy's face was cut and the Dundee lad laughed. He said he had sharpened the tip of it so that it was as sharp as a knife. I couldn't believe it! No wonder the lad's face was cut. It was one of the first proper scraps I'd had at the football and left me hoping it wasn't to be the last. I was buzzing for hours after it.

I later found out that the Perth lads had some of the Huddersfield Town firm with them, which explained the lad with the English accent. It also explained how the Perth lads felt able to steam right into a Dundee firm of over 200. After the match, our mob had risen to around 200–250, and we immediately went looking for the Perth lads again.

We had to pass the home end, but they were standing on a hill inside Muirton Park and wouldn't come out of the ground for a second pop. We ended up getting

*escorted back to the train station without further
incident and were put back on the next train home. The
friendly between Dundee FC and St Johnstone was
never played again after that.*

For the next year or so, I reluctantly floated in and out of
the scene. Thinking I'd grown up, I met a girl and settled
down, leaving the lads and some of the new Under Fives
to get on with it and learn the ropes. I passed the time on
Saturday afternoons acting like I was 47 instead of 17. In
early 1989, I finally came to my senses and rejoined what
was left of the party.

One of the first weekends back ended up with one of the
most vicious street fights I've ever seen. After spending a
great Saturday night out with lads I felt I'd nearly lost
forever, we decided to venture along to the city centre to
hang around for an hour, as we did back then, before we
headed up the road. Earlier that day, two local amateur
football teams, which included some of the so-called local
hard men, had been out on a bender together. After
playing one another in an important cup semi-final, they
passed through the town and the usual nonsense started.

'Casual wankers,' was the shout, but this was par for
the course on a Saturday night from the older pissheads
passing through. This time, we were a bit hesitant to go
ahead as we knew it was the amateur football lads giving
out the abuse. I can't exactly remember how it kicked off,
but within seconds around 100 lads were going at it
hammer and tongs. We were taking casualties all over the
shop, with little battles going off everywhere you looked.
There were lads running about with blood pouring from
head wounds, but we were getting fired right in. We had

already gone past the point of no return, so we went for it big time. I found myself halfway up Reform Street, near the Old Bank Bar, and all the punters from the surrounding pubs were out on the street watching the show. Fuck knows where the ever-reliable coppers were, as they were usually on the scene within seconds, and this had now been going on for almost 10 minutes. Maybe they'd left off deliberately, hoping that some of us would come a cropper.

I started running down the street when I saw this big cunt backing off a few mates. Just as I got near him, I took him clean off his feet with the best punch I've ever thrown. No sooner had he hit the deck than the Old Bill arrived and it was time to scarper. We bolted in the direction of the Perth Road and the further we got from the town, the more my arm throbbed. We sat down at a bench to take a breather, by which time my hand was fucking aching.

'Fuck sake, mate, your hand's like a balloon,' said Rory.

'I think I've broken my fucking arm,' I replied. 'Fucking great, eh? First weekend back with the lads and this happens.'

'Aye, welcome back, mate, we missed you!' said Dean, and we all burst out laughing and headed up the road.

A visit to the hospital was put off until the next day, in case we bumped into any unwelcome guests after the battle. When I did go, I found that I'd three broken bones in my hand and a busted knuckle. I was put in plaster for the next three weeks.

The town was a bit of a no-go area for a couple of weeks after that, in case any gangster-type revenge was handed out. But nothing ever came of it, as I reckon they'd enjoyed it as much as us!

THE BEGINNING OF THE END

After a couple of weeks, I was keeping the fingers crossed that I could get the cast off and be back to full fighting fitness. It was due off the day before Scotland played England at Hampden, so I got myself to the local hospital to have it removed. Once it came off, my hand felt worse than before, really weak and sore, but at least the thing was gone. Although I was in a bit of pain, I decided to get myself to Hampden anyway for the visit of the auld enemy. It was a game I didn't want to miss; I'd missed enough in the past year and a bit already.

CHAPTER 24

THE AULD ENEMY

Times had changed, as had most of the mates. I was now knocking about the town instead of Stobie, as most of the mates had moved on. One of my best mates from the town, Dean, had hired a bus for the trip to Glasgow to take on the English. It was arranged to board it around the corner from the train station, at 11:00 am, so most of the lads would meet in the city centre beforehand. On the morning of the game, I met my old sparring partner Steve in the centre, then had a walk down to the station and met up with the rest of the lads. There were a lot of lads milling around, as some were getting on the train and had arranged to meet us in the centre of Glasgow. Also going was another bus-load from Ardler, so it looked as though Dundee would have around 150 representatives.

When the bus got going, it was time to get the beers open and get tanked up for the journey ahead. All that was spoken about from the minute we left until the minute we got there were stories from the lads who'd been to Wembley, and whether or not the English would appear mob-handed. Up until 1985, our friends from the south hadn't dared make an appearance in Glasgow, which was the complete opposite from the 70,000-plus Scots who invaded the English capital every other year. In 1985, a small mob of English tried it on in Hampden, only to get leathered. A few more braved it in 1987 and fighting all over the centre of Glasgow was reported in the tabloids the following day.

The mood on the bus was at fever pitch as we arrived in Glasgow, especially for me. This was new territory, our meeting up with the mobs we'd battled for years in order to team up and take on the mighty English football hooligans.

As soon as the bus stopped in Glasgow, we were off and into George Square, where there was already a fair amount of Dundee lads sitting around and drinking in the blazing sun. We mingled with the rest of the lads and asked them if they'd seen any English. We heard there were a few holed up in a boozer called the Lorne Bar, just off Argyle Street. Around 50 of us decided to go for a browse. Just as we got past Argyle Street and into the bus station at St Enoch Square the pub emptied and this was it: game on.

For years we'd seen all the footage of English mobs on the rampage, and now we were face to face with them. Around 50–100 of them, all looking over 30, came charging across the road towards us. They seemed content to just throw pint glasses and bottles at us and not come any closer. After the first barrage, we moved towards them and a few punches were thrown as neither side backed off.

As we geared up to charge across the road, the Old Bill come tearing round the corner in cars and wagons and we split in different directions. John and I ran back on to Argyle Street and temporarily got lost and separated from the rest of the lads.

Just as we decided to walk up the street and try and go back to George Square, a firm of what looked like 300-400 came walking towards us in the distance.

'Who the fuck is this now?' asked John.

'Fuck knows, mate, but stand in this doorway until they get close,' I replied.

Just as we got ready to disappear into the shop, the shout went up: 'Scotland, Scotland.' It was our boys and we crossed over the road and joined in the march. Right away I spotted one lad from Arbroath that I knew. Big Danny was a regular visitor to Dundee and ran with us from time to time. I asked him where this little lot was from.

'All right, Kenny, how's tricks?' he asked. 'Most of the lads here are Aberdeen. They've around 300, and around 75 of us got on the train they were on.'

'We just had it with the English around the corner, they must be about here somewhere,' I told him.

The word went around quickly and everyone quickened up and broke into a jog.

As we moved around the corner, the rest of the Dundee lads joined in. With lads from Celtic and St Mirren tagging on, the numbers were up above 600. This was now the biggest mob I'd ever been in and, just as we were getting away from the Old Bill, a mob of English appeared and it went off again. It was now almost out of control as around 1,000 lads were bang at it in the middle of Glasgow. I tried to swing at this big cunt with my left hand, as I was trying hard to keep my hand that was just out of plaster safe.

We continued the long walk to the ground. Every minute it seemed as though a roar went up followed by a charge, a few blows exchanged and more arrests. When we got into the big park just down from the stadium lads from all over the place began to appear, each one telling tales of the battles he'd had on the way to the match.

We eventually got into the stadium after what had seemed like hours after Queen Street. We were in the section right next to the English, who had brought around 2,000–3,000 fans with them. It felt a bit weird to be in the ground in that situation: we had the English to our left, 200–300 Aberdeen above us and above them a load of Hibs. It was strange mixing in with all the lads we'd battled with over the past five years, but hostilities were put to the side for the day in order to take on the English.

A pretty forgetful game ended 2–0 to the auld enemy, with Wolves striker Steve Bull coming off the bench to win the game for England. As soon as the final whistle went we made our way outside to have another pop at the English. Hundreds of lads gathered at the top of the steps to wait for the English, not realising that they were being held back in the ground until it cleared. Mounted police started trying to push us back down the huge stairway at the back of the terracing and after a minute of pushing someone threw a full tin of juice at one of the coppers on a horse and nearly knocked him off. This sparked a mass riot, with around 800 lads fighting the Old Bill. At the same time, a bunch of lads was trying to get over into the English end.

Bricks and cans were hurled at the Old Bill and every

time they charged at us hundreds of lads fell down the steep terracing and then ran back up again. With the horses jumping around out of control it was a miracle that no one was seriously injured. After around five minutes of battling, the Old Bill got on top and forced us out on to the street and back towards the town. If the English had come out then, I reckon they would have got murdered, but I suppose we'll never know for sure.

We started the long journey back to the centre, knowing that that would probably be the end of the fun for the day. Once back at Queen Street, we hung around for a while until everyone else arrived back. Apart from some English walking past with a huge escort, it was game over. We set off home minus five lads, who'd joined the more than 150 who were arrested that day.

As soon as we got back, we couldn't wait to tell the lads who hadn't made the trip all about what had happened. It had been a great day out and on top of everything else I'd avoided getting nicked and hadn't damaged my hand. Later on, I went up the road with a bird I'd had my eye on for ages. Happy days!

Walking up the road that evening, I thought of how the next season could be a return to what things had been like in the mid-1980s. Little did I know at the time that, within a couple of weeks, the exact opposite was going to happen.

PART 2

A NEW DAWN

CHAPTER 25

DANCING WITH THE DEVIL

During the summer, dance music swept throughout the country and ecstasy turned football hooliganism completely on its head. Battling non-stop for years with places like Aberdeen and Perth was swapped for nights dancing with them. Ducking down to avoid the hail of missiles when passing through their towns on the train was replaced with meeting them off buses and welcoming them into our clubs. Trading blows with sworn enemies was turned into hugging and sharing nights out with our new best friends. You really couldn't have made it up!

I must admit, that summer was right up there with the best I've ever had. I wish I had a camera for the first few times the Old Bill appeared at 7:00 am to witness dozens and sometimes hundreds of battle-hardened football thugs dancing on beaches and in forests, blowing whistles and wearing funny gear. Even my dress sense, which was more important to me than anything else, went right out the window as I spent the next few months walking around looking like a fucking Teletubby!

Unlike most of the converted lads, I still couldn't completely get my football head off. I was always being told, 'chill out, they're cool' by my mates, who had now completely forgiven all the old enemies. As much as I did enjoy my new Saturday pastime, I was never completely at ease at raves away from Dundee. When my gut instinct was proved right one night, it put an end to my straying too far from home when it came to dancing the night away.

Wayne from Dundee and Zammo from Perth got a spot spinning the discs in a club called Kronk in Dunfermline once a month on a Friday night. A car full of us decided to take it in and support the local lads. From the moment I walked in the club I felt uneasy. Even though the place was jumping, there was something not right. 'Settle down, man, everyone's all right,' I was reminded, but I wasn't convinced. After the night finished, we got back in the car and headed back to Dundee. I thought that maybe I had been paranoid, but the next time we went I felt even worse about the place and decided not to go again.

Four weeks later, the fun was interrupted when the back door was smashed in and a few members of the Hibs CCS steamed in and ran riot about the hall, attacking the ravers with baseball bats and other weapons. It was so bad that jail sentences were eventually handed out, with their alleged top man getting five years. It just goes to show how the old casual instincts were right after all. All this love and ecstasy nonsense was turning my mates' heads to mush!

CHAPTER 26

CAN'T STAY AWAY FOR LONG

Just after the New Year 1990, with a new decade upon us, I couldn't decide if I wanted to dance in the clubs or at the match. The word in the town was that the new, young and eager firm of Under Fives was up for a trip away. Dundee were struggling to escape relegation and decided to put on free buses for the fans to travel to Motherwell to get behind the team. This was something United had done a lot in the past as well, so it was agreed that the young team would cut their teeth at the home of the Fir Park club.

I twisted my old mate Steve's arm into coming, as he'd practically given up on the football scene. DJing was now his thing but he agreed to give it one last bash. We got on one of the supporters' buses and settled down at the back with a few other old faces.

As soon as we got to Motherwell we were off the bus and looking for the rest of the lads. This was in the days before mobile phones, so we had to wander around the

161

centre of Motherwell and try to find the rest of the mob. We bumped into a few of the old mates, and just as we stopped to speak a couple of lads from my young brother's school walked past and told us that a mob of Dundee had chased a few Motherwell and had headed to the ground.

I reluctantly agreed to go off to the game with the lads, as I had little interest in watching a struggling Dundee. The game had already kicked off when we got to the ground and as we approached the away end we bumped into a couple of young Motherwell lads. We had a laugh, winding them up about their invisible mob and left them to head towards the turnstiles. Just then, a shout went up behind us to come ahead. A quick look showed us that the five or so Motherwell lads were closing in on us fast – and they were all tooled up. We spread out a bit to present a bigger target as the Motherwell launched their bottles at us. This meant that they were now unarmed and we began to move in on them. Just as we did so, the Old Bill arrived and got us all up against the wall. Thinking that they would throw us into the ground, we were shocked when the coppers nicked all six of us – and let the Motherwell lads go.

Sitting in the back of the meat wagon, I couldn't believe how for years I'd evaded arrest when here I was at the first game back for a year and I'd been picked up for a shitty little battle. We were dubbed up in pairs in the station, which wasn't so bad, and we settled down in our new accommodation, hoping we'd be out soon. A couple of hours passed and it started getting busy. Looking through the small hole in the cell door, I recognised a few faces walking past. We found out that more than 100 Dundee had stormed the Motherwell end after the game and that another eight lads had got lifted.

The Dundee Under Fives on the march to the ground before the first game of the 86/87 season, v. Aberdeen.

Above: Tackling the hill at Aberdeen in the early nineties.

Below: The re-birth of the Alliance Under Fives, on their first away.

Above: The Cup semi-final in 1994, under attack from the Rangers as soon as we arrive in Glasgow.

Below: The police disappear and it's back for round two with the ICF.

Above: At Euro '96 against the auld enemy. Here we are, firming up in High Barnet.

Below: Charging the Motherwell end.

Above: 1992 – leaving the station in Aberdeen, calm and confident.

Below: Kev, Jim and Big Steve having a dip in Slovakia.

Above: Trafalgar Square is once again the backdrop as we are confronted by Middlesbrough.

Below: Under the watchful eye of London's finest.

Above: In Utrecht with Scotland.

Below: The late nineties – on our travels again as Dundee gain promotion back into the Premier League.

Above: Victory! Enjoying the walk to the ground after the rout with ASC in 1992.

Below: Holburn Street, Aberdeen, 1994 – the demolition begins.

Around 10:00 pm, the door opened and we were told to get up and get out. At first we were happy as fuck, thinking we'd be getting out. However, our thoughts of how we were going to get home now that the last trains and buses for Dundee had already left were interrupted by the announcement that we were not to be freed – we were being transferred to the main police station in Glasgow's London Road, as the Motherwell nick was getting overcrowded. This was now turning into a nightmare. It meant that we were to be held all weekend and were to appear in court on the Monday.

Sunday morning, we were taken into a room, quizzed by the CID and had our photos taken. On Monday morning, we were put five to a cell and told we'd be heading to court soon. It was a relief to see the mates and we had a bit of a laugh at the lovely hospitality of our Glasgow friends. Around 9:30 am, we were handcuffed together and taken on the jail bus to Hamilton Sheriff Court. We also had a few weegie arseholes with us on the bus who had been nicked for the usual house-breaking and so on. They were getting lippy on the road to court, saying we'd all get remanded and that we'd get it tight in Barlinnie, Glasgow's notorious jail. The thought that we might have to spend a couple of weeks in Barlinnie really hit home. I'm not afraid to say that my arse was now twitching!

All the lads from Dundee were put into one of the holding cells under the court building. One at a time, we got to see a duty solicitor. He told me that he'd do his best, but that as there were 14 of us there was a good chance we'd all get remanded. When I went back to the cell I paced back and forth like a headless chicken.

AFTER THE MATCH, THE GAME BEGINS

'Gonna sit down Kenny, you're making me nervous,' said one of the mates.

'You're fucking nervous? I'm fucking shitting it!' I replied and we all had a bit of a nervous laugh.

A couple of hours passed and the first lad from Dundee, young Colin, was sent up. We all stood at the door and waited for him to come back so that we could find out what had happened. A few minutes later, he came back down and was taken to another cell. One of the lads shouted to him, 'What's happening Colin?'

'Two-week remand,' he yelled back, and was led away.

'Fuck this!' I said and was told to sit down and calm down.

Another young lad, Tam, was up next, and the same two-week remand was handed out. He was followed by 16-year-old Dean, one of a pair of twins, who was given the same treatment.

Next up was the six of us who had been nicked outside the ground. I'll never forget us trying to get up those stairs all handcuffed to one another. It was like we were on death row and were being led to the electric chair. Up in the dock, it was hard to make out what was going on. Anyone who's been there will tell you that all you hear is mumbo jumbo from all the solicitors and judges. I could have sworn I heard the judge say 'bail opposed', and my heart sank. But, as we were led away, my mate Steve C turned around and said to me, 'Thank fuck, Kenny. I thought we were off to Barlinnie there.'

'What the fuck are you talking about? We've been remanded, have we not?' I replied.

But we hadn't. We'd been given bail.

I had to control myself as we walked back down those

stairs. I was almost doing handstands, even with the cuffs on! We couldn't get out of the court quick enough and ran out on to the street, flagged down some taxis and got ourselves to Queen Street Station.

I felt like a tramp on the train home, sitting next to a load of high-flying businessmen with their laptops and suits, while us lot hadn't washed or shaved for three days. Charming! As we neared Dundee, all I could think of was the three young lads who would be in for a hard time in the jail. Fucking shame. At least if we'd all been remanded they'd have had a bit of back-up.

As soon as we got home, it was up the road in a taxi. I got the compulsory hard time from the old man, but, after a little sob story, the old dear stuck on my favourite tea and ran me a boiling hot bath. Ah, to be home!

We had to travel back and forth to Hamilton Sheriff Court a couple of times, which was a pain in the arse, as the 200-mile round trip and days off work were sore on the wallet. At the third time of asking, we stood trial and, after a bit of bargaining from our solicitors, three of us pleaded guilty and three of us pleaded not guilty. The three that pleaded guilty were only fined £300, so we split it £150 each.

After all the nonsense of nearly going to the Bar L, it all ended up as a game between the solicitors and judges and a measly £150 fine each. That's the great British justice system for you. A crappy fine for us and huge fees for the lawyers. No wonder they drive around in the best cars and have houses the size of Southfork.

There was a buzz about the town for the start of the 1990/91 season. There weren't many of the original lads left, but there was a fast-growing, close-knit and violent young team coming through in their place. Only lads like Stu, Sammy, Big Steve, Jim K, Glen, John Mac and around another 30 or so had survived the pill-popping era. Together with an ever-growing Under Fives mob, we had a nucleus of just less than 100.

John had kept me informed over the summer that Lochee, one of the biggest areas in the city, was going to bring a good 50 young lads to the party. The talk in the town was that they had rediscovered the buzz as well and had a lot of young lads eager to join up and take on the rest of the country. It was arranged that some of them would come into the town centre the Friday night before the season started and organise what was going to go down. After a night out on the town, I decided to wander along and see what was happening.

When I got there, there was only around half a dozen lads about, including John, Fraser, the twins and a couple of others. I asked John what had happened and he told me that they hadn't yet appeared. Just as he said that, they came down Reform Street, at least 40-handed, singing their Lochee songs. Fraser walked up to greet them – and, instead of them returning the favour, they proceeded to start punching fuck out of him. I couldn't believe my eyes at what was happening. At first, I thought he must have done something out of order for them to tear right into him like that. To give Fraser huge credit, he got wired right into them and never went down once. The rest of us seemed to freeze for a minute, not knowing what to make of it, but we soon regained our senses and ran into them and they backed off. The Old Bill appeared and the Lochee mob disappeared up Reform Street. For our part, we walked back down to the centre, trying to figure out from Fraser what it had all been about. He said that he was at as much of a loss to know as we were. However, what we did figure out that night was that revenge was on the cards and that the Lochee lads would not be welcome in the firm.

After that night, Lochee – and a load of lads from Fintry, for similar reasons – were never to run with the firm again. This meant that we'd lost lads from around 40% of the city. For 10 years afterwards, there were some horrendous beatings handed out on all sides, in tit-for-tat revenge attacks. These have affected everyone. Even my younger brother was found by my mother outside the house after getting a serious tanking. We know who the lads who did it were, and we'll never forget.

But, instead of this incident decimating the firm, it actually made us more close-knit, spurring us on to be the best in the country.

The fun wasn't over yet. Far from it!

CHAPTER 27

BACK HOME FOR AFTERS

The start of the new season saw United at newly promoted St Johnstone, in Perth, for the first game. In years gone by, this would have been a hooligan's dream, as not only were they our arch enemies but they were also the closest, only 20 miles down the road. There wasn't the same buzz though, as the vast majority of their top boys – and a good few of ours – were still dancing in a field somewhere and popping pills. Not knowing who would be there to greet us, or who would be going, I'd arranged to go in a mate's car. We drove into the town early doors to find out the arrangements for the day ahead.

A lot of old faces were about and they agreed to get taxis down to Perth in order to avoid the Old Bill and to meet up in a certain pub. When we arrived in Perth, we had a drive around and decided to have a nose at the ground. Our driver and the mate he had with him weren't lads, but they agreed to take me and Steve down there, as long as they got to the match. We got the ground and parked up and just as we walked through the car park seven Perth lads came towards us looking for it, so we duly obliged. Steve and I went straight into them and actually backed them off. I remember turning around to get my bearings and saw that the two lads who had come in the car with us were frozen to the spot.

After a brief few blows, the Old Bill came running up, so it was time to split. Steve and I headed up through the car park, to the top of the hill, and had a look back down to where the Old Bill had a hold of the two lads, who were still rooted to the spot. Laughing our heads off, we jogged along the road and kept an eye out for the rest of the lads. We later heard that our driver and his mate were let off with a warning, which was good news. Funnily enough, they never gave us a lift to the game again!

We got another 100 yards along the road when we bumped into Bell, who was driving around in his motor looking for any lads. He stopped and rolled down his window. 'What are you two up to?' he asked.

'Just had it, with a few Perth, in the car park. We had to scarper, as the Old Bill arrived and nicked the two lads who took us through!' I replied.

'Jump in then, and I'll take you back to the boozer where I dropped the rest off,' he said. So we drove back into town and met up with the rest of the lads.

When we got into the pub, there were around 100 Dundee lads drinking there. None of them was bothered about going to the game, so we got a round in and asked if anything had been going down. 'A couple of young lads have been out for a browse and seen a few Perth lads. They told them where we are, so they could come at any time,' said Kingy. So, we settled down and waited for them to arrive. A couple of pints later, and just as the lads were getting impatient, the familiar shout went up: 'Here they are. Let's do it.' It was time to forget about the pint, squeeze out the door and game on! We went through them like a knife through butter. This to me was the day that the new wave of Under Fives came of age. After a brief stand from Perth, the young lads, aided by a few veterans, were all over our old rivals and they were soon on their toes. It was a sight to behold, to see a firm that always gave us a run for our money get run like that on their own turf – especially as our numbers were a bit depleted because of the ecstasy craze.

Perth in the 1980s were in my opinion the best of the rest. Easily the gamest firm of the smaller teams, but on this day they were no match for the young Dundee Under Fives. When they turned and ran away we heard the familiar sound of cop car sirens ringing out, so everyone about turned and headed back to the pub. Bell grabbed my arm and we ran into the car park at the back and into his car. 'Come on, let's see if we can catch some of them in the car. The Old Bill will be all over the pub like a rash,' he said.

So, we waited a second and then casually drove out past the police and down the road to look for any Perth. No one seemed to be around, as they looked as if they had retired for the day, embarrassed. Instead of going back to the pub, which was heavily guarded by the police, we went back to Dundee to try and catch the end of the Dundee v Partick Thistle game at Dens.

As soon as we were back in Dundee, we had a drive around town to look for any Partick. There was no one at the train station, so we decided to head up the road. Passing the bus station on the way home, we noticed there was a mob hanging around so we drove around the block. As we neared the station, a few lads walked into the middle of the road towards the car, as they must have clocked us driving round. Bell slowed down, and as I thought he was going to stop I jumped out and ran towards them, only for him to drive away. Now, I'd a quick decision to make. There were now more lads coming towards me and a quick estimate took their numbers up to around 50. I exchanged a couple of blows with the first lad to come towards me and then I turned and legged it.

I managed to escape into the Wellgate shopping centre and mingled in with the shoppers. With time to reflect on what had just happened, I was raging at my mate for driving away.

I waited a couple of minutes until I thought the coast was clear and then headed back out. Instead of walking back towards the bus station, I headed off towards the centre of town – and there was the fucking batmobile coming round the corner. 'Where the fuck did you go, you prick? I nearly got my life taken!' I angrily said to Bell.

'Sorry, mate, I didn't fancy getting the car wrecked and I thought you'd jump back in. Look get in, there's around a dozen of them walking from the bus station to the train station,' he told me.

Against my will, I hopped back into the car to see if I could take my anger out on someone. We stopped on the way and picked up a couple of lads in the centre, who'd no idea that the Partick were in town. Just as we turned the corner across from the station, there was the dozen or so Partick away to get the train. We stopped the car and ambushed them. Still boiling about the earlier incident, I was the first out and into them. But, before we could get a good toe-to-toe with them, they turned and ran like fuck. Instead of giving chase, we got back into the car. Just as we closed the doors, about half a dozen cop and CID cars came at us from all different directions. They trapped us and we were nicked.

'Fuck sake, that's all I need,' I shouted.

They dragged us out one by one and put us in separate cars. On arrival at the police station, we were charged with the usual breach and affray and led down to the cells.

I settled down to prepare for the monotonous weekend ahead, but at around 10:00 pm I was taken from my cell and told to put my shoes on. I thought that I was going to get my picture taken or be interviewed, so I couldn't believe my luck when I was taken through the front door to where my grim-faced old man was standing. He'd obviously been down there asking if they'd let me out. Even though I would be in for a grilling from him, it was a whole lot better than spending a weekend in that shit hole.

Up the road, a telling-off, quick shower and then back into town for a night on the tiles. Fantastic! It was a much better end to the night than when we got nicked at Motherwell I can tell you.

The court date was a couple of months after the Motherwell one and was over in less than an hour. The witnesses from Partick, to their credit, all told different stories and the case was thrown out, much to the annoyance of the coppers at the back of the court. After a quick 'Thank you, your honour' and a nice grin at the boys in blue, we went off down to the boozer for lunch and a few celebratory drinks.

CHAPTER 28

THE RISE TO
THE TOP

The next big away for me was Aberdeen in March 1992. It came almost exactly six years to the day after my first journey to the Granite City.

This was a fixture that, in the past, we wouldn't have wanted to travel to with anything less than 150 lads. But helped on by the super confidence of the new Alliance Under Fives, aided by 30–40 battle-hardened lads who were now out of their teens and into their mid- to late twenties, this was to become a fixture that held no fears for us.

We were joined on the trip north by four lads from Colwyn Bay in Wales, who a few of the lads had met on holiday, to take the total to around 80–100. This was the first time I'd travelled to Aberdeen for a while and was the first time I went with the young lads. The mood was so relaxed it was unreal. It wasn't as if we were away to take on Aberdeen, it was more like going to some small Third Division outfit.

AFTER THE MATCH, THE GAME BEGINS

I sat beside Stu, Sammy, Kingy and Glen for the journey. Ronnie, who I hadn't seen at the football since the days when he walked about with that cagoule on, was also there, sitting beside the Welsh lads. I remember thinking, 'This young team isn't half bringing out all the old boys.' We talked about whether or not the ASC would be out and about and one of the lads said that they knew we were coming, as phone calls had been exchanged telling them that we were on our way.

After a couple of tins, we passed Stonehaven and began to ready ourselves for getting off. As the train pulled into the station, we piled out on to the platform and, instead of running and singing like a pack of wild animals like we'd done in previous years, we seemed to calmly walk out of the station and on to the street.

Surprisingly, there were no police about and we headed off up the hill towards Union Street. We decided to settle down in a bar called Clarkies, which is situated in a back street just off Union Street and is perfect for seeing if any opposition are on their way. The young lads had certainly done their homework.

Everyone was in great spirits as we had a few beers, and the bar staff seemed to not mind us being there as we weren't giving them any hassle. I had a walk about the pub, speaking to all the lads and ended up sitting down beside the older mates. A couple of coppers walked past but never came in and gave us any hassle, which I found surprising. Usually, they'd be down on you like a ton of bricks in Aberdeen, especially as they'd had more practice at it than any other police force in Scotland. We weren't complaining, anyway.

After an hour of sitting in the bar, the young lads started

to get agitated. Just as they were starting to think about going to look for the ASC, they came to us. 'They're here, they're here. Come on, Dundee,' was the cry that echoed around the pub. This was it. Time to go to war! The doors weren't wide enough to allow all the eager lads out and it took a few minutes to get us all on the pavement. As soon as I got out there was no holding back. We spread out across the street and went down into them. Just before we got to them, I noticed my best mate, Stu, flying head-first down the street. At first I hesitated, wondering what had happened to him, but it turned out he'd tripped over something as he was too eager to get into them. Typical Stu, always first in. But not this time! I think he was more bothered at missing out on the action than the skinned knees he now had.

We continued without my horizontal mate and absolutely routed the once famous Aberdeen. They'd come to the pub with around the same numbers as us, about 60-strong, but couldn't cope with the ferocity of our attack. A token stance and a few blows were exchanged before they turned as one and ran for their lives. I couldn't believe my eyes as the young lads kept chasing them like a pack of wolves hoping to catch a stray. They soon gave up and we walked back up to the pub, ecstatic at our comprehensive victory. The Old Bill finally decided to arrive, but, as the fighting had ended and we were walking back to the pub quietly, they didn't know what to do. We didn't try to rock the boat by trying to run away from them, so an escort to the stadium it was. The walk to Pittodrie was surreal. Instead of being pissed off at the presence of the boys in blue, we laughed and joked all the way there.

AFTER THE MATCH, THE GAME BEGINS

We hung around outside the ground when we got there. The Aberdeen Old Bill were happy to let us wander around as long as we were still in sight. A few young lads started to drift away, looking to see if they could find any ASC. A few of us stayed outside the ground and were soon confronted by small groups of Aberdeen. They were trying to save face by attempting to catch us unawares but they were soon chased off.

We were split into three groups now: the young lads on the roam; a mob that went off to the boozer, not interested in seeing the game; and the rest of us entering the ground to take in the match. Before, being split up like this would have bothered me, but today was different.

This was the last game at Pittodrie I went to where the away end was the big Beach End behind the goal. It was soon knocked down and a huge stand was built in its place to house the home support. The game was a bit of a blur to be honest, but I do remember United's controversial Argentinean striker Victor Ferrara scoring, and Jim McInally scoring near the end, to round off a great day. When McInally's goal went in, a few of us jumped on to the track behind the goal to celebrate the winner, rubbing it in even more with the deflated Aberdeen fans and casuals.

After the game finished, we made our way out of the Beach End and over the big hill. The police escorted around 50 of us away from the ground, keen to keep an eye on us. We figured that the rest of the lads would make their own way to the station, so we concentrated on trying to escape the clutches of the law, but they weren't having any of it. At the halfway point to the train station, we came to some pubs that the ASC was known to frequent and from where they would launch their ambushes. As we passed one of them, the Swan Bar, it was clear that it was full of ASC. Ignoring the Old Bill, we calmly walked across to the front door, chasing a few of them who were standing outside away up a side street. With them gone, we then concentrated on the others inside the pub.

A few things were thrown at the door and then we stood back and waited on them to come out. I wish I'd had a camera then, as you should have seen the once-proud ASC fighting one another to get out. NOT! Honestly, it was pathetic. It was also hilarious in our eyes. They were actually holding one another back from coming outside. There were only a few coppers there, too, barely stopping them. We gave it a couple of minutes, waiting on them and laughing, but we ended up just walking away and shaking our heads. The rest of the walk was negotiated without any more hassle. A few of them threatened to try it on but didn't even come close.

Back in the station, we laughed and joked about the day and were joined in dribs and drabs by the rest of the lads who all had similar tales to tell. After a short wait we were on our way home on the train.

There was no chance of the train getting wrecked this time, as we didn't fancy getting the jail and spoiling a good day. When we got back to Dundee, we went on one big bender to celebrate the day's result and partied into the small hours. The Welsh lads that were with us had had their eyes opened. They'd probably heard all about Aberdeen this and Aberdeen that – and here was little old Dundee turning them over. This would have them raving about us for years to come. They certainly enjoyed the Dundee hospitality that night as we showed them how we partied.

The 1990s were beginning to belong to us and that day proved that the myth and reputation that Aberdeen once carried was well and truly in tatters. Scotland's number-one firm was no more.

In late 1993, we ended another myth, as the 'unbeatable' Hibs CCS were next up to be put to the sword. Around late October/early November of that year they came to Dundee around 60-handed. I'd been up late the night before, so I didn't surface until well after dinnertime. We'd all been at the funeral of one of our best-known and best-liked lads, Lenny. An emotional night was had, as a huge mob of lads gathered for a night he would have loved. We planned to see it off the following day with a result against the Hibs in his memory.

When I got my act together, I phoned and asked Tony if anything was planned for after the game. He told me that there was a good mob of around 50 lads in the Cally and around 30 more in town, waiting on the Hibs making their way down from the game. I got my gear on and picked up my mate Billy and headed into town in my car.

As the game had just finished, I had a quick drive past to see if the Hibs were on their way. I couldn't find any of them, but as I was driving down the Dens Road I thought I saw them walking down a path. I decided to head for the Caledonian to try to find a parking space and meet up with the lads. As I got to the top of Union Street, I was just about to turn down and try and park the car when it all kicked off. Around 40 of the CCS were walking through the town towards the top of Union Street. I pulled over at the side of the road and got out of the car in time to see them attacked from behind by about 20 young Dundee. Surprised at the ferocity of the attack, Hibs started backing off. Just as I was going to run across and join in, I looked to my right and saw that the Caledonian had emptied. As the 40 or 50 lads who had been in there charged up the street, I shouted, 'There they are, come on!' and everyone fired right into them.

For the first time in a long time, they were coming unstuck in Dundee, as they were backed off down Whitehall Street. The compulsory flashing blue lights and the familiar sounds of the police sirens soon meant it was time to scarper. Forgetting for a second that I had the car, I almost ran in a different direction, but quickly turned and sat in it without driving away. I gambled that if I drove away they might try to stop me. I waited a few seconds until after the cops had arrived and then calmly pulled away. As soon as I'd passed the coppers, two mates, Tony and Gary, jumped in front of the car and I stopped and let them in.

'Go mate, go,' Tony shouted.

As I drove away, I told him, 'Calm down, mate, we'll bring attention to ourselves. What's the rush?'

With that, Tony pulled out this small stick-like thing. 'Fucking hell, check that!' he said.

'What the fuck's that?' I asked him, thinking it was a small cosh.

'It's the handle of my hammer. I hit a Hibs cunt right over the skull and the head has come right off! Some cunt's got a sore head tonight,' he laughed and we drove away from the scene.

We later heard that young Dean and a Hibs lad had been nicked – and that the Hibs lad that had been 'hammered' had been taken to a nearby pub, where he was cleaned up and let home.

We were on a roll – and it would continue throughout the 1990s.

Another small but violent victory was just around the corner. It came in late December 1993, and the visitors were Aberdeen. I'll let John take it from here.

John's story, part three

We met in the Centenary bar on the Clepington Road, as we knew the Aberdeen sometimes went there for a drink. We got in early and tried to surprise them. It's only about five minutes from the ground and has a function suite that caters for away fans, so we knew that the chance of a bit of action was good.

We only had around 20 lads at the time of the arranged meet, but knowing it was still early we hoped a few of the lads were still to rise or were already on their way. We made a few phone calls, to try to boost the numbers, as we knew they could appear at any moment. One of the lads managed to get hold of Jimmy and Paul from Fintry, who said they were on their way, and would try and round up a few of the lads from their end of town.

As the morning went on, it didn't look as if our numbers were going to get any better, and we started to rethink our plans, as we knew they'd soon be coming mob-handed. Kingy then looked out of the front window of the boozer to see if the Fintry lads were on their way, only to see 40–50 ASC standing right outside the window and being refused entry from the bouncers. This was all their faces. We couldn't believe it. This was our perfect opportunity.

The only problem was our poor turnout. It was all good lads that were in the pub, though, and one of them took the initiative. 'Come on, Dundee, let's fucking do it!' he said, and we all stood up and got ready to go.

We looked out of the window again and saw them heading around the corner of the pub. Assuming that they'd been told that there was a social club round the back of the Centenary, we made our way to the side exit of the building, right where they were passing. Picking up anything we could get our hands on, we stood behind the fire exit door, ready for the ambush. Heavily outnumbered, we waited until we were all together and barged open the fire-exit door and steamed into them. You should have seen the looks on their faces as we charged out into the street, taking them out as they stood astonished at what was happening.

One of the ASC lads went down by the door that we came out of and got a savage kicking. I think every lad who came out of the door had a go at him as he lay there abandoned by his 'mates'. It was a sad sight to see them leave him like that. We gave chase along the back of the street behind the Centenary, which was the perfect place to kick off, as it's off the beaten track. As they kept running, a few of us started to shout to the others that we'd better get out of there as the Old Bill were sure to arrive any time. With the ASC lad lying pole-axed in the middle of the street, arrests would certainly be on the cards.

We jogged back and on to the Clepington Road and headed towards the ground, mingling with the scarfers that were making their way to the match. We passed the Aberdeen lad, who was still lying outside the pub.

AFTER THE MATCH, THE GAME BEGINS

Realising things were getting more jail-friendly by the minute, we decided to get out of there pronto. Myself and Benny jogged along to the top of Hindmarsh Avenue, which runs from the Cleppy to Tannadice. When we got there, we turned to see if the Old Bill had arrived and noticed that the ASC were pursuing us, trying to save a bit of face.

We were now spread out all over the place, and with the Old Bill due to arrive any minute we kept going in the direction of the ground. They could have had it earlier, as the numbers were in their favour two to one. We got down Hindmarsh a bit and looked around to see seven Dundee standing the 40 Aberdeen. As we made our way back up the road, the lads, who were well outnumbered, backed off and we ran back to behind Tannadice. They later claimed this as some sort of result, which amused us, as we know what had happened earlier behind the Centenary.

CHAPTER 29

ON THE ROAD AGAIN

1994 was to be the pinnacle for the Dundee Utility off the park and for Dundee United on it. It started with the third-round of what would turn out to be a memorable Scottish Cup campaign. Here's the third round story in John's words.

John's story, part four

January 1994, and it was third-round Scottish Cup day. This is the round that the big guns enter the draw and where everyone, fans and casuals, prays for an away tie for a carry on, preferably in some obscure town that you'd never usually visit, or, failing that, a game against one of the big guns or your bitter rivals.

This is where being from Dundee has its advantages, as it means we've got two chances of getting a plum draw with both clubs going into the hat.

The third round of the 1993/94 season saw myself as a

AFTER THE MATCH, THE GAME BEGINS

Dundee fan, and Kenny as United, watching the draw unfold, with Dundee coming out of the hat away to lowly Clydebank and United away to Arbroath. Bingo!

If you were ever to sum up what Dundee's mob was all about, the third round of the cup would do it perfectly.

The links between Arbroath and Dundee had more or less finished, so the tie gave us the chance to go and see if our near neighbours were still up for it. Likewise, the trip to Clydebank would be seen as a laugh. They didn't have a recognised firm, but with it next door to Glasgow you never knew if there would be any visitors.

In the 1980s, with there always being a firm in Dundee on a Saturday to entertain, the away days were a rarity. In the 1990s, however, we travelled a lot more and the third-round draw meant two aways to choose from.

On the day of the match, the Utility lads that supported Dundee United made their way to Arbroath, 60-strong, with a few Dundee lads going with them for a carry on. Dundee, meanwhile, took 50 on a bus to Clydebank, aided by a few United lads who fancied the trip west. We're a strange lot. Not many mobs in Britain can say they've had two firms, in two different towns, watching two different teams on the same day, can they?

The Utility lads that were in Arbroath set themselves up in one of the local bars down the high street, not expecting any trouble, when suddenly the Arbroath casuals decided to have a pop. Around 30 of them appeared. Small in numbers, but well up for it! One thing we knew from the days that they ran at our side was that the lads from Arbroath were game as fuck and were well battle-hardened from fighting with the marines every weekend from the nearby army base.

ON THE ROAD AGAIN

The Dundee lads ran out of the pub and on to the street to confront the Arbroath mob, to see what they were all about. To everyone's astonishment, they were all bouncing about the middle of the high street, ready to have a go. The two mobs steamed into one another and it kicked off big time. The Arbroath were holding their own, until the sheer numbers of Dundee overpowered them and the Arbroath lads took to their heels. The Old Bill appeared and the lads headed for the nearest boozer without a single arrest being made.

Meanwhile, the 50 Utility that were on their way to the Clydebank arrived safely, half pissed after a few beers on the way, and were looking to head to the nearest boozer rapid, as it was chucking it down in that dark and dismal little town. Clydebank's ground was a shit hole, with hardly any cover, so all the lads decided that, instead of watching a boring match on a freezing cold day, the best option would be to find the nearest watering hole and stay warm. We eventually all got settled in a bar, with all the usual banter flowing, when word spread that Dundee were 1–0 down.

What a fucking disaster it would be if we got knocked out of the first round proper and not even having seen the game. The lads were now getting rowdy in the pub and were dying to start a fight. But the only chance of a fight in Clydebank it seemed was with old men and the local Neds. We decided to drink up and make our way to the ground for the last 10 minutes of the match.

With the gates at grounds usually opened with 10 or 15 minutes to go, we knew there would be no problem walking straight in. Inside the ground, we noticed a couple of thousand Dundee fans taking shelter under the one stand that ran the length of the ground. With the rain stopping almost as soon as we walked in, we decided to stand behind the goal, all 50 of us, and get behind the team and try to stop this fucking disaster from happening! With the game entering injury time, Dundee pushed forward in one last attempt at getting an equaliser and winger Paul Tosh curled the ball over from the left-hand side of the pitch, straight into the top corner of the net. Goal! The whole Dundee end went absolutely mental. All of the Utility, out of pure relief, jumped the small barrier at the side of the pitch and bounced on to the park.

We were now jumping around the pitch, with all the Dundee players happy as fuck that we were still in the cup. What followed shocked Scottish Football to the core. The tabloids reported that it was the worst football violence that had happened in Scotland for 20 years.

As all the Dundee lads were celebrating with the team on the pitch, the Clydebank players started to get some of the lads off the park. Pissed off, we turned and squared up to all the Clydebank players and it kicked right off! Lads were bouncing about toe-to-toe with the Clydebank players, including ex-Rangers and Scotland legend Davie Cooper. Next, one of the lads was now rolling around in the net with the Clydebank goalkeeper. I ran into the net and tried to help my mate off the keeper, but had to scarper as the police were on their way after us with their batons out.

Things eventually calmed down and we jumped back into the terrace behind the goal as the players looked on astonished, trying to calm us down. The keeper lay in the box getting treatment and the police arrested 16 lads from Dundee. Right away, I knew there would be more arrests to follow as they would be hell-bent on nicking as many lads as possible. After the game, those of us that had escaped the clutches of the Old Bill for the time being got back on to our bus and made our way back home to Dundee.

Meanwhile, the Dundee United Utility contingent that had had a day out in Arbroath were also making their way back home to the city, happy with their day's events after having had some aggro with the Arbroath casuals. When they heard on the radio on the bus home that one of the Scottish Cup matches had been marred by crowd trouble involving one of the Dundee teams a cheer went up on the bus as they thought that their antics had made the headlines! When they turned up the radio, they soon realised it was their closest allies, the Dundee FC contingent of the Utility, that had made the headlines.

Back in Dundee, the whole mob met up and exchanged stories of the day's events at both cup ties. At the start of the day, none of us could have ever imagined the outcome of the day's events. The next day, I got up early in the morning and went to get the Sunday papers and usual morning rolls. When I walked into the shop I couldn't believe my eyes. Splashed all over the tabloids were pictures of myself and all the lads under the headlines: 'THUGS MAR SCOTTISH CUP DAY'. When I got home, it wasn't long before the phone started to ring and all the lads were saying the same thing – that the tabloids were blowing things out of all proportion.

Later that day, I sat down to watch the highlights of all the cup action from the weekend, but the show was more interested in showing the events of Clydebank than any actual football. They played the incident over and over *again in slow motion, and highlighted all the suspects in what was the start of a witch hunt. The presenter of the show, Dougie Donnelly, went on and on about how it was a black day for Scottish football and that the morons that had run on to the pitch must be brought to justice. They even had a hotline to phone if you knew any of the hooligans. It was the same again on the Monday morning when I was making my way to work. All the papers were covered, from the front page to the back, with the events at Clydebank and again asking the public if they knew any of the culprits.*

This dragged on all week and started to get out of hand. It was worrying the lads who had been there and we were all waiting for the dreaded knock at the door. I personally thought that there had been a lot worse incidents in Scotland than what happened in Clydebank. Fair enough, we did run on to the pitch, but only in celebration. Then things turned daft, mainly through drink. If you take Celtic and Rangers, for example, when these two meet each other for an Old Firm game there are hundreds of arrests. People are slashed and stabbed and sometimes even lose their lives – and most of the time it just gets brushed under the carpet.

The Dundee–Clydebank replay eventually had to be played in front of a controlled crowd, with only a certain number of season-ticket holders allowed in and the general public kept out.

Six months later, when I had all but forgotten about Clydebank, there was a knock at my door. When I opened it two plain-clothes police officers were standing there and looking rather smug. One of them, grinning like a Cheshire cat, said, 'Hello, John, you know why we are here.'

To which, I obviously replied, 'No, why are you here?'

They told me that they wanted to interview me at the station about an incident that had happened six months previously. My mind was racing as I walked out towards the car, trying to think what had happened. I really didn't have a clue what they wanted to talk to me about. Dundee was a violent place at the weekends, so it really could have been anything.

At the station, I was taken to one of the interview rooms. As I wondered what the fuck was going on, the two CID that had brought me down to the police station walked into the interview room and pulled out a folder and showed me three large photographs that they had blown up.

Suddenly, I was sweating like fuck as I looked at the images that seemed to show me running along the goal line at Clydebank and then hitting the goalkeeper! I couldn't believe it had taken them six months to come and interview me about it when at the time it had been all over the papers. I thought that by now they'd forgotten all about it. I had. The CID asked me if I recognised anybody in the photos and I admitted that it was me as there was no point trying to get out of it. I was well and truly fucked! They went on about how one of the photos they had made it look as though I was hitting the goalkeeper. I tried to explain to them that the picture did look like that, but that I was only trying to split up the fight. The CID were having none of it and charged me there and then with breach of the peace and assault of the Clydebank goalkeeper.

After being cautioned, I was about to leave when the CID asked me where my yellow jacket was. I told them I didn't have it any more. I couldn't believe it – I was actually wearing it! The coat was a yellow and blue reversible Lacoste jacket. When the Old Bill came for me I just grabbed the nearest jacket to hand. It was the same one that I'd been wearing at Clydebank, but I had turned it inside out when I got into the police car. Just as I thought I'd got away with it, one of the CID noticed the yellow lining on the inside and asked me to take my jacket off. They soon realised it was the one I'd been wearing that day and kept the jacket for evidence.

A year passed, and thankfully the case against me got dropped as they didn't have enough evidence. It was a huge weight off my shoulders, as a few of the boys had already been up at court for only running on to the pitch and had received massive fines. Funnily enough, after all the hype in the papers at the time, no one received any jail sentences. I did eventually manage to get my Lacoste jacket back, but with a few extra holes cut out of the arms. Apparently, there was blood on the sleeves and the forensics had to cut samples out for evidence. Luckily enough, the Tayside police had the fucking jacket that long that by the time I got it back it was out of fashion anyway!

The next round saw me on the road, after a chance meeting that came about after an accident.

I'd saved up and bought myself a car for about £3,000 and had been driving around thinking I was the dog's bollocks. I'd only had it for a couple of weeks and, one Friday after work, myself and the mate Billy decided to go into town for a quick couple of pints before we went on to a party.

ON THE ROAD AGAIN

We went into the Old Bank Bar on Reform Street and met a few of the lads, including my old mate Sammy. After a couple, we headed up the road and agreed to drop Sammy off. Just before we got to his house, I switched off for a second and ploughed right into the back of another car and smashed mine to bits.

Luckily, I didn't fail the breathalyser, as I was right on the border line. But I was still pissed off at the three-grand car lying in bits around me. Instead of going home and getting changed to go to the party, I about turned and headed straight back to the pub I had come from and got absolutely bladdered.

In the pub I met a couple of the older lads, Glen and Big Steve, and they asked me if I fancied going to Airdrie the following day, as United were playing them in the Scottish Cup fourth round. There was a space in the car, as Kingy was also going. It was a far better alternative than going on the supporters' bus, as I didn't think any of the lads were going and I was right in the mood for some action after writing off the motor. I agreed to meet them in the Caledonian Bar on Union Street, just up from the train station at 11:00 am.

When I got up to go the next morning, I had the hangover from hell. I very nearly didn't go, as spending an hour and a half in a car didn't really appeal. Then I remembered about my car and that cheered me up even more! I got myself changed anyway and got a taxi into town and made my way down to the Caledonian Bar, where I met the other three. A swift pint was negotiated with ease and we made our way out to the car and I sat in the back with Kingy, who looked even worse than me! 'What's up, mate?' I asked.

AFTER THE MATCH, THE GAME BEGINS

'I lost my job yesterday. Got paid off, so I went out and got steaming drunk and I'm feeling like a bucket of shite.'

'Sorry to hear that, mate. Fuck, here's me thinking I had a sob story to tell too. I wrote off my car that I'd just bought, but it's fuck all compared to that.'

With that, we just slumped back in our seats and Glen took off. 'This is going to be a barrel of laughs,' I thought to myself.

The first 10 miles or so I was really wishing I'd not come as I was struggling to stop myself from being sick, especially when Big Steve cracked open a bottle of Merrydown cider and proceeded to drink it like it was a bottle of water! He then passed it to Glen, who took a swig and then cracked open a can.

'What's Glen doing, Kingy?' I asked. 'He's driving.'

'He does it all the time, he doesn't give a fuck,' Kingy replied.

I sat back and laughed nervously. If I wasn't feeling bad enough already, here I was, in the hands of this big mad cunt behind the wheel, getting pissed and driving like Michael Schumacher. Next, the old punk band Stiff Little Fingers was stuck on and turned up full blast, which made Glen drive even faster. 'Oh, well, if I'm going to go, I might as well get pissed and enjoy it!' I thought to myself, so I cracked open a tin and joined in the sing-song.

When we arrived in Airdrie we parked the car not far from the centre of town and had a walkabout. Being a bit older and full of the beer, we didn't care about their nasty reputation and we swaggered around their turf without a care in the world. We soon decided to go for a pint and picked a pub right in the centre. A few pints later, and a few funny looks as well, we left to go to a pub closer to the ground. We got there only to be turned away as the pub closed down during games. Pissed off that we weren't getting another pint, we turned and made our way to the ground.

We bumped into a few older lads from Dundee as we walked back. One well-known lad had obviously been attacked and when we asked him what had happened he told us he'd been jumped by around 20 Airdrie. Knowing they were about and up for it, we quickened up to see if we could find them. Just as we neared the ground, it was going off. We ran down and jumped over a wall to find around 30 young Dundee and 40 Airdrie bang at it outside the ground. After a few blows and a brief exchange, the coppers were right on top and we were pushed into the ground.

The game was a bit of a non-event to be honest, so as soon as it ended we went outside and we were escorted out of the ground and down towards the car and the buses. We were tailed all the way by Section B, but every time we turned and offered it to them they weren't up for it.

The journey home in the car was an escapade and a half, as a now pissed Glen took about four hours to get home in a journey that usually took an hour and a half. We kept going the wrong way and stopping in weird places for a pint. We had a right laugh winding up the normal fans on the way home. Every time we passed a bus, we directed a barrage of abuse at it for a laugh and a huge Utility Union Jack was unfurled, much to the disgust of the head-shaking scarfers, who didn't see the funny side of it!

When we finally got home we continued our bender well into the next morning. Even though there hadn't been much violence to write home about, it had been a brilliant laugh and cheered me and Kingy right up after our mishaps the previous day. This was also the beginning of the road to Hampden, which for once wouldn't end in tears.

The replay at Tannadice on the Wednesday night would see United canter through to the quarter-finals against Motherwell, with an easy 2–0 win, with Airdrie not bringing any lads of note. The quarter-final versus Motherwell would also go to a replay, with a cracking game at Tannadice ending 2–2, with United's striker Craig Brewster scoring two cracking goals, only for Motherwell to score a last-minute equaliser to break United's hearts and force another replay, this time at Fir Park. United won with a late great strike from centre-half Brian Welsh, to take us on another trip to the National Stadium – where we would face Aberdeen, old rivals on and off the park.

CHAPTER 30

A CRAZY DAY

Once again, arrangements were made to meet early in the town and catch the train just before 10:00 am. I'd talked to one of the young Stobie lads called Billy into going, as I'd been with him to a couple of games that year but he'd never really been into the casual side of things. However, I assured him that he'd enjoy himself!

We met at the top of the Hulltoon at 9:00 am and had a stroll into town to meet Stu and Mattie. The four of us then had a walk towards the train station. We met a few other lads on Union Street.

After a quick drink, we made our way to the station and boarded the train, around 80-strong. One of the lads told us there were a few lads staying in Glasgow and that a couple of cars had also headed on their way and would meet us in the pub opposite the door of Queen Street Station in Glasgow. Also coming for the trip were the four or five Welsh lads from Colwyn Bay, who we'd not seen for a while. This would take our numbers close to the 100 mark.

AFTER THE MATCH, THE GAME BEGINS

When we arrived in Glasgow, the mood was as always one of excitement. As well as our old friends from the north, we knew we'd probably have a pop at some of the Old Firm lads if any of them showed. We headed into the pub and welcomed our Welsh mates to the party. No sooner had we drank our first drink than some of the younger lads told us that the Rangers lads might be drinking in a pub called the John Street Jam across George Square. Everyone was rounded up and we went off to look for the opposition.

Halfway across the square, the shout went up: 'Here they are, come on, Dundee.' We sprinted towards the pub and were met by a smaller but game as hell Rangers ICF firm. They charged out of the pub and launched a volley of glasses and bottles at us. At the same time, we heard the police sirens wailing in our direction. We tried to make a run from the Old Bill but they collared us and took us to a pub a couple of minutes away. As soon as we got into the bar, it became apparent right away that it wasn't any ordinary pub – it was a fucking gay joint! I'm not sure if the Old Bill were trying to be smart arses, but putting 100 football hooligans in a gay bar was maybe their idea of a joke!

The bar was littered with baskets of condoms and KY jelly, much to our amusement, but I don't think our bent-looking barmen were too happy when they started getting thrown around the boozer. They didn't know where to look as we became more and more boisterous. The next things to be lobbed around were packets of fags, as one of the lads had ripped a fag machine off the wall beside the toilet and emptied it. We had so many cigarettes that even the lads that didn't smoke were having a fag. Just as it was getting out of control in our poofy pub, a rumour went round that the Old Bill had disappeared from outside and had probably gone off to the train station. This, of course, was our cue to have another pop at our Glasgow friends around the corner.

We were greeted at the John Street Jam by the usual volley of glass and bottles, but with no Old Bill around we had time to avoid the hail of glass and this time scattered the small but game mob of Rangers ICF. As we legged them everywhere, one of their lads got caught and got a bit of a hiding. As the belated sound of the police sirens neared, I turned as we left the scene to see the lad pole-axed in the middle of the road.

This time, the Old Bill weren't so tolerant. Instead of taking us back to the pub, they frog-marched us to Central Station and put us on a tube to Mount Florida, beside the National Stadium. A couple of the lads had been nicked at the second fight and this led us on the train to discuss how the Glasgow Old Bill always seemed to disappear then reappear during a battle and arrest a load of lads. We were used to the opposite tactics in Dundee, where the Old Bill tried to avoid trouble at all costs. It may well be that the Glasgow coppers were on some kind of arrest-related bonus. I wouldn't have been surprised.

We got to the stadium and made our way to the end we'd been allocated. As we sat about waiting on the match starting, some of the lads had a walk around and some went to the pub instead of staying at the match. Around 30 or 40 of us decided to hang around and see if we could find the Aberdeen, who'd still to make an appearance. After around half an hour, we saw around 100 of them walking down the hill towards us. We calmly stood up and braced ourselves for the attack. Even though we were depleted – under half strength – we just stood and smiled. They seemed to stall as they got close and didn't seem to know what to do.

Just as they got right beside us, a couple of coppers appeared and it seemed to frighten them into making a move. For a second, there was a weird stand-off as no one made a move. Just as they were right among us, Jim F, who'd been up in one of the apartment blocks having a piss and was completely oblivious to what was going on, walked out and straight into the situation and steamed right into them. This was the cue for us to go into them from all angles. Even though we were well outnumbered, we backed them off. As usual, the Old Bill arrived en masse and another handful of arrests was made, bringing our numbers down even more. After this brief exchange, we decided to make our way into the ground to watch the semi-final. We all sat down in an area at the front that wasn't meant to be sat in, but rather than try and move us in the Old Bill left us where we were. Then, what seemed like 75% of the coppers in the ground stood around us in an over-the-top show of authority.

As the game looked to be heading for another disappointing defeat for United at Hampden, a last throw of the dice resulted in the quarter-final hero big Brian Welsh throwing himself at a cross in the dying seconds and scoring a last-gasp equaliser. This led to a final few minutes of absolute bedlam before the final whistle went.

Coming out of the ground, it was the first time in God knows how many trips I could remember leaving Hampden a happy man. But, of course, the day wasn't over yet. As we always say: after the match is when the game begins! We rounded up the troops for one last pop at whoever wanted to take up the challenge. As we walked towards the big park down from Hampden, a meat wagon pulled up at a scuffle between scarfers and nicked a United fan and also pulled in my mate Billy. We couldn't believe he'd been nicked for nothing.

Another 50 yards further down and it was on again. The Aberdeen ASC came screaming down this hill towards us and without a moment's hesitation we grouped together and ran up the hill towards them. The amount of Old Bill around made sure the battle was short but sweet, as again the ASC took to their heels and we sent them back in the direction they'd come from.

Once again, some lads were arrested, including my good mate Stu, and this time the Old Bill didn't fuck about. There were almost as many police in the escort as there were Utility lads. Coppers on foot, coppers in cars, coppers in vans, four mounted police and even a helicopter took the 75 or so of us on the long walk back to Queen Street Station.

As we approached George Square, we walked past the Rangers HQ, the John Street Jam pub. They watched from inside this time as we wearily marched past. One of them, who'd been scouting around, went by and informed us that there was Aberdeen in the station. This perked us up as we knew they could get the same train home as us, which would be interesting. This time, though, the Old Bill were leaving nothing to chance and we were lined up along the back of the station, while the Aberdeen lads were grouped in a corner of the platform. Then we were marched into the station in single file – and were clapped in by the Aberdeen. Nice to see that they acknowledged our efforts on the day.

Later on that evening, the lads that had been arrested were all released without charge, which was a result for them. Young Billy wouldn't live it down for a while, though, as not only did he get nicked on his first venture into the world of the soccer casual, but he would also have the lads laughing all the way home on the last train. As they all stood at the charge desk in the police station, the lads were asked to empty their pockets. As the usual keys and fags and loose change were put on to the charge desk, Billy was left red-faced as he turned out his pockets. Littered across the counter were dozens of packets of condoms and KY jelly, lifted from the earlier visit to the gay bar. Even the hard-nosed Glasgow coppers found it funny. 'Where are you planning on going, son?' asked the sergeant, as the lads all doubled up with laughter.

Billy didn't know where to look or what to say! It's fair to say he didn't hear the end of that one for a while.

I didn't make the replay, due to work commitments. Another trip to the National Stadium for both clubs resulted in a poor attendance. Hardly any lads made the trip, but it still resulted in a few skirmishes before and after the game in which United triumphed with a late rare goal from midfielder Jim McInally. This meant another final, this time against treble-chasing Glasgow Rangers!

CHAPTER 31

AT LONG LAST

The rest of the season passed in a flash as cup final fever set in. It was to be a strange final for a few reasons. The main one being that the old man decided that, after travelling to the National Stadium over a dozen times in the previous 20 years and never having seen them win, he was going to give this one a miss.

If he had gone, I would have gone with him. Even though you'd think this would have been a game that would have brought together a huge firm of lads, in Dundee it usually meant the opposite. Even though we ran together as one, as I've mentioned before, we still dislike one another's team to the point where we wouldn't want to be present at the other's final. As a United fan, the thought of being there as thousands of Dundee fans were celebrating winning the Scottish Cup doesn't rank high among the things I'd most like to do, and I'm sure they feel the same. It's always more of a family occasion anyway, so most of us take the opportunity to bring our kids along with us.

AFTER THE MATCH, THE GAME BEGINS

Also, for the first time that I could remember, United were massive underdogs. Walter Smith's Rangers had won the last five major trophies in a row and were expected to run over a United team who couldn't buy a win in a cup final at Hampden.

With 1994 probably being our biggest year – as far as off-the-field activities went – I decided to get in touch with Big Steve and Kingy to find out how they were getting there, as I'd travelled to a few games with them that season already. A van was hired for 15 of us older lads and tickets were bought and paid for. We arranged to leave from the Smugglers, as that was where a few other buses were leaving from. A few good lads were going, so we knew that we'd be in good company. On the morning of the big match, Mattie picked me up in a taxi and we made our way down to the Smugglers, where the place was jumping. We got everyone together and, after a couple of drinks, got ourselves a carry out for the journey. Then, the 15 of us piled into the back of a hired van and made ourselves comfortable on our luxury milk crates. The journey was an uncomfortable one, but a great laugh as we got stuck into the drink. After a few stops, we eventually got to Glasgow and now we had to try to find a pub called the Black Bull, where the rest of the Smugglers lads were drinking.

We had trouble finding the place but eventually got the area where we knew it was. We decided to park up and look for the pub on foot. As we got out of the van a couple of Rangers fans walked past and Kingy and Glen kidded on they were going to do them in. The Rangers boys legged it as Kingy and Glen approached.

'Fucking leave them alone, you fucking bullies,' we all shouted and laughed.

'We were only fucking around. I was only gonna ask him for a light!' said Kingy.

We all laughed and walked up the hill towards the dual carriageway. As we walked away, I kept an eye on the two lads, who'd sprinted down the road and had gone into a boozer.

'Fucking hell, lads, here we go,' I shouted to alert the rest of our group as the boozer suddenly emptied and around 50 raging Rangers scarfers came running up towards us. We ran down towards them and a vicious bottle fight started between us. After a minute or so, they started to make their way back to the boozer and we pulled each other away from it, as we didn't fancy getting nicked before the game. I shouted to Mike, who'd been driving the van, that we'd better move the car or else it would end up smashed to smithereens. As he drove it away, the Rangers came back out after us but we got away just in time.

It wasn't until we'd reached the top of the hill that someone pointed out that we'd left Fraser and Kingy behind and that we'd have to go back and get them. Mike turned the van around and drove back towards where we'd come from. As we got back to the point where we'd parked before, two Rangers lads appeared from nowhere and threw this big fuck-off paving slab right through the windscreen. We absolutely shit it and Mike, who was driving, did well to keep control of the van and park it at the side of the road.

Kingy and Fraser ran across towards the van as the Rangers lads disappeared and we got out and cleaned the front of the van. As we were standing around, we noticed the Black Bull pub was just across the other side of the carriageway – and was not too far away from where we had been in the first place. We took the van down the road and phoned a windscreen-repair place and arranged for the van to be fixed while we were at the game.

At last, we got settled down into the Black Bull. The place was jumping with lads from the Smugglers in Dundee and the party was now in full swing. The drinks were flowing and I walked around, having a crack with all the lads. Football violence wasn't on the agenda for me that day. After a couple of hours, I couldn't find Mattie. Mattie's always been a bit of a free spirit and could be anywhere at any time. He's as likely to be on a plane to the Himalayas as he'd be in a taxi on his way to the match, so I decided to go walkabout and try to find him. Everyone I asked hadn't seen him for a while. Knowing him, I thought there was a good chance he'd be speaking to some complete stranger about some bizarre subject.

On the way down the stairs, I was stopped by Big Kev. Kev's a big likable lad, who'd not long been in the casual scene, but was a big and game and was pretty obsessed by it. 'I've just been on the phone to the Rangers. They've got 150 lads on their way and they know where we are,' he told me.

'What the fuck did you do that for?' I replied. 'The pub's full of scarfers and families.'

'If we gather together a squad, we could take them. There's 15 of you lot in the van and we could get another 20 or so,' he said.

'Listen, mate, to be quite honest, I'm not bothered today, but if it comes my way I'll not turn away, but I think you'll find most of the lads will tell you the same,' I told him, adding, 'By the way, have you seen Matt?'

AT LONG LAST

He told me that he hadn't, so I went off and continued my search. When I walked outside, I got that weird feeling that you get when you've been inside a pub for hours and then walk out into the blazing sunshine. You know, that sort of spaced-out, floating feeling. As I walked about for a couple of minutes looking for Matt, trying to get my bearings, I noticed that there was another couple of pubs further down the road, so I decided to float on down there and have a browse.

I opened the door of the first pub and had a look but there weren't many people in, so I about-turned and went to the next pub. When I opened the door I saw about a dozen lads I go to Tannadice with on a regular basis, including some great mates that ran with the firm. There was John L, Ronnie and Greg. So I sat down with them and had a couple of drinks and laughed and joked about the vanishing Matt. They agreed that he could be anywhere, so I forgot about him for a bit and settled down where I was, as it was a lot quieter and cooler than the Black Bull, which was at bursting point.

After around half an hour, I decided to go and look for Matt and agreed to keep an eye out for the lads and walk up to Hampden with them. When I walked outside again, I got that weird pissed feeling again as the fresh air hit me like a ton of bricks. As I staggered towards the Black Bull, I couldn't believe my eyes. I soon sobered up, as around 150 Rangers ICF came charging towards me across the dual carriageway.

A quick look around told me it was time to scarper quick, as around a dozen people, some lads and some ordinary scarfers, were running for their lives and all trying to get in the narrow doorway of the Black Bull at the same time. I quickly decided that I had no chance of making the pub, so I turned and legged it as quick as my pissed legs could take me. The last pub on that stretch of road was my port of call, as I knew my good mates were all in there. Even though it was only around 100 yards, it seemed like miles as my heavy legs struggled to get me there.

As I finally got to the pub, I kicked open the door and screamed at the mates to get out and give me a hand. Ronnie was first through the door and crashed a bottle off the first lad that ran past. We fanned out on to the street and tried to have it with the ICF. Just before it came on top, each pub emptied with a few hundred United scarfers and a few lads and the Rangers backed off across the dual carriageway. Even though the Old Bill arrived in huge numbers the anger of everyone from Dundee was there to see. A couple of lads had been slashed as they'd tried to flee up the stairs of the Black Bull, in what was a blatant liberty. Everyone was trying to get at them but they wouldn't cross the fence that separated the road and a few arrests were made.

As the Old Bill got to grips with the situation, they pushed everyone back towards the pubs and took the ICF away from the scene. As we walked back to the Black Bull, I noticed the back door of our van opening and out fell Matt, looking like he'd been dragged through a hedge backwards!

'Where in the fuck have you been?' I asked. 'I nearly got my life taken looking for you, you daft cunt!'

'Stop fucking moaning and chill out,' he answered. 'I was starting to get a bit pissed, so I went for a sleep in the back of the van. I pulled up a few milk crates and had a nap. Why, what's been happening?'

I told him, 'It's kicked right off. 150 Rangers attacked the pub.'

Matt was his usual laidback self. 'Just as well they didn't look in the van then,' he laughed, and I shook my head and laughed too.

Everyone from Dundee was then escorted to the ground. I was annoyed at our poor showing for a huge Rangers firm, but it was the norm for us at a cup final. In their defence, they were phoned and told where we were, which in hindsight wasn't the cleverest thing to do, but such is life. We forgot about it soon enough as we walked the long road to Hampden in glorious sunshine. What was on our minds now was whether United could upset the form book and finally win the Scottish Cup at the seventh time of asking.

On arrival at the stadium, football hooliganism was forgotten about for a couple of hours as we sat down to take in the final. As usual, we were outnumbered massively by the Rangers support, by about three to one. We'd sold all of our ticket allocation, as had Rangers. Trouble was, ours was 12,000 tickets and theirs was around 40,000.With them getting to sit in their own traditional end and us having to sit in the 'Celtic' end, it was the usual backs-to-the-wall job.

The United fans were in great voice as the game kicked off in glorious sunshine. I asked Kingy if he reckoned the van would get fixed in time and he reminded me that the windscreen guys were fixing it as we left the Black Bull.

The first half ebbed and flowed, with Rangers doing most of the pressing and United trying to hit them on the counter-attack. Big Brian Welsh and Yugoslavian Gordan Petric were doing a great job at the back, marking

AFTER THE MATCH, THE GAME BEGINS

Rangers' international strikers Mark Hateley and Ally McCoist out of the game. The first half came to an end in a flash and both teams went in locked at 0–0. We stood around talking at half-time about the game and whether or not the ICF would make another appearance afterwards, as they'd know where we were drinking and where the van was parked. We shrugged it off and decided that we'd cross that bridge when we came to it.

Just before the teams came back out, Mattie disappeared up to the shop for his compulsory Bovril. So, we sat down just as the teams came back on. Two minutes after the restart, United scored an incredible opener. What started as a long punt up the field was flicked on by Craig Brewster. Christian Dailly chased the lost cause after Rangers' centre-half Dave McPherson rolled the ball back to 'keeper Ally Maxwell. Maxwell then panicked with his kick and hit it straight at Dailly, who calmly rounded the outstretched 'keeper and shot towards the goal from a tight angle. His weak shot seemed to crawl along the line and eventually hit the back post and trickled back out – to where Brewster was following up to slam it into the back of the net. The 12,000 United fans behind the goal went absolutely bananas.

As I was sitting at the end of a row beside Kingy, we both dived out into the walkway, where the first person within hugging distance was Mattie, who was swaggering back to his seat with his Bovril. Before he'd even had a chance to sip it, I leaped on to him and the next thing we knew we'd both landed about 20 yards away – with me wearing Mattie's red-hot Bovril all down my arm.

The goal was ironic to say the least. In this day and age

of foreign players who are just here for a payday, the goal was made and finished in Dundee. Brewster and Dailly were both brought up in Dundee as United fans. Having Dailly involved especially meant a lot to me, as he was brought up across the park where we played football as kids.

The rest of the second half seemed to take forever. Rangers threw everything at United, who defended for their lives. Countless trips up and down the stairs to the bogs and the pie shops were a must, just as an effort to waste time in what must have been the longest three-quarters of an hour in my life.

Right at the end, a miraculous tip over the bar from our Dutch 'keeper, Guido Van De Kamp, stopped the game from going into extra time and a couple of minutes later the ref finally blew for time up. Finally, at the seventh attempt, we'd won the Scottish Cup! The next 20 minutes or so were fantastic, as the players celebrated with the fans. I remember walking out with a lot of mixed emotions, though, as I thought about the old man, who'd taken me to so many finals in the past. With this being the first one he'd missed, it had to be the first one we'd win! I also thought about my young mate from Stobie, Si, who'd been a great United supporter all his life, and who had also missed the final because of a daft fight in the town earlier in the year that had resulted in him getting sent to jail.

Obviously ecstatic at winning the cup, I also thought it a bit weird that our celebrations at winning the cup were cut short after just 20 minutes. It was like the ground staff were, 'Right, you've had your fun, now get out.' I wanted to enjoy the moment a bit more. After all, the pain of all the finals we'd lost in the past seemed to stay with me for weeks at a time, so a few minutes of pleasure wasn't asking too much, was it? 'Fuck it!' I thought to myself. 'Let's get back to Dundee and party!' I phoned the old man and he was as happy as Larry. He told me to have a ball and to behave myself. As if I wouldn't.

When we got back to Dundee, the town was going crazy. Every pub and club was packed and we celebrated well into the next morning. The following day, the players paraded the cup in the city square in front of thousands of happy Arabs. This brought down the curtain on another great season, on and off the park.

CHAPTER 32

A CAPITAL START

The following season started off badly for United on the park as we lost a lot of games and fell into the relegation zone. But, off the park, we got a dream fixture to begin the campaign.

Because we'd started to turn the tables on a few of the 'bigger' clubs, including Hibs, they were especially keen to get it on and they didn't have long to wait. The fixture list came out and the first game for United was Hibs away. John will tell the story.

John's story, part five

A couple of weeks before the season started, a few of the older Dundee went to Edinburgh to meet a few CCS faces and hatched a plan so that we could have it in the centre of town without alerting the Old Bill. It was agreed that only one Hibs lad would know our meeting place and would call us when we arrived to tell us that they were on their way.

We also decided that, instead of travelling to the capital mob-handed, we would make our own way there and meet up at the arranged pub. So, with lads travelling through in cars and vans and some on the train, me and a few of the lads decided to go by bus and met up at the station in Dundee. We caught an early Citylink and settled down for the journey ahead. Once we arrived in the capital, we made our way to the Melville Bar in William Street. Lads were now arriving in small groups, swelling the numbers to around the 60 mark. We were quite disappointed at the numbers, but, with it being the first game of the season and some lads still on holiday, it was to be expected. Even though we only had 60 lads it was possibly our best 60, which usually is better than, say, a couple of hundred lads, some of whom you don't know or trust. This was as close-knit as it comes. As the day went on, we couldn't wait for them to turn up.

We started to get impatient and seven of us went outside to see if they were about. Just as we got outside, a car with a couple of their lads drove past and the driver nodded at us and said they'd be back soon. We took it with a pinch of salt, as they'd promised to phone the pub when they were on their way. We went for a stroll down the street and, just as we got down a bit, I turned to see them running towards the pub. They were here and it was on. They hadn't stuck to their side of the plan, which was to tell us when they were on their way. They'd obviously planned to try to ambush us as we sat in the pub. They came charging down the street, around 50-handed, with their mates from Oldham. One of their lads right at the front had his hand behind his back and, as he neared, he pulled out a baseball bat. They meant business. The seven of us tried to run at them and get to the pub and warn the rest of the lads, but their sheer numbers – and the fact that they had an array of weapons that would have put the army to shame – meant that we got backed off to where we had come from. We seemed helpless as it kicked off at the door as the rest of the lads from Dundee tried to get out.

They seemed to spray what looked like CS gas at the door, which had the lads doubled up as they tried to get out. Just as we made another attempt to help the lads, they came bursting out of the doors behind a huge table. Big Ian had picked it up and charged out of the door, using it as a battering ram, with the rest of the lads behind him. It was now game on, as the lads fired straight into them, fuelled by the fury of being attacked and stuck in the pub. The street was like a war zone, with all sorts of weapons being used, including a load of road signs that were being thrown back and forth. We had them on the back foot now, as their surprise attack had gone pear-shaped and we were all out and going for it big time.

The cops arrived and everyone split. The seven of us who were cut off from the rest of the lads were cornered by the Old Bill and nicked. As we sat in the back of the van we saw the street, which looked as though a bomb had hit it. There was broken glass and tables and chairs lying about everywhere. People looked on in amazement, including a bus-load of Japanese tourists who were snapping away and loving every minute of it. Just the right advertisement for the Edinburgh Festival!

We drove past the Hibs lads and noticed that one of

their top lads was giving it to the rest of their firm with both barrels, obviously pissed off at the result. I also noticed that one of their mates from down south was covered in blood.

We were driven to the nearest station, where we were convinced that we were in for the weekend. With the festival about to start, it was definitely not the type of thing that the authorities wanted to allow. We kept our heads down and kept quiet, hoping that they'd go easy, except for Eddie, who was a bit worse the wear for drink. He started getting lippy with the Old Bill and was taken away. When the coppers came back we got a dressing down and were told that we were being released without charge – and that we had to leave Edinburgh immediately. If we were seen again, we'd certainly be nicked. Result!

We walked out of the station grinning like Cheshire cats and made our way to the station to catch the next train. When we got back to Dundee, we headed to Jack Daniels, where the rest of the lads were celebrating our result. We thought that they'd be back for revenge after that, but they never seemed to be the same again. The following day our 'little' battle with the CCS was splashed all over the front pages of the Sunday tabloids.

CHAPTER 33

OUR GREATEST DAY

One Saturday night in the town in September 1994, I met up with a few of the lads and arranged to go to Aberdeen, as Dean, one of the twins, had organised a double-decker bus. I wondered to myself, 'Is there any life left in the casual game? Can we still raise the numbers after all these years?' Little did I know that we were about to have our best result ever!

For the weeks leading up to the game there was a buzz around the town like I hadn't experienced for years. Everyone who was anyone was speaking about the trip to Aberdeen. I tried to play it down any time I spoke to anyone about it, though, as with Dundee being the biggest village in the world it would get back to people that we didn't want to know about it. I was convinced that, with the Old Bill becoming better and better at policing games, and preventing days like this happening, they'd definitely have this one sewn up. Even though I was of the belief that it wouldn't happen, I still tried to round up the troops for another crack at our rivals from the north. The younger brother and I, along with Tony, Ryan, Steve, Bill and a few others, would make sure my old stomping ground was well represented as usual.

The lads that had organised the bus had been up to Aberdeen a couple of times before the big day, sussing out the best places to go and even getting a boozer sorted out and making sure the manager was all right with a bus full of lads. They'd convinced the manager of a pub called the Malt Mill in Holburn Street that we wouldn't be any bother. With the prospect of a healthy pay day, he happily okayed it. Holburn Street is just off Union Street, the main street in Aberdeen, so we knew that if we could pull it off we'd be right in the heart of Aberdeen territory. Another stroke the lads had pulled was that John had told his Aberdeen contact we were definitely coming by train, which had them waiting in a pub down by the station, giving us time to get organised away from the watchful eyes of the Aberdeen Old Bill, who'd be keeping an eye on their lads for sure.

Having organised the Aberdeen side of the trip with military precision, the bus was arranged to leave from the Ellenbank Bar in Alexander Street in Dundee, which was right in the heart of the Hilltown area, as central as you can get. It's also a five-minute walk from the grounds and Stobie, which was a handy stroll along the road for us.

On the morning of the match, the usual wide-awake club were making their early-morning Utility alarm calls! When there are days like these planned, there are always lads in the firm that have either never been to sleep or are up with the crows because of the excitement. My alarm was set for 8:30 am, but my phone began ringing at 7:00

am. 'Wakey wakey, this is your early morning Utility wake-up call! Time to rise and shine!' said the friendly voice on the other end of the line.

So, I got up and had a shower and then put on my best gear, which had been washed, ironed and laid out for the best part of three days. This is when the butterflies start and the excitement kicks in. I was out the door and bouncing off down the road to meet the mates who, same as always, had been hanging around from early doors, waiting on the rest of us appearing so that we could all set off together.

When we got to the Ellenbank Bar it was clear this was going to be one of those days. Every game that I'd ever been to with the lads, especially if it's pre-arranged, will have a turnout of less than expected. As with every firm, if it's been talked about for weeks, the numbers are nine times out of ten exaggerated. Every lad that's involved doesn't want to be seen to let down the rest, so when he's asked if he's going he always gives a positive answer. The hard core will always be there, but there are lads who, for whatever reason, either want to go but can't manage it or bottle out at the last minute.

Today was different. In the mid-1990s, numbers had dropped for every club by as much as 50–75%, so taking anything up to 75 lads would be a result. It had been rumoured that there could be 100 lads out for the trip, but I'd have settled for 75. A quick head count in the boozer, which was now buzzing, told me that there was as much as 120 lads ready to go. We hadn't taken as many as that anywhere for nearly eight years!

Fake £10 notes were getting handed around, so a free day out was adding to the buzz. One of the lads would become the butt of the jokes on the bus, as he didn't realise that we all had fake tenners. He handed over a genuine £20 note to the barman in the Ellenbank, only to get a fake tenner back in his change!

As you can imagine, 120 lads don't fit on to an 80-seat double-decker, but we managed to squeeze around 100 on, with 20 or so lads jumping into a van and a couple of cars that three of the lads offered to drive. The off licence was also hit with the fake tenners, as fags and carry outs for the journey were bought. The journey itself was a right laugh, as the drink flowed. As seats were few and far between, getting up for a piss meant yours was a goner from the minute you left. This hooligan version of musical chairs continued right up to the minute we arrived in Aberdeen.

As we exchanged seats on a regular basis it gave me the opportunity to speak to most of the lads. Older lads like myself, Benny, Tony, Jim, Glen and Dave, were discussing what we should do on arrival. Should we stay put and wait for them to arrive? Or should we go on the hunt as soon as we got there? We agreed to settle down in the boozer and play it by ear. Also, the young lads, some of whom hadn't been on a trip like this before, were asking all sorts of questions about what lay ahead and what had gone on in previous trips over the years.

How we never attracted the attention of the Old Bill I'll never know. From our leaving from the centre of Dundee, the fake money, the overcrowded bus, the drunken carry on we had on the bus and getting into Aberdeen undetected – well, we had to make the most of this opportunity.

The Utility express rolled on and on, into the Granite

City and up on to Holburn Street. The driver pulled up into a lay-by about 50 yards from the pub and we knew it was time to quieten down as we didn't want to blow a plan which had already gone like clockwork. So, we quietly departed the battle bus and made our way up to the Malt Mill bar. The owner seemed a bit surprised at the numbers entering his pub, but the prospect of an early payday helped him to paste on a smile and serve up whatever the lads were after. The mood in the pub relaxed a bit as we all settled down around the bar and waited to see how the day panned out. Myself, Ian and another couple of lads went over to the dartboard and had a chuck of the old arrows and a few beers.

A couple of younger lads and one of the older lads went out for a scout about to see if the ASC were having a sniff around. Young Dean reminded me that they'd told the ASC that we'd be travelling by train, so we'd have to make a move at some point and go and hunt them down. I was dying to go at this point. I'd not felt like this for years. Coming up here as a young kid and expecting to come up against possibly 1,000 ASC was enough to put the shits up anyone. Now, as we were all 10 years older and wiser, and the numbers were on a more even keel, the nerves had gone and had turned into pure adrenalin and excitement.

The three lads returned from their scouting mission laughing and struggling to contain their excitement. We all gathered round, trying to get them to calm down and tell us what had happened. 'We bumped into a mob of them and they asked us where our lads were. We told them we were in the Malt Mill down Holburn Street. They then asked how many lads we had and we told them 30 to 40.

They told us that they'd be down soon and then they pissed off.'

This just added to the buzz, as we were now itching to go. I pictured the Aberdeen lads getting back to the boozer and spreading the word that there were only around 40 of us just around the corner in Holburn Street. I imagined the conversation would be along the lines of: 'Let's do these jute bastards once and for all.' They must have wanted to wipe us off the map and put themselves back to their old top spot as Scotland's number one.

They were in for the shock of their lives!

The darts were put back and we waited on the call to go. The relaxed atmosphere was now gone, as coats were zipped up and we began to gee each other up with the usual 'No one run, let's fucking smash them' comments getting barked around the boozer. The front door of the pub was crammed with lads wanting to be the first out and into the old enemy. It was like a scene from *Braveheart*, as we were all shouting at one another to hold on and wait until they got close or we'd fuck it right up if we got out too early.

'Here they are, here they are,' shouted the lads at the door excitedly, as the tension became unbearable. This was it – about 60–80 of Aberdeen's finest, their top boys, the lads that had started the casual movement. They looked impressive, as they fanned out across Holburn Street and came charging down the hill towards us. We were holding one another back and waited until they got closer. Once they were within 50 yards the pressure of bodies behind became too much and we burst out and on to the road.

Our numbers kept building as we charged up the road

towards them. Over 100 lads were out now and you could see them putting the brakes on. In 12 years of being involved with the casual scene, I'd never felt anything like it – and still haven't since. Every single lad was now running at full speed. This was no pavement dance today.

The front 15 or 20 of the ASC stopped and bounced, about to go ahead as their mates behind them started to melt away in the opposite direction. There was no dancing from us, though, as we ran through them like they weren't there.

As game as the front of the Aberdeen firm were, it counted for nothing as they got punched all over the street. We were fighting over one another to get a piece of the action as the demolition continued. When it's going off like this it's hard to keep your wits about you, with bodies jumping about all over the place and punches being thrown from all angles. I saw young Paul having a straightener with a big ASC lad and I jumped in front of him and landed a cracker on the side of the lad's head. As he stumbled backwards and tried to turn and retreat, I grabbed hold of the hood of his coat and landed another four or five blows. No sooner had I got hold of him than there were half a dozen lads raining blows on him as well and he went down. I took a quick look around and saw this same scene happening all over the street. Lads were going down everywhere, while others were disappearing fast and leaving their lads to take one of the biggest hidings I've ever seen.

It was becoming brutal now, as we were really going to town on the once proud ASC. As I jumped about in the street I heard a lad screaming. This distressed sound stopped me in my tracks and I looked around to see two

AFTER THE MATCH, THE GAME BEGINS

Dundee lads literally carrying an Aberdeen lad across the street towards a shop. One lad had him by the head, while the other had his feet and they bounced his head off the window and tried to put it straight through the glass. After about three, thankfully failed, attempts to introduce the ASC lad into the world of the shop-window dummy, they dropped him and, after a couple of boots, left him to join the rest of the rout.

Everyone now turned their attention to the rest of the Aberdeen and we chased them up Holburn Street. I was still thinking about the lad that was nearly decapitated, but as my old man always said, 'You fly with the crows and you get shot.' Or beheaded in this case. We ran them right up on to Union Street and with each step their resistance crumbled. Not one of them fancied it. All they wanted was to get out of there. Before we got right down the famous Union Street, we were surrounded by Old Bill and pushed down and held in a side street. With only one lad arrested for continuing to run down the high street, the whole thing was turning out to be one serious result in the heart of where it all began.

We had to stand around for a few minutes as they waited for reinforcements. When they came, we were marched down a street that looked out on to Union Street. As we passed we could see the Aberdeen lads looking down at us, almost astonished at what had just happened. There wasn't even the usual baiting. They just stood and watched us march past as we sang, 'Scotland, Scotland's number one.' This time we meant it – and they knew it!

The police never left our side for one minute – and the Aberdeen never resurfaced for the rest of the day. The Old Bill made sure we didn't get to wander about this time and forced everyone into the ground, whether they wanted to go or not. This pissed off the Dundee lads in the firm, as sitting watching United, as opposed to being in the boozer for the afternoon, didn't appeal to them. The blow of having to go into the ground was softened for them by their paying for it with the fake tenners that had been handed out earlier in the day.

I'll never forget walking into the ground. We were housed in the corner of the south stand, right beside where they sat. The baiting was merciless, as for once they couldn't even muster a reply and had to sit through the game and take it on the chin. Moments like that have to be enjoyed to the full. These were the founders of the casual movement in Scotland and they'd been almost untouchable for a long time. Aberdeen as a city had always looked down its nose at Dundee as some sort of poor neighbour. Today we were going to milk it for all that it was worth and we would have happily sat there tormenting them for hours.

The game was irrelevant. Even though we lost it 3–0, we still laughed and smiled as we left the ground. We tried as we left to get around to the Aberdeen end of the ground, but a massive police presence made sure we weren't to have another pop at our old rivals. We were soon to be disappointed again as we walked over the hill outside the ground. We thought we'd get another chance to have a go at them where we'd parked up, but it wasn't to be. The police had moved the coaches to the ground, so that we could be put on them and driven off as quickly as possible.

The journey home was the usual laugh, as stories were swapped and, as always, exaggerated. The Old Bill escorted the bus out of Aberdeen until they felt we were far away enough not to bother coming back. After a quick stop for a carry out, we were off down the road again and even had the hard neck to have a whip-round for the driver, handing him a fine sum, albeit a fake one.

As always after nights like these, when we got back to base, a bender around town was on the cards. A mass pub-crawl ended up in our favourite club, Fat Sams. The day's events were replayed over and over again as we celebrated well into the next morning.

CHAPTER 34

TAKING THE BAIT

A few weeks later, Rangers were in town. Over the past 18 months we'd had a few ding dongs with the blue half of the Old Firm and we expected them to come out to play for this visit.

The game had been put back to the Sunday as it was to be screened live on television. This meant that I would possibly miss the action. At the start of the season, I'd started playing football again on a Sunday for a team that the young lads in the firm had started. The first couple of seasons they had the team were a right carry on. They'd named themselves after the nickname of the Under Fives, the Dundee Alliance, which caused no end of trouble.

With all the in-fighting in the city with the other schemes, such as Lochee and Fintry, having the name of the team in the paper every week and saying where they were playing meant that more often than not the games would end up with mass fighting in the middle of the pitch. The lads faced changing the team name or being booted out of the league, so they decided to call themselves after our HQ at the time, the Caledonian Bar in Union Street. In return for the manager of the pub sponsoring the team, it was renamed Dundee Caledonian.

We had an important Scottish amateur cup game that afternoon and so weren't there for all of the action. I'll let John tell the story of what unfolded that day.

John's story, part six

Rangers had been in contact with one of our lads, saying that they'd planned to come to Dundee for the game at Tannadice that Sunday afternoon. After the attack at the cup final, which resulted in a couple of lads getting slashed, we weren't taking any risks. Both the big two from Glasgow had reputations of not playing the game and weapons were always used when they were in town. So we decided to take them on at their own game, and planted a few bats and table legs outside the pub and in a couple of alleyways on Union Street.

We sat patiently in the Caledonian Bar, around 70-strong, waiting on the call. When the lads from the football team came in, the numbers swelled to around 90. The longer the afternoon went on, the more impatient we became. Lads were going walkabout, trying to see if they were coming, and we were also trying to phone them to see where they were. They then phoned to say they were on their way and would phone again when they neared the town. The lads were now champing at the bit. We knew that the longer we had to wait the more chance there was of the Old Bill making an appearance and fucking it up.

Next thing, they phoned to say they weren't coming into

the town but were heading for Broughty Ferry instead. The Ferry, as it's known, is joined to the outskirts of Dundee, five miles away from the centre of town and is home to the city's wealthier residents. We couldn't believe the hard neck of the ICF. We knew that they didn't carry the huge mobs of the 1980s any more, but, even though they only had around 40 lads on a bus, we fully expected them to come into Dundee and give it a go.

This was like us playing Rangers at Ibrox and stopping at another town like Coatbridge or Motherwell and refusing to budge unless they came to us. It wouldn't happen. Aberdeen or Hibs, for example, wouldn't dream of pulling a stunt like it. They always brought it to the table. As we had around 90 boys confident of a result, hearing that they weren't on their way after two hours of waiting pissed off the lads, to put it mildly, and threw our plans up in the air. A lot of the firm weren't entertaining the idea of taking it to the ICF, rightly complaining that, being at home, why should we have to travel out of town to play their game? They should come looking for us. A lot of arguing started, as we couldn't agree whether or not to go. In the end we decided to stay where we were for the time being.

The longer the day went on, the smaller the firm got. Fed up at the no-show of the ICF, most of the lads starting drifting away. Some went home to get ready for the night ahead and some moved on to another pub. When the mob was down to around 25, we decided to give it a bash. Taxis were phoned and we arranged to meet up in a pub in the Ferry. Our cab was first to arrive, so we went in and got a drink up while we waited on the rest. As the lads started to arrive, it began to be *questioned whether or not this was a good idea. A lot of the boys there were young lads who didn't have much experience of Saturday matches, far less daft missions like this. But after a couple of swift pints we agreed that we'd come too far to turn back.*

As we finished our drinks, one of the lads phoned his contact from Rangers and found out that they were in the Royal Arch pub. This was just around the corner, about 100 yards from where we were, so it wasn't long before we found out what we were up against. We turned the corner on to the main drag and saw a coach parked up outside the pub we believed they were drinking in. Knowing we'd be up against it, we ran towards the pub to try and catch them on the hop. It was now or never, as we neared the Royal Arch, and just as we began to think we'd pulled it off, it emptied.

They came charging out of the pub with whatever they could get their hands on. As we were already unsure about the attack, seeing them with twice our numbers and tooled up put us on the back foot right away. After a brief stand and a couple of punches thrown, we turned and legged it. As we ran, I heard one of the Rangers shouting, 'Fucking stab them.' 'Fucking typical,' I thought. We got split up in different directions, so before the Old Bill appeared we jumped in a taxi and headed back to a pub in Dundee.

No one said a word in the cab back home, as we were pissed off at what had just happened. When we got back to the pub, lads starting drifting back in dribs and drabs. It got worse when we heard that one of the lads had got caught and had been kicked senseless. Not happy with giving him a bit of a slap, they broke his ribs, which punctured his lung, and stabbed him in the back as he lay on the road.

As the pub still had Rangers fans in it, having a drink before they got the last train home, things got a bit heated. We even heard one of the Rangers lads bragging on the pub phone about the result and about the lad from Dundee who'd got a hiding. Once things calmed down, we agreed we'd have to get revenge for this.

CHAPTER 35

PAYBACK

We agreed to try and exact some sort of revenge the next time one of the teams played at Ibrox. With Dundee playing that season in the First Division, we'd have to wait until after the New Year for United's next visit to Rangers. The date of 4 February 1995 was pencilled in and a bus was organised for the revenge trip.

Tony, the lad that had been given the going over by the ICF, was one of my longest-serving and best-ever friends – it was me that had taken him to his first-ever game as a kid – and this meant that I was right up for the trip. The Sunday before the game I had being playing for Dundee Caledonian. We were cruising in against our rivals, 5–0 up with five minutes to go, when I snapped my knee in a completely innocuous challenge and was rushed to hospital. Three days in hospital and an operation on a ruptured cruciate ligament meant that the trip to Glasgow for me was a non-starter. My days of running around on and off football pitch were to be few and far between from now on as well. The trip to Glasgow would go ahead without me, so here's John's version of events.

John's story, part seven

We had been in contact with them for weeks leading up the game and had arranged to meet them in the Gallowgate area of Glasgow. We thought this was a bit strange, as this was in the heart of Celtic territory. Itching for revenge, we went along with it.

The Saturday before the game, a few of us met in Jack Daniels in Dundee and one of the lads, Steve, took us outside the pub to show us a flare gun he'd 'acquired' for the trip. We were having a laugh about who'd have the bottle to fire it into the Rangers, when young John from the Hulltoon came barging out of the pub, grabbed the gun and pointed it in the direction of the busy traffic coming down the dual carriageway. Young John, who's a crazy bastard, turned to us, gave us his mad cackle and then proceeded to fire the gun into the cars. We ran back into the pub, pissing ourselves laughing. With the pub being so close to the waterfront, the flares had sparked a rescue mission, with the lifeguards thinking a boat was in trouble. We'd found our Saturday sniper!

The Ellenbank was again agreed upon as the point of departure, this time minus the fake tenners. We'd had a lot of good results against what we'd seen as two of the big four – Aberdeen and Hibs – the other two being ourselves and Rangers. With them claiming that we never came to Ibrox, it made us even more determined to complete our own 'treble'!

We hired a double-decker bus again, but only around

40-odd lads turned up. This left a lot of empty seats in a bus that held 86. A bigger problem was that, with a lot of boys turning up with little or no money, it meant we were short of cash for the driver. Looking like we'd maybe have to call the trip off due to lack of funds, mad young John got on the bus and sat at the front, threatening to go on his own! Knowing he'd probably do this, we had to do something. One of the lads suggested going into the bookies next door to the Ellenbank and sticking our money on a horse. This was agreed, so some of the lads piled into the bookies to try and salvage the day. You can imagine the laugh when the horse we'd bet on romped home. John would have company on the bus after all!

Once it got going, we forgot about the poor turnout and got stuck into our carry outs for the journey. The usual carry on was next, up at the service station piss-stop. The shop was emptied of its goods as the lads went on a help-yourself spree. The manager of the shop phoned the Old Bill and they appeared before we left, leaving us on a bit of a sweater, before we were eventually allowed to leave and continue our journey to Glasgow.

On arrival, we told the driver, who was under the impression that we were going to Ibrox, not to bother and to take us to the Gallowgate. We phoned the ICF to tell them we had arrived and they told us to sit tight in a pub and they would come. We settled down in the famous Celtic supporters' pub The Bairds Bar.

We seemed to sit around for ages and the lads were getting very impatient. They finally phoned to say they were on their way. Knowing they wouldn't play by the rules, we got tooled up with ashtrays, bottles and even a stool that we broke up. As soon as one of the lads started to fill his pockets with pool balls the barman went mental. 'Fucking leave the pool balls, they cost a fortune,' he barked at the young lad.

'Let's fucking do it,' was the cry as we piled out on to the famous Gallowgate, expecting the Rangers to appear at any time. We hung around for a while, only to be disappointed again at a no-show from our big city rivals. Not wanting to attract the attention of the Old Bill, we decided to go back into the pub and discuss what our next move would be. As it was getting late, with the match long over, our chances of action were disappearing fast. We tried again to make contact with them, but with no answer. We disappointedly made our way out on to the street and towards the bus. The weapons were ditched and we boarded the bus for the journey home. Most of the lads went upstairs and sat at the back as the driver started the engine. At that moment, I looked out the back window and saw a lad with this big fuck-off yellow bin above his head, running at the bus and trying to stick it through the back window.

We couldn't believe it! After waiting all day on them, they finally appeared as we were leaving. We got up and made our way down to the front. 'Fucking stop the bus, fucking stop!' we screamed at the driver and he pulled on the brakes. The emergency exit was pulled and we piled out of the doors and ran at the ICF. As expected, the Rangers were tooled up all right, but it didn't stop us. We steamed right into them. Young John pulled out the flare gun and pointed it straight at a Rangers lad, who seemed to freeze. He tried to call John's bluff and shouted at him, 'Go on then and fire it!' Bad move.

BANG! It was off! Luckily it never came out straight and whistled past the lad, who looked as if he'd seen a *ghost. As we charged them, John reloaded and fired another one right into them and it bounced through and set a bush on fire at the back of them. They weren't putting up much of a fight, as we had them backing off up the Gallowgate. After a third charge, they dropped their weapons and took to their heels.*

As a fire was blazing from the flare, we thought it better to fuck off from the scene before the Old Bill appeared. As soon as we got back on the bus, they reappeared; again, we got off but they never put up a fight and disappeared. They'd tried to save face but had failed.

When we got back on the bus this time we never even had a chance to move before we were surrounded by police cars. John stuffed the flare gun down the back of a seat, trying to hide it from the Old Bill, and as I looked out of the window I saw that the coppers had a few Dundee lads lined up against a wall. Plain-clothes police were also picking up the weapons from the street as our chances of getting away with this one got less by the minute. Our chances decreased to zero when the coppers got on the bus, nicked all 44 of us and took us to the station. They also found the flare gun.

The coppers were having a field day. As well as the 44 of us, they'd also nicked four Rangers and we were all taken in one by one for photographing and questioning. They tried to wind us up by guessing who the leaders were and who were the foot soldiers by the way we dressed. More seriously, the CID then came in carrying plastic bags filled with weapons retrieved from the scene. These included a sword and an array of sticks and coshes. I remember thinking, 'Thank fuck John had that flare gun or we could have got cut up badly.'

AFTER THE MATCH, THE GAME BEGINS

With it being Sunday and Glasgow being what it is, the cells were chock-a-block, so we were thrown in there four at a time. We weren't complaining though, as it was a bit of company. Being in a cell on your own, especially in Glasgow, isn't much of a laugh. The usual banter went on all night between ourselves and the weegie Neds.

I couldn't wait until Monday morning when they would hopefully let us out. It was doing my head in. When the day came, we were all put into those armoured vans with the small windows that you see on the TV – the ones that terrorists get taken to court in. When we arrived at the sheriff's court, we were all handcuffed to one another and led into the building and told that the breach of the peace charge was likely to be increased to mobbing and rioting. With Glasgow known for not tolerating this sort of thing, 44 of us up on a mobbing and rioting charge wasn't looking too clever.

When we were taken down into the holding cells under the court the banter started again. The weegies took great delight in reminding us where we'd be going if we got remanded and what to expect. Young mad John was taken to a cell on his own, because of his previous, and when I was taken from the cell to speak to a solicitor I had to walk past the cage he was in. As I went by, I saw him sitting there as if he'd not a care in the world, smoking what looked like a joint, with his feet up and with these four young weegies in the cage with him looking like petrified hostages. 'Fucking nutter!' I whispered to myself. I laughed and shook my head. He didn't give a fuck.

The solicitor wasn't much help as he didn't know when or if we'd get out. He said the court could be open until 10:00 pm, so we had to expect a long day. When I got back to the cell the rumour was that we were getting PF releases, but that seven of us were getting remanded and done with mobbing and rioting. This meant that the ones getting released would get home, with the charges most likely dropped, but that the ones charged would be looking at two to three years inside.

We were all sitting wondering and worrying who would be the unlucky seven to get jailed. We were left to stew for what seemed like forever and when we eventually faced the judge we were released without charge and let out. Seven were charged, along with four Rangers, but were released as well to reappear at a later date.

When we were outside the court, a few Rangers were there, including the mouthpiece who had phoned the pub after the Broughty Ferry carry on. Give him his due, he and his mates came over and admitted they got smashed and they also warned us that there was a load of newspaper photographers waiting around the corner to take our pictures. Not wanting to be the next day's headlines, we thanked them for the warning and headed off. A little bit of respect was given back to them then.

The seven Dundee lads and the four Rangers lads had a bit of a scare, as they were told there was video evidence of the fight. Luckily for them, it was only a fixed black and white camera from a shop. All it showed when they went to court was lads running past the camera and the flare flashing past. There was nothing to incriminate anyone.

The charges were thankfully dropped to breach of the peace and massive fines were handed out. One of the Dundee lads was hit with a £750 fine, which back then was well above the normal £200 or £300 you'd expect for *a football breach. Still, it was a lot better than the prospect of two or three years in Barlinnie.*

And so, the treble of 1994/95 was complete.

CHAPTER 36

COMING DOWN WITH A BUMP

John's story, part eight

During the 1994/95 season, Dundee FC had to visit St Johnstone in the league. Our old rivals had almost disappeared completely from the football hooligan map, so a trip along the road to Perth was no longer undertaken with the anticipation of previous years. From about 1991 on, it was seen as no more than a day out on the lash and this day was no different.

Our usual hardcore of 50 or so lads got the train to Perth for the match – and a day on the bevvy. On previous trips to Perth, we didn't even make the effort to go to the game. We would rather sit in a pub and get pissed. The fixture had just become an excuse to go to another town and have a drink with your mates. And Perth town centre was the ideal place to have an all-day pub-crawl. It had plenty of bars and the last train home usually didn't leave until about 11:00 pm. Even if you missed the last train you could always split the cost of a taxi ride home as it was only 20 miles or so.

We had been sitting drinking in Perth city centre all day, unbothered by any Perth casuals. Later in the evening, well after the game had finished and with everyone a bit worse the wear from drink, our mob started to head back to the station in little groups of twos and threes. When there were just about 15 of us left in the pub, one of the lads who had left earlier suddenly burst back through the doors and told us he had been jumped. He had banged into around 30 Perth MBS lads when he was making his way to the train station. This infuriated us. We didn't understand why they had turned up with 30 decent lads at 11:00 pm when we had been sitting in their pubs all day with an equal number. By this late time, our mob had split up into small groups of lads making their way home. Rightly, as one of the lads angrily pointed out to me, if a mob had come to Dundee with 30–40 lads and was sitting drinking in our city centre, you could bet that, as soon as the Utility had gathered a decent enough mob, we would be straight around to where they were to have a go with them.

We wouldn't wait until they were all pissed, heading home in twos and threes, before we tried to take any liberties. The 15 of us were raging and decided to go looking for the Perth mob. We knew we would be well outnumbered, but the lads who were left were good boys and trusted one another 100%. We were so wound up that we just had to have a pop at them. As it turned out we didn't have long to wait. We left the pub and spotted them just a few minutes later. As soon as we started up our chant of 'Utility, Utility!' there was no turning back. They charged down the middle of the road to meet us and we spread out as much as possible to make it look like we had a bigger mob than just the 15 of us.

As the MBS got closer, they saw that we weren't going to budge and this threw them. They stopped right in their tracks. I couldn't believe it. We were outnumbered two to one and they still bottled it! They were bouncing around the middle of the road giving it the big one, but not actually coming anywhere near us. So, we decided to charge into them and they immediately started to back off. At that point, two police vans arrived to split the fight up. The MBS got pushed down a side street and we were escorted to the train station to catch the last train home.

This sort of thing began to happen more often than not in Perth and it fast became a waste of time going there. On a couple of other occasions when we tried to arrange a meet with the MBS they appeared not to want to know but would then still try to pick lads off on the way home. This started to seriously piss us off.

The final straw came when one of the Utility's older and well-liked lads went to Perth for a non-football-related night out at a club called the Ice Factory. They had a regular night at that club called the Rumba, which had started in Dundee and so was popular with Dundee lads. On this particular night, the Perth mob once again took a liberty and the Dundee lad, who believed he was in good company, ended up getting a hiding and was left with a nice little scar on his face. For us, this was the limit. They were taking the piss and the Utility had to take action!

It was planned that we would go to the next Rumba night and pay them a visit.

We found out that there was an upcoming Rumba night

in Arbroath – and that a bus-load of Perth lads was going to it. Perfect! On the night in question, we kept ourselves sober and headed up there for 2:30 am, knowing that the club ended one hour later. It was time for revenge!

We all turned up in dark clothing, with hooded tops and scarves to cover our faces. We parked our cars and mingled with the clubbers outside the nightclub, trying not to look like a mob, and discreetly checked everybody out to see if we could spot any of the MBS. Meanwhile, one of the young Dundee casuals walked around the coach park and told the bus drivers that he had lost his coach and asked which one was going to Perth. Bingo! He found it. We now knew where to find them.

There was only one way out of the club, via a small ramp at the entrance, so we lined up either side of it and checked each clubber as they came out of the place. Their faces were a picture as they came out, off their heads on Es, and wondered what the fuck was going on.

The doors of the club opened again and this time we recognised some of the Perth lads. More and more followed as they walked right into the middle of us. They had no idea what was going on as they were too busy chewing off their faces. The Dundee lad who'd got the nice little scar on his face put his arm around one of the Perth boys and said, 'Remember me, mate?'

An eerie silence followed and you could have heard a pin drop in the few seconds before the Perth lads realised what the fuck was going on.

One of the Dundee lads shouted, 'Fucking do the Perth bastards,' and that was our cue. They tried to run down the middle of the ramp and jump the railings, but we pulled them down. There was no getting away from our *well-planned chicken run. A couple of the Perth lads got booted to fuck when we caught them and were screaming for their lives. A couple tried to have a go back at us but had no chance. The rest of the Perth mob had taken to their heels and were running for their bus. There was only a couple of Old Bill there, old boys up for retirement by the look of it, and they could do nothing.*

The Utility made its way to the coach that the Perth lads were on and started to smash in the bus windows. The MBS were shit scared and cowering in their seats. By this time, the two old coppers had called for back-up, so we decided to make haste and get back to our cars before more Old Bill arrived. We made our way back to Dundee happy with a good night's work. Result!

A great season was coming to a great end, on and off the park. Dundee, who had dropped down into the First Division that season, were building a decent team and were pushing for promotion back to the Premier League. They also went on a great run to the final of the League Cup, where they met our old rivals Aberdeen. United, on the other hand, were in complete freefall! After the highs of the previous season, we were losing games at an alarming rate and looked like we could go down. Here are a few stories of how the season ended.

CHAPTER 37

DUNDEE'S TURN

John's story, part nine

Dundee, languishing in the First Division, went on a run in the League Cup and got Airdrie in the semi-final. The game was played at a neutral venue, McDiarmid Park in Perth, the home of St Johnstone.

With Dundee yo-yoing up and down the divisions in the 1980s and 1990s, they never had a settled team and struggled for cash. It was suggested that, if Dundee did not beat Airdrie and reach the final, the club would fold and die. Something I hoped would obviously never happen. The manager of Dundee FC at the time, Jim Duffy, was basically running the club and paying some of the players out of his own pocket. The fans did not know the true extent of the trouble the club was in, but it turns out that a win over Airdrie in the semi was financially a must for the club. There was also the possibility of a cup final day out in Glasgow, which we don't see very often.

AFTER THE MATCH, THE GAME BEGINS

Before the semi, we'd taken one of our biggest mobs of the 1990s up to Aberdeen, about 120-strong. We were hoping for similar numbers for the Airdrie match, but you could never be sure. Being from Dundee was a hooligan's dream. If you were so inclined, as I was, you could follow both teams, but not all the lads were like that. The week after the Aberdeen game, we only got about 80 for the trip to Airdrie.

We knew Airdrie would be there in good numbers and would be well up for it. We'd travelled by coach and managed to get to a city-centre bar without the attention of the police. A few stragglers arrived later, late no doubt due to the hangovers they were nursing from a heavy session the night before. Well, there can only be one cure for a hangover, and that's more bevvies, which we duly supplied. After an hour, with everyone settled and having a few laughs and getting pissed, the police raided the pub. Unknown to us, the Old Bill had been watching the place and were waiting for us to make a move. When it never came, the police decided to take matters into their own hands.

It was probably no surprise after the events of Aberdeen, which had virtually been a riot. To make matters worse, the police had laid on a big operation to stop trouble that day – and it kicked off anyway. To say they were pissed off would be the understatement of the year. There was no way the police would ever let it happen again. They were on to us, big time.

All the boys were removed from the bar, filmed and then had their names taken. Was that over the top or what? Nothing had even happened yet.

McDiarmid Park was about two miles from where we were. Since it was sunny, we decided to walk to the game, hoping to bang into the Airdrie boys on the way. As we got closer to the stadium there was still no sign of them. Why hadn't they come into Perth city centre? It doesn't matter where you play: you always go into town for a drink before the match, hoping to see the opposition.

I got talking to a couple of Dundee fans at the stadium who said there was a large group of Airdrie casuals hell-bent on causing trouble and to stay well clear of them. They were attacking innocent fans, people who were there with their kids just to see the football. That was well out of order! What's the point in taking liberties on fans, when you have 80 soccer casuals who are dying to meet you in the city centre? I know for a fact that Dundee would never take liberties on fans, never mind if they were with their kids.

Half of our mob decided to stay away from the match and hit the boozer, seeing as they were Dundee United fans and had no interest in Dundee FC. The rest of us, Dundee FC through and through, would not miss a semi-final for anything. As we entered the stadium we could see the Airdrie casuals behind the goal singing their usual chants. The match ended 1–1, so extra time had to be played. Five minutes before the end of the match, Neil McCann sent a high ball into the box. It caught the 'keeper out and sailed into the net. The Dundee fans went wild! We had three sides of the stadium that day and they were all jumping. The goal had been a total fluke. McCann said in the papers the next day that he'd meant it, but I'm sure it was a cross. Who cared anyway? We were going to our first cup final in a long time!

After the final whistle a few Dundee fans and some of the lads ran on to the pitch to celebrate with the players.

AFTER THE MATCH, THE GAME BEGINS

They were followed by a few Airdrie casuals, who took it upon themselves to join the party. Dundee's French goalkeeper was standing at the Airdrie end of the ground with his hands in the air when one of the Airdrie boys jumped on his back! Turned out that he picked on the wrong player, as our 'keeper just threw him off his back and wrestled him to the ground. I loved every minute of it. Dundee were in their first major cup final in years and had possibly been saved from extinction.

Back to business, we decided we would meet up outside the stadium in the car park to have a pop at Section B. As we came out of the ground, there were only five of us and we had to pass the Airdrie end. Suddenly, I heard some shouting and these lads came running towards us. I jumped straight into the one in the front, grabbed him by his hooded top, swung him around by the neck and slammed him into the side of a car. 'Come on then, Airdrie,' I shouted as I fronted the rest of them.

It turned out that the lad was a Dundee fan who was being chased by the Section B. I let him go and started laughing. The Airdrie lads who were chasing him had seen what had happened and backed off. We then walked around the ground to where we were meant to meet up with the rest of the Dundee firm. There were only around 50 of us, but it was a very strong mob and a lot of good lads. We were now ready to see what Section B were all about! It was getting dark now and we started walking up a small path with buses on one side and a steep hill on the other. Suddenly, there was lots of pushing at the front and then a cheer went up: 'Section B! Section B! Section B!'

The cunts were right in front of us, giving it the big one. They steamed right into us, expecting Dundee to back off.

No chance. Not this mob. Airdrie soon realised this and backed off themselves, but we then charged them and knocked a few of their lads to the ground. They were now up against a bus with nowhere to go. The police started wading in with their batons, getting right into us. They weren't facing the Airdrie, they were facing Dundee. It was as if they were protecting them. You could see the fear in some of their faces and I think the Section B were glad that there was a line of police separating us from them. I am pretty sure that if the bus hadn't been in the way the Airdrie would have been right on their toes.

After a couple of minutes, Airdrie were put on the coach they had been cowering beside, while we were pushed further up the road to the top of the car park, where we met up with the other Dundee lads. The police had stopped them coming into the stadium car park but it was too late anyway. Airdrie were now unreachable, being on the bus, and had a massive police escort. A couple of Airdrie boys did run up through the cars to try to have another go but kept getting pushed back down by the police. They'd had their chance and should have taken it when it mattered. So, we had a cup final to look forward to and another day in Glasgow against Aberdeen.

The cup final wasn't long in coming around. It was something I personally had been looking forward to for some time, as this was the first final we'd reached since we played United in the League Cup Final in 1980. The last time Dundee had actually won the League Cup was in 1973, when Gordon Wallace scored the only goal of the game, to beat Celtic 1–0.

This time though it was Aberdeen we were playing, which gave us something to look forward to off the pitch as well. With Dundee playing in the First Division at the time, reaching the cup final was an achievement in itself and it meant that Aberdeen were huge favourites to win the cup. Off the park, we'd had the upper hand with Aberdeen for the past couple of years and looked forward to continuing that run.

Some of the Dundee lads who knew Aberdeen lads kept in touch with them before the final to try to arrange for us to get it on in Glasgow. There were also rumours that a mob of Tottenham Hotspur were coming up to Scotland for the final. Aberdeen had had connections with Spurs for a number of years, so this was no surprise. However, Dundee also had an English connection with Stoke City's Naughty Forty. We knew a lot of their lads from the Fenton area of Stoke-on-Trent and they were also anticipating the trip up north for the final.

We told the Stoke to try to keep the numbers down to around 10, as we wanted the majority of our mob to be from Dundee. Not that we wouldn't have welcomed any more, but we didn't want to be seen to have relied on another mob. It adds that little bit extra when you know that there will be a couple of English firms present to see what Scotland was all about. It makes for a more interesting and excitng day all round.

On the day of the match, we decided not to travel as one big mob. We would split up and catch different trains throughout the day. That way there was also a better chance of meeting the ASC on our journey, as their mob had to pass Dundee to get to Glasgow. Therefore, there was a chance that both mobs could end up on the same train. Half of our mob decided to catch the 7:30 am service train to Glasgow Central Station. We hoped to catch the

DUNDEE'S TURN

Old Bill out by going that early – and to our surprise there were no police at Dundee Station when we arrived.

Forty Dundee turned up for the train; however it was all Dundee's old mob. Some of the lads had not been to the football for years and would only come out for the big games. Well, they certainly did not come any bigger than Dundee versus Aberdeen in a major cup final in Glasgow. The two Dundee teams had previously played Aberdeen in semi-finals in Glasgow and they always turned out to be mental occasions. Something always kicked off, either with Aberdeen or with Rangers. You could never anticipate what was going to happen and this added to the whole buzz and fun of the day.

As the train pulled into Glasgow Queen Street Station, everybody was buzzing, excited at not knowing how the day would unfold. As we got off the train we were greeted by 12 Stoke lads. They had travelled up overnight, on an eight-hour journey in a transit van. Fuck that for a joke! Nevertheless, they were there and we were all happy to see our English friends. It was about 9:30 am in the morning and there were about 50 of us in Glasgow.

There was now only one problem: none of the pubs was open yet. I thought Glasgow city centre would have had at least one pub open at that time, considering the size of the place. I got talking to an old man, who told me there was a social club that was open 24 hours a day. You just had to knock on the door and they would let you in, he told me.

It sounded all right. To be honest, it was the only option we had. The door of the club was already open when we got there, so we all trooped in. Not expecting any customers that early in the morning, there was only one *barmaid at work. Not wanting to knock back our custom, she phoned for help.*

On a typical Saturday, they probably just have the usual alcoholics lying about the place, particularly as this was quite a rough part of Glasgow. A couple of hours had passed, so I phoned to check where the rest of the lads were and to find out if they had all managed to catch the train. Great news: another 50 were coming on the next train. I just hoped that they'd be able get out of Glasgow Queen Street without the Old Bill spotting them. I advised them to all split up in taxis and gave them directions to the club we were in. Then we would be ready to take on the ASC and their Tottenham friends!

It was now about 2:00 pm. All the lads were well tanked up, chanting the old football songs. Everybody was hyped up and it was decided that it was time to leave for the match. Hampden Park was 20 minutes away, so we decided to walk, hoping to bang into the ASC on the way to the stadium.

We had to walk through a big park as we got near to Hampden and all of our mob mixed in with loads of fans from both teams out to enjoy the occasion. At this point the only thing on our minds was looking for – and turning over – the ASC.

In the distance, it looked as though there was a mob of lads, but they were too far away to tell so we just left it. We came out at the top of the park and walked into a side street. There were a few lads just in front of us and they certainly weren't Dundee, so I shouted over to ask who they were. The lads started shouting down the street and to my surprise I realised that the whole fucking Aberdeen mob was walking down the road in front of us. By chance,

*our mob had walked out into a street right behind them.
It was away to kick off big time.*

*The two mobs charged right into one another in the
middle of the street and went toe-to-toe. I took a swing at
an Aberdeen lad and completely missed him because I
was so fucking pissed! He swung back at me and I wasn't
so lucky. He clocked me right on the chin and he got me
a cracker.*

*By this time, it had fully kicked off all over the road.
Lads were rolling about everywhere, with no side willing
to back off. It was battlefield central! The police eventually
arrived on horses. They charged right down the middle of
the two mobs, splitting them up, then drew their
truncheons and started whacking anybody in their way.
The ASC mob got put on one side of the road and Dundee
on the other. We were escorted towards Hampden Park
and as we got closer to the stadium the Aberdeen mob was
pushed down a side street away from us to make sure there
was no more trouble.*

*Most of the Dundee mob went inside the ground to
watch the match, but a couple of us stayed outside while
one of my mates tried to get a ticket off one of the touts.
Suddenly, out of nowhere, a couple of Aberdeen casuals
who fancied their chances ran into us. Total jail bait!
There were police everywhere. To make it worse, Big
Robo, who was standing with us, got arrested for
nothing. He was one of the original lads, who only
comes out now and again and was only interested in
going to see the football.*

*He would have been pissed right off, as he was a
Dundee diehard and would not miss a cup final for
anything. Unfortunately, he would now be missing this*

one, due to a couple of hotheads. Thinking back, I suppose he would not have been too downhearted in the cells when he heard that Dundee had lost 2–0. Worse still, they never even gave Aberdeen a game.

After the match, we met outside the stadium and regrouped, only to be spotted by the police. We got a massive police escort back to Queen Street, where they put us on the next train home without any further incident. Coincidently, we later found out that the street where the fight had occurred was called Battlefield Road.

CHAPTER 38

GOING DOWN

The season was ending fast and disaster was on the cards for both clubs. Dundee, even though they reached a cup final, looked to fall short in the race for promotion back to the top flight. United, on the other hand, were in freefall and were in serious danger of being relegated for the first time in my lifetime, only 12 months after lifting the Scottish Cup. A season which had started with so much promise on the park as cup holders – and off it as arguably the country's number-one firm – was in grave danger of going tits up.

From the start of March, United lost six and drew one. In the meantime, our relegation rivals Aberdeen started to win games every other week. Everything came to a head with two games to go!

The penultimate game of the season would see us having to travel north to old rivals Aberdeen and needing a win in order to keep our destiny in our own hands.

On the day of the game, I decided against travelling with

257

the lads as I was still barely able to walk from my injury. Instead, I went north on a supporters' bus. The atmosphere before the game was superb, as we were confident of getting the result and avoiding the unthinkable. I hobbled about, talking to the mates about the game, but I couldn't stop thinking about whether or not the lads would be having it with the ASC.

As it got closer to 3:00 pm, it was time to drink up and get on the bus to the game. The streets on the way to Pittodrie were jumping with fans from both sides. This was probably the most important game ever between the two sides and a full house was guaranteed. However, we were up against it from the start. Not only was our confidence low from the bad run that we'd been on, but three or four of our better players were also suspended. Right from kick-off, you could tell that Aberdeen, having been on a winning streak, were in a completely opposite frame of mind and they attacked United from the start.

Disaster struck less than 10 minutes before half-time, when Billy Dodds put Aberdeen in front. Things got even worse with 20 minutes to go, as Duncan Shearer rifled home to put the Dons 2–0. This practically condemned United to the drop. A late Robbie Winters goal gave us a little hope, but it was too little too late. Barring a miracle on the final day of the season, we'd be playing in the First Division the following year. With United to play Celtic in the final game, and Aberdeen at Falkirk, it was more or less a certainty that we were relegated.

I've never felt so down in my life as when I walked out of the ground that day. As we made our way back towards the buses, heads were down and everyone was so quiet you could have heard a pin drop. Just as we walked out on to the huge grass area at the back of Pittodrie, a huge mob of Aberdeen ASC came running towards us. A quick look around told me the day could get worse. With over 200 Aberdeen getting nearer, and a rough head count of 30–40 of our lads, along with me just off crutches, it looked like disaster was about to happen. United's normal fans pride themselves on their good behaviour, so we knew that we'd get no help from them. There was nothing else to do but go for it.

I couldn't have run away even if I'd wanted to, so I yelled at the lads to come on and get into them. The next thing that happened will live with me forever. Our normally boring normal fans turned as one and got stuck into the ASC along with the lads. It was fucking hilarious, as old men rolled up their sleeves and piled in. And so started one of the best battles I've ever seen.

Around 1,500 United fans and 200–300 Aberdeen were having it in the park. Blows rained in from all angles as the Old Bill struggled to get it under control. Big Kev and a few of the lads started fighting with the Old Bill and Kev caught one of the coppers a cracker as he tried to nick one of them. They let the dogs go and one of them was soon rolling around on the deck with an Aberdeen lad who'd been felled by a stray missile. It was going off all over the place. I was going toe-to-toe with this big lad as the adrenalin began to pump and I forgot about the leg for a minute. After what seemed like ages, the coppers eventually got it under control and forced us back to the buses. But we were off and on those buses like yo-yos as the Aberdeen, to their credit, wouldn't give in and kept coming back for more. Eventually, around 45 minutes after the match had ended, we were given a huge escort out of Aberdeen. At least a bit of a carry on after the game had made us forget for a while that we were in the shit on the park.

The next Saturday came and the inevitable happened. We were officially relegated, after Celtic beat us 1–0 at Tannadice and Aberdeen cruised to a victory 2–0 at Falkirk. This would more or less see the end of the second generation of casuals, especially in Dundee, as with both clubs being stuck in Division One, our chances of playing against the bigger clubs would have to rest on the cup competitions from now on.

CHAPTER 39

FIRE AWAY

Season 1995/96 would see me semi-retired from the casual scene, but I actually ended up going to more games that season than I'd ever done before, most of the time as a fan. With United stuck in the First Division, the action off the park was non-existent. I travelled to nearly every away with the Smugglers boys and, even though the majority of them weren't lads, some were ex-lads and the rest, if push came to shove, would get involved. Knowing this, it was a chance to get round to the grounds that I'd never usually go to as if trouble came about I would have some sort of back-up.

We did have a bit of bother at some games, though, especially Airdrie. Here's a story from John of how a brief battle with them before a game at Tannadice ended up with the jailing of Ronnie, one of our best lads.

AFTER THE MATCH, THE GAME BEGINS
John's story, part ten

The match at Tannadice was a perfect opportunity to take on Airdrie and the Section B. Word was spreading fast that that the Section B were definitely coming to Dundee for the game. One of the Utility lads was in touch with one of the Airdrie boys and they were mouthing off about what they were going to do when they got to Dundee. We had heard all this before and nothing had happened. However, on this occasion, we decided to mob up anyway, just in case this Airdrie mob was as good as their word.

We met up in the Hilltown area of Dundee, where some of the lads came from. It was the nearest place to the football stadiums and, most importantly, it had plenty of pubs. As far as we were aware, Airdrie had been making a lot of noises again in the lower leagues and had a decent mob – but they hadn't shown in Dundee as a serious force for a long time. The Utility would never usually meet up so close to the football grounds on match days due to the concentration of police activity, but, thinking Airdrie wouldn't come into the city centre of Dundee, this didn't leave us much of a choice. Back then, there was always more chance of a battle in the town centre, as the Old Bill policed the grounds more than anywhere else. If the Airdrie lads came by train or parked their coaches in the town centre they would have definitely got a fight within half an hour of arriving. We knew that would never happen and that we would have to go up by the ground if anything was going to take place.

It was now about 1:00 pm and we were firming up nicely, about 60-strong in a bar just off the Hilltown and five minutes from the stadium. One of the young Dundee lads got off a bus on the Clepington Road and saw about 50 Airdrie Section B going into the Centenary bar. Once we knew that they were definitely there and where they were, we decided to let them get settled for a while before making the call. Soon they would find out what we were all about!

One of the Utility lads who was in touch with Airdrie, gave them a call and told them to leave the pub they were in and walk along to Provost Road where we would bang right into them, but they refused to do it. I couldn't believe it. They said they wouldn't do anything that we told them to do. You have to ask, what was the point of them coming with a mob in the first place? All the Utility were totally pissed off and had had enough of this bullshit. We ordered taxis and decided to go straight to their pub. If they were not willing to walk five minutes along the road to meet us, then we didn't have much of a choice but to go to them.

The taxis arrived and we made our way to the street behind the Centenary, where we knew we could mob up out of sight of the Old Bill. We were now buzzing, 60 Dundee Utility ready to do the damage. We all walked around the corner to the front of the pub and one of the lads walked in to tell our friends that they had a welcoming party outside. A minute later, he walked back out looking bemused. The Airdrie weren't there. The bar staff told him they'd already left for the match.

It was only 2:30 pm, with half an hour remaining until kick-off. Why the fuck would they want to leave the pub early and go down to the stadium? Once again, we gave the Airdrie lad a call and asked what the fuck they were up to. He told us that they were looking for us. The situation was now starting to seriously piss us off. Did they think Dundee would be hanging around the streets outside the stadium? They certainly knew how to get our backs up. What else did we have to do to meet these cunts? Firstly, we'd given them the opportunity to walk five minutes along the road in order to bang right into us. Secondly, having refused this offer and thinking, fair enough, it was our town, we decided to go up to the pub they were in. Then we find out that they had left the pub to look for us down by the match, despite knowing fine well that Dundee's mob was nowhere near the ground. It was totally unbelievable. Were they really that stupid?

We started to walk down to the stadium, hoping to eventually bang into them. As we walked into Sandeman Street, the main road between Dens Park and Tannadice Park, we spotted them walking up the road and chanting their songs. Like on every other match day, there were about four or five Old Bill standing outside the away turnstiles. The police also had a surveillance camera pointing into the street from the stadium, which was always manned on match days. By this time, the two mobs had seen each other and were now on collision course.

The police ran into the middle of the two mobs, trying to stop the chaos that was about to unfold in front of them. The policeman with the video camera also spotted what was going on and pointed the camera straight at us. 'Let's fucking do it,' everybody shouted. One of the Dundee lads had a golfing brolly and whacked the first Airdrie lad that came near him. All the Dundee followed suit. Next thing I heard was this whizzing sound above my head and realised that one of the Utility had discharged a flare gun right into the middle of the Airdrie.

FIRE AWAY

The police, who were in the middle of the maul and trying their best to stop the fight, hit the ground, shouting and alerting the others that one of us had a gun. All the Utility were just as shocked as the Airdrie that someone had fired a flare gun outside the stadium with the place swarming with Old Bill. I looked up at the stand to where the policeman with the camera was and noticed that he had turned his attention to us. Everybody started to split up, running into different streets, while the police escorted the Airdrie Section B into the stadium.

The police got their hands on one Dundee lad and accused him of being the ringleader. He was also charged with firing the distress signal. We all knew he hadn't done it, but he had hit one of the Airdrie lads with the golfing brolly. Fair play to him, though: he got a three-month jail sentence for it but kept his mouth shut. Later, the Dundee lads who had decided to go into the match said that all the Airdrie lads were singing, 'You ran! You ran!' What a joke. If the Section B were really interested in meeting the Utility and testing themselves against us, we'd given them umpteen opportunities. To tell the truth, they went right down in my estimation after this and didn't match up to what Kenny had told me they were like in the 1980s. One thing remained the same, though: they liked to make a lot of noise in and around the ground. But, unlike their previous generation of lads, they didn't seem to be able to back it up with brains.

CHAPTER 40

TROUBLE ON THE TERRACES

United struggled to break away from the rest of pack and the run to the end of the season was a tense one. Promotion was a must for a team like United. Another season stuck in the First Division would absolutely cripple our once famous club. With around 10 games to go, we took huge support to every ground as we tried to get the club back up. Hamilton, Airdrie and Paisley were all visited and with four games to go it was back to our old stomping ground of Perth.

The day of the game, we left as usual from the Smugglers with a full bus. There must have been something in the air, as more old faces than normal were on the bus. We'd no sooner cracked open a can than we were in Perth. We plotted up in a bar that we'd pre-arranged to go to in the city centre and were joined by a few lads who'd made their own way. A couple of hours before the game – and a bit pissed and thinking about the old times in Perth – I went out for a bit of fresh air and to have a nose about to see if they had any lads around. I was soon joined by one of the mates, who seemed to have had the same idea as myself.

'What are you up to?' he asked. 'Just having a browse, mate. Fuck, I remember the time you couldn't walk about here for five minutes before you had some cunt on your case. I've a feeling something is gonna happen today. Too many old faces about,' I said.

'Come on back in the boozer,' he replied, 'it's your round, you miserable cunt!'

By about 2:45 pm. a couple of the lads were trying to round us up to go to the game. Their pleas fell on deaf ears as we'd had too much to drink by then and were happy to forget about the game. Finally, with about five minutes to go, we made our way to McDiarmid Park, getting there about 15 minutes later.

We all walked down towards the United end behind the goal, only to be met with closed turnstiles. 'This end's been full since well before kick-off, lads, try the main stand,' said the steward at the gate.

We made our way around the ground but the story was the same at the next stand. Then someone said, 'Come on, lads, let's go in their end.'

Now that sounded like a good idea!

We made our way around to their main end and quietly made our way through the turnstiles. Being one of the first through, I waited on the rest of the lads to get in. Once we were almost all in, I was buzzing like fuck. I hadn't felt like this since before I'd done my leg in. Being back to almost full fitness, I was raring to go. We decided to make our way along to the end where they usually sat and walked up the stairs into the seats.

BANG!

As soon as we walked up the stairs and came out into the stand, we were attacked from all angles. Punches were being thrown all over the place. Their lads had recognised us as soon as we'd walked in. We stood our ground, even though it seemed as though every cunt from Perth was having a pop at us. The police came charging around the pitch and up the stairs, trying to gain some sort of control and nicking some of our lads. Those of us they didn't nick, they frogmarched to the other end of the stand and made us sit down. It was funny as fuck going along that walkway, as every man and his dog gave us no end of abuse and we just lapped it up and laughed right back at them.

They had the last laugh, though. United, as usual, crumbled in a crunch game and went down to a single goal. There was no more trouble after the game, as the cops kept us in for 10 minutes and made sure we went straight back on the bus. I remember thinking on the way home that, even though I thought that football violence was on its way out, it never really went away. I must admit, it was all I thought about for the rest of the night. I'd missed the Saturday buzz.

As per usual, United did it the hard way. A midweek win at Hamilton was ruined by a 1–0 defeat by Dunfermline at Tannadice the following Saturday. It meant that with a game to go we had to go to Morton and win – and that Dunfermline would have to slip up at home to Airdrie. For a while in the last game, it looked to be swinging our way, but our game ended up 2–2. With Dunfermline winning at home, it meant that the Fife team would go up as champions and United would have to go into a play-off with Partick Thistle.

AFTER THE MATCH, THE GAME BEGINS

The first leg in Glasgow ended up 1–1, while the return leg at Tannadice saw one of the most memorable games ever. Halfway through the second half, Partick went in front and led 2–1 on aggregate. With seconds left, they were denied a stonewall penalty. Then, United raced up the park and, when all looked lost and with the ball bouncing around the penalty box, up popped old Hampden hero and centre-half Brian Welsh and headed home the equaliser. In extra time, striker Owen Coyle tucked away a cross to put us 3–2 up on aggregate. After a nail biting last 10 minutes, the whistle finally went and we were back in the Premier League. Cue a mass pitch invasion as we celebrated with the players.

PART 3

TAKING IT ABROAD AND INTO THE MILLENNIUM

CHAPTER 41

VISITING AN OLD FRIEND

As we looked forward to the new season, there was a little matter of the 1996 European Championships down south to be dealt with, which saw us drawn against the old enemy, England.

John's story, part eleven

Scotland games are usually low on our list of priorities, but when we drew England in the 1996 European Championships this all changed. This had once been the oldest annual fixture in the world, but had been stopped because of crowd trouble. Well, there was no way of stopping this one. As England were also the tournament hosts, it was an even bigger challenge for all the hooligan firms across Europe to have a pop at England on their own doorstep.

Four months before the big match and there was already talk in the papers about potential trouble at the tournament – of how the Dutch and the Germans were supposedly coming over to do the business. But, deep down, England knew who they wanted: Scotland. The big one! We were up for it big time and were ready to invade London. All the Scottish mobs were talking about it and could not wait for the match. The two countries had not played each other for seven years.

Scottish firms knew they could not travel down to London on their own as we would be well outnumbered. We had to put our differences aside and join together to form a national firm. A meeting was planned in Dundee, with Aberdeen, Rangers, Hibs, Falkirk and ourselves. We met in the Beefeater, just off the Kingsway, with four casuals from each mob present. It was kind of funny sitting there. It was like it was going to kick off at any minute among us 20 shaven-headed, battle-hardened football thugs. We must have looked a little on edge as we sat there surrounded by families having their dinner. But this was where the foundations for the Scotland mob were made. We were all as one – well, for a couple of weeks at least! Scotland now knew they would stand a much better chance against England. We were all a lot older and wiser than the last time Scotland had played them in 1989. This time we were ready for them.

A couple of weeks passed and the top boys from Scotland met for one last time to finalise our plans and travel arrangements. If all our mobs met up as agreed, it was estimated that there would be at least 600 or 700 hardcore lads in London. It would be the elite of the Scottish casuals, lads who would not budge from anyone– especially our English counterparts!

In the week leading up to the game, there were stories in

the press saying that anyone who didn't have a ticket for a match should not come to the game or they would be arrested. We were also told that the police would be trying to deter mobs by stopping coaches en route. On the Friday before the game, I was sitting in work when I heard on the radio that the police had stopped a coach-load of known hooligans in Edinburgh. The bus had been impounded, so that was at least 50 Hibs fucked!

To this day, I still do not know if any of them made it down to London. All the other mobs knew not to travel in such large numbers. The lads from the Utility were either travelling down in cars, flying in twos and threes, or going down to London a few days before the match to stay with friends in various parts of London and keeping our heads down.

The day of the match could not come quick enough. It was time to see how many of the lads had made it to London. The group of lads I'd travelled down with set off for the meeting point in High Barnet, in North London. The journey on the train took about 45 minutes, but it seemed like eternity. Every step of the way, at every tube stop, we looked out of the windows to see if there were any English about. The buzz and the excitement of just sitting on that train for the small journey is one of the main reasons for going to football. You never knew what to expect next.

The five of us eventually reached High Barnet and saw a few lads hanging around. We found out that they were Celtic and they told us that the Scotland firm were meeting up in a pub just up the street. We got there to find a fairly large Scottish mob gathered, but not as many as I expected. Nevertheless, it was a good mob. A lot of known faces were there from all the firms and it was still early doors at this point. By about midday, we were about 300-strong, with about 60 of them from Dundee – a hard mob, with all our main boys who had been going for years. Hibs had around the same numbers and the rest of the mob was made up of Celtic, Rangers and Falkirk. There was no Aberdeen, which I couldn't understand. What was the point in meeting up months in advance, saying all the mobs would go as one, and then not show?

As the afternoon progressed, the whole Scottish mob grew restless. The Hibs main boy was in contact with a mob of English and he told us they were definitely on their way. With Oldham and Man United being friendly with the Hibs lads, I assumed it was them he was talking about. However, he also told us that the Old Bill were on them and that they'd have to try to shake them off first.

A few of the Dundee lads went around the whole mob, telling everyone to put money in a pint tumbler for a small bet. The first Scottish lad to hit an Englishman would win the money. Not that anyone needed any encouragement to do that in the first place. We were all itching to get at them!

A while later, a car pulled up outside the pub with a few English in it. One of the Hibs boys that knew them went over to talk. It was Oldham's top boy, with a few of his cronies. He said their mob would be here soon, but we had been hearing this all day. I had had enough of these delaying tactics, so I smacked him in the face and told them to fuck off. We had been there for hours and were getting pissed off. The Hibs lad was not amused by my punching the Oldham boy, but by this time all the lads from Dundee's patience was wearing very thin – especially *with the Hibs for arranging to meet on the outskirts of London with no result. One outcome of the little fracas was that I won the bet about being the first one to punch an Englishman, so I used the winnings to buy the Dundee lads a round of drinks.*

Once again the phone rang. It was the English and they said that they were five minutes away. It was on, so all the Scottish lads went outside and started to break up a fence to get together some ammo. By this time, they were all steaming drunk and fired up with anticipation. Yet, once again, nothing happened. All the Dundee lads had had enough now. Even worse, we'd had word back about loads of trouble at Trafalgar Square. There was a mob of 200 Scotland there and they were fighting like fuck. There were about 20 Dundee, Aberdeen's mob and some other small Scottish firms and they were having a ball. That just topped it off for everybody who was stuck up at High Barnet. Maybe Aberdeen had been right not to meet up with us after all. The Dundee Utility decided to leave and asked if any of the other lads wanted to come with us. Celtic agreed, as did a few Hibs, leaving behind their main mob. It proved to be the best move we made that day.

About 80 of us made our way into central London. We decided to get off the tube for a drink at Camden Town and headed to a pub called The World's End to watch the match. As soon as we got off the train, there was a scuffle with a few lads who I think were Cardiff boys out for a nose. We knew that this would draw attention to ourselves and that the lads we'd just had it with would probably come back later with a few more boys.

Suddenly, a van pulled up beside us and out jumped the plain-clothes police from Dundee's Football Intelligence. I could not believe it! They must have been watching us the whole time up at High Barnet, sneakily waiting for something to happen. They had cameras with them and started taking everybody's pictures. We decided to make for Trafalgar Square, getting back on the tube and then off again at Waterloo. Everyone made an effort not to speak, so that we could remain inconspicuous and nobody would be able to identify us as Scottish. There were no tartan fuckwits among us, just Scottish casuals blending in with our deadliest rivals and ready to kick it off at any time.

As our mob neared Trafalgar Square, we could see that it was surrounded by English casuals with Scotland stuck in the middle. There were fights in every corner and it was complete mayhem. I loved every minute of it. This is what we had travelled 500 miles for. There were that many different English mobs that none of them even batted an eyelid at us. They must have just presumed that we were another English mob heading to the square. How wrong they were. As we got to the square, we charged the English from behind and they certainly did not know what had hit them.

When we turned up, the Scottish casuals were trying to fight their way out of the square just as we started to fight our way in. It was complete chaos. By now, there must have been 400 or 500 Scottish casuals in the square, all together as one and ready to take on any English mob who wanted to have a go. On top of this, there was at least a 1,000-strong tartan army. Usually, they wouldn't get involved in any violence at matches but today they were up for it. An international match against England is always a totally different story. Everybody hates them!

The police did not know what was going on and were

losing control. It was probably the worst football violence I had ever seen or been involved in. It went on all day. There were also a couple of little scuffles between Dundee's mob and Aberdeen, because they hadn't bothered to show up at High Barnet. That was always going to happen. To put it mildly, we do not like each other, but it was eventually sorted out. We had a couple of thousand English casuals to deal with, which was a little more important than a little argument with the ASC.

The police were now charging into the square with their batons and spraying CS gas to try to break up the fighting, but with no effect. I was standing near one of the monuments, when these five guys walked into the square, game as fuck, and started to confront a couple of us. They were not giving a fuck. I walked over to one of them, stood beside him and gave him a nod. He must have thought I was English. I then put my hands against the monument for balance and kicked him straight in the face. He fell back a little and then shouted that they were Millwall. We started rolling about on the ground, until the Old Bill came over and split up the fight. They didn't even get arrested, but were just told to fuck off out of the square.

By now, me and a few other Dundee lads were starting to sober up and wanted more drink. We made our way across a road to a small off licence on the edge of the square. We were standing outside the shop, me with a few cans of lager in a bag, when some English lads who'd spotted us leaving the square decided to pull us up. 'Who the fuck are you?' they shouted, to which we readily replied: 'Dundee Utility.' This was followed by the carrier bag I was carrying being smashed over a lad's head. Next thing I knew, he took his belt off in response and whacked me in the head with it. They eventually retreated, so we headed back into the square.

Once there, we gathered the Dundee together and decided to leave by a set of stairs in the corner. We then walked along the top of the square, past where the English mobs were standing. There were about 50 of us, but we remained inconspicuous, blending in with our English counterparts as we did not wear any colours. This allowed us to take them by surprise, as they were still occupied with the Scottish who remained in the square.

We ran into any English mob we could see. I do not even know who the English mobs were that we were fighting that day, but I suppose it did not matter. The Utility, happy with the day's events, then made their way towards one of the tube stations for our journey back to Kings Cross.

When it comes to football violence, it was one of the best days I personally have ever had and is one that I will always remember. It was an achievement in itself, to go down to England and hold your own the way we did. When we got to Kings Cross, most of our mob had split up and gone its separate ways. I later heard that there had been fighting well into the night and into the next day, but that was always going to happen when we crossed the border for a match with the auld enemy.

CHAPTER 42

GOING ABROAD

Scotland games were never really our thing, but there were a couple of times that we had lads in the national team when we went to see them play. Once again, John takes up the story.

John's story, part twelve

In May 1994, Scotland played Holland in a friendly match in Utrecht. All the Scottish firms were talking about it, how it would be a good trip that would really test our mob. Holland has some of the hardest mobs in Europe, such as Ajax and Feyenoord. These two clubs have had a bad reputation throughout the years of football violence, especially when they played each other. In fact, the hatred would rival that of Celtic and Rangers at Old Firm games. In the past, people have lost their lives in some of the trouble.

Excluding the English matches, this was probably the

first time Scotland's top mobs had ever joined together. Undoubtedly, the Dutch would be a massive test for everyone. I don't know why the Scottish casuals didn't follow Scotland abroad more regularly. To me, causing trouble abroad was something more associated with the English. For Scotland, it was very rare and the tartan army was probably the best behaved in the world. However, we couldn't resist having a go at the Dutch on this occasion. Playing Holland also offered the added bonus of staying in Amsterdam, the sleaze capital of Europe. It was just the extra incentive that we needed.

The Utility decided to travel by coach to Amsterdam. We left Dundee on a Thursday evening and travelled down to Dover. At that time, no football fans were allowed to travel on ferries due to all the trouble the English teams had caused with each other, including the infamous riot between West Ham and Man United all the way across the English Channel. Following that, the authorities vowed never to let it happen again and enforced a ban. When our bus reached Dover, it was stopped and we were asked where we were going and if we were football fans. Aware of the ban, the lad who was running the bus said that we were going to a Phil Collins concert. I nearly pissed myself when I heard him say that. The bus was full of seasoned football hooligans and none of us looked like Phil Collins fans, that's a fact!

To my amazement, it did the trick and they let us on our way. Once on the ferry, we were able to stretch our legs and relax after our 12-hour journey from Dundee. Twenty-two hours later, with splitting headaches, we arrived in Amsterdam on a Friday morning. We looked for digs and found a few hotels in the red-light district, *which suited us just fine. That afternoon, the Scotland firm met up just around the corner in the Grasshopper Bar, a famous drinking and smoking joint in Amsterdam. When I walked in, it was already packed with lads. There was about 80 Aberdeen – they always manage to get the numbers – plus 50 Hibs and now about 20 Dundee. This was quite a poor showing from Dundee's point of view. Nevertheless, we were there with a few good lads and that's all that mattered.*

Altogether, it was a decent turnout for Scotland, considering the fact that we don't usually travel abroad with the national team. I walked into the Grasshopper, ready for my first drink of the day, thinking I was the business in my open Lacoste cardigan, with a Dundee Utility T-shirt underneath. An Aberdeen lad told me to close my top, to which I told him to go and fuck himself. If he wanted it closed, he could try and close it himself. The whole place fell silent, until one of the Hibs lads I knew shouted over to ask me if I wanted a drink. Things quickly settled down after that, which was just as well. We were there to fight the Dutch, not each other.

The match was being played in Utrecht, which was about half an hour on the train from Amsterdam Central. On Saturday morning, the day of the match, all the lads met again in the Grasshopper and planned to get the train together as one Scotland mob. This was it, what we had travelled all this way for. We left the Grasshopper and walked up to Central Station. The Scotland mob were looking very impressive and ready to take on the mighty Dutch.

As we boarded the train, everybody kept quiet and tried not to draw attention to ourselves. Half an hour later, the train pulled into Utrecht Station. Everybody was really filled with anticipation. The Dutch had been aware for some time that we were coming over to Holland, so we were expecting trouble.

As soon as the train stopped in the station, we tried to get off. However, the train doors didn't open. Suddenly, loads of police appeared and ran on to the platform with dogs, forming a line that stretched the whole length of the train. The Dutch police were a little different from what we were used to in Scotland, as they carry guns and CS gas. I thought to myself, 'This is it, we're fucked. We've come all this way for nothing.' None of us even had tickets for the match. The police didn't let us off the train and I thought they were going to turn the train back to Amsterdam Central. One of the Hibs boys started to try to force the train doors open and everybody joined in. We were all going mental. We knew that we had to get off the train or the whole trip would be ruined.

To our surprise, the train doors opened and we all charged out on to the platform. It took the police completely by surprise. I even noticed one of the Dutch coppers reaching for his gun while trying to hold on to a big fucking dog. It was complete chaos. Two Hibs casuals started rolling around the platform with the policeman who went for his gun. Another of the Hibs lads was lying on the platform with handcuffs on, with all the rest of the Hibs trying to set him free. The Hibs guys were fucking mental.

The rest of the Scotland ran out of the Utrecht train station. There were a few Dutch lads waiting outside and they got chased down the street. I don't think they expected 150 Scottish casuals to run out of the station towards them. A few shop windows got smashed in the process, but the police were quick on the scene and rounded up most of Scotland's mob. However, me and Gilky from Dundee jumped into the nearest bar we could find. A couple of minutes later, another couple of Scotland's lads came in. I couldn't believe my eyes, as it was the Hibs boy who had been lying face down on the platform with the handcuffs on. His mates had managed to rescue him. However, there was only one problem – he still had his hands behind his back with the cuffs on! He put a jumper over his shoulders to hide them.

The four of us decided to stay in the bar for a while, until the police cleared off. All the Scotland lads were getting rounded up, so it seemed a good idea to lie low. It was a hot day, so I asked the barmaid for four of the finest Dutch lagers they had, which were much needed after all the running about that we had just done. The barmaid put the cold pints down on the bar and they never touched the sides. The Hibs lad asked me if I thought I was being funny – how the fuck was he supposed to have a drink while he still had the cuffs on?

The rest of us looked around and burst out laughing. I had forgotten that he was cuffed. I just didn't think. Shortly after, I phoned one of the other lads to see what had happened outside. He said 46 Scotland had been detained by the police and were all going to be deported. There was now no way I was going back to Utrecht Station, especially not with that daft Hibs cunt still having cuffs on. We would all end up getting nicked and deported too. The four of us decided to get a taxi back to Amsterdam.

We arrived safely back in Amsterdam, but we now had

the little dilemma of getting the handcuffs off the Hibee. We walked around the centre of Amsterdam looking for a hardware store to see if we could buy a hacksaw to try and get the fuckers off. We went into a couple of stores and explained to the shop assistants that we were on a stag night, had put handcuffs on him and then lost the key. One shopkeeper gave us a funny look and then said he couldn't help us. We left the shop, but the shopkeeper had obviously already phoned the police. Just our luck, there was a police station right across the road from the shop and the police were quickly out into the street and looking for us.

The Hibs boy legged it. However, he got caught further down the road and was arrested. We tried to help the boy as much as we could, but didn't want to end up getting arrested ourselves. There was only so much we could do. The three of us that were left ended up staying out for the night, doing the things that you would usually get up to on a night out in Amsterdam! The only thing about the trip that I was disappointed with was that the Dutch didn't show. To this day, I am unaware of the reason for this. They knew we were coming and it was not like their mobs to turn down an opportunity for a battle. Nevertheless, it was a trip that will long be remembered!

CHAPTER 43

PUTTING THE DRAGON TO THE SWORD

John's story, part thirteen

In May 1997, Scotland played Wales in a friendly at Rugby Park, the home of Kilmarnock Football Club. The match was played on a Wednesday night, so some of the lads decided that we should go. Kilmarnock was a good two-and-a-half-hour drive from Dundee, so most of the lads who worked took a half-day holiday or just pulled a sick one. I took the names of all the lads who were interested in going to the match. It came to 30, so two minibuses were hired.

In Scotland, there was now a mob called the National Firm, which was made up of lads from Hibs, Rangers, Hearts and Airdrie. I didn't mind joining up for a Scotland match, but this National Firm concentrated only on the national team and stopped going to their domestic games. Fuck that! I was Dundee through and through and a lot of my mates were Dundee United fans. None of us would ever dream of not supporting our club on a weekly basis and just solely concentrating on the Scotland matches. I would imagine it would be the same for Aberdeen. I could never imagine Dundee playing Aberdeen, or any of the other teams that made up the National Firm, and the match passing off peacefully with no lads in attendance. If they were through as a mob, then they would always get a fight.

All the lads met in a pub at midday for the Kilmarnock trip. There were rumours that Wales were bringing a big mob to Scotland. The Welsh had never come to Scotland with a mob before, but I knew they had a couple of tasty mobs in Cardiff and Swansea, so we were all looking forward to the trip and any surprises that may be thrown up. The minibuses arrived in Kilmarnock about 3:00 pm and most of the lads were half pissed already. Three hours in a minibus is a long time and the only thing that kept us amused was plenty of drink. We parked the minibuses in Kilmarnock city centre and made our way to a pub.

An hour or so had passed and we noticed a car kept passing the pub we were in, obviously checking us out. The car eventually stopped and asked us who we were. They were Kilmarnock casuals and couldn't believe it when they realised that there was a mob of Dundee in Kilmarnock. They were even more gobsmacked when we told them a Wales mob was expected, too. God only knows how all the other Scotland firms knew what was going on in Kilmarnock, but the local soccer firm was oblivious and didn't know anything about it.

We heard that the National Firm was in a boozer just up the road from us. They were 150-strong, which is not bad considering it was a midweek friendly and the venue was miles away from all the main cities in Scotland. The Killie lads decided to tag along with us to see if there was any action. Kilmarnock usually have a good mob at home, but it very rarely travels.

We were all just getting settled in a pub, when one of the Kilmarnock lads came in and said there was a Welsh mob about 30-strong just up the road. This was it! We couldn't have asked for any more: even numbers of Dundee and Wales. We didn't see the need to phone the National Firm. That would be a total liberty, outnumbering them big time. If there were 150 of them, the Old Bill would be with them anyway, no doubt. As we reached the pub where the Welsh mob were supposed to be, one of the older Dundee lads, Big Gary, went in for a look, while the rest of the Utility stood across the street.

A few Dundee lads walked into the pub and Gary told the Welsh lads that if they were there for trouble they were to get outside now and have it. We waited across the street anxiously for five minutes until the Welsh lads started to come out of the pub. I couldn't believe our luck. Thirty on to thirty, with no police presence, on a Wednesday afternoon in Kilmarnock! It was ready to go off at any minute!

One of the Welsh lads shouted, 'Let's have it,' instigating the rest of them to follow. The Welsh lad that charged into us first got put right on his arse by Ryan and another few of them hit the ground after him. It was a big mistake on their part. If you could pick 30 Dundee out of our whole mob, you would be hard pushed to pick a better 30 lads than the ones taking the trip that day. The Welsh got absolutely demolished. However, they were game, so fair play to them. Later that day, we heard that the lad who ran into us first was Swansea's top boy. I *don't think he would do that again in a hurry! We also heard the National Firm were raging about what had happened, saying we had fucked the fight up for them. But there had only been 30 Welsh, so it had been an even fight. It was probably just as well that the Welsh lads banged into us and not the main Scotland firm. There would have been far too many of them. As I said earlier, it would have been taking a total liberty.*

The rest of the day passed off peacefully and we didn't see our Welsh friends again. We did bang into the National Firm and had a couple of drinks with them, but it was a tense atmosphere so we just drank up and left. They were obviously pissed off with what had happened, but that's just the way it goes. If you're not fast, you're last!

We decided to make our way back to Dundee, happy with the day's events. The next day I woke to receive a phone call telling me that one of the lads, a good friend of mine who had been in Kilmarnock with us the previous day, had passed away in his sleep. It was the last time that any of us saw him but he will always be remembered!

May DM rest in peace.

CHAPTER 44

THE NAUGHTY FORTY

In the late 1990s, the Dundee Utility had formed strong links with Stoke City's Naughty Forty. It came about when a group of Dundee on holiday met some Stoke lads in a bar and got chatting to them. They ended up exchanging numbers and our lads said we would maybe pay them a visit one day. The casual scene had died down in Scotland, due to the introduction of CCTV, the NCIS (National Criminal Intelligence Service) and improved policing at games. At that time, the Old Bill were right on top of our mob and we couldn't even sneeze without getting nicked. It was like that all over Scotland, so the mobs were deteriorating fast. Meeting the Stoke lads was a breath of fresh air. It couldn't have come at a better time. This was our chance to go and mix it with the English, where no one knew us – especially the police. It was a fresh start. It was like being reborn into the world of soccer violence. Here's John's story of the lads' first trip down south.

AFTER THE MATCH, THE GAME BEGINS
John's story, part fourteen

This was Dundee's first trip down to Stoke and it was a match that will stay with me forever. Fifteen of us set off from Dundee in a minibus. We didn't want to travel down with too many lads, just in case things turned nasty. None of us knew what to expect but we were all ready and willing to find out.

We left Dundee in the early hours of Saturday morning. All the usual banter was flowing as we travelled down. Six hours later, we eventually arrived in Stoke-on-Trent. The mood on the minibus quickly changed, with everybody now sitting quiet as we did not know what to expect. A phone call was made to a Stoke lad called Martin, whom the Dundee boys had met on holiday, and he gave us directions to an area of Stoke called Fenton.

When we met up with him, he told us he had booked us into a hotel. It was a bit of a hole, but from what I had seen Stoke was a bit of a dump anyway. In the morning, the lads got up, showered and made themselves ready for the day's events. In those days, Ralph Lauren jackets with Polo Sport T-shirts and Adidas Stan Smith trainers were all the rage. All the lads had on new gear, as we wanted to make a good impression for our southern allies. Martin and his brother were waiting for us in the hotel reception area, ready to go and meet up with the rest of Stoke City's Naughty Forty firm down at Stoke Station.

We entered the train station and there were at least 100 lads already there. That just wouldn't have happened back in Dundee, as it was only 8:00 am. The majority of the Stoke lads just looked at us, wondering who the fuck we were. However, we were with the Fenton lads, who are well rated within the Stoke firm, so everything was OK. It was 9:00 am by the time the lads boarded the train and there were now at least 200 Stoke lads. They looked really impressive, and most of them were a lot older than us. We were all in our mid-twenties, but the Stoke lads were in their mid-thirties and they had been going to the football for years. That just seemed to be the normal thing to do down in England.

The train journey to Wolverhampton took about 40 minutes and, by the time we arrived, the Dundee Utility were well mixed in with all the Stoke lads. We told them stories about what it was like in Scotland, while the Stoke lads told us all about what had happened the last time they had played Wolves. The two mobs had had a right good fight on a dual carriageway that lasted for ages without any Old Bill being about to stop it. It sounded too good to be true. If that happened the last time these two teams met each other, there was definitely going to be Old Bill on top of us this time.

As the train pulled into Wolverhampton Station, the Stoke lads sat quietly, trying not to bring any attention upon themselves. We disembarked the train and there was some police on the platform with dogs but, to my amazement, they didn't follow us out of the train station. They just left us to walk into the city centre and head straight to a bar. You would never get away with that in Dundee. The police would have rounded up our whole mob, taken our names and escorted us to the match, even though nobody had done anything yet.

We all managed to cram into a bar and got the drinks in. The pub was just off a square in the city centre. We noticed some Wolves already checking the Stoke mob out, by passing the pub and looking through the pub window, but so far it had stayed quiet. Suddenly, the Wolves firm was outside the pub and they were trying to block us in. We Dundee lads couldn't hide our excitement but nothing seemed to be happening. So, we took it upon ourselves to kick it off by throwing a couple of bottles through the pub windows. The Stoke lads were trying to calm us down but we hadn't seen action for ages and it was like the 1980s all over again: big mobs, hardly any police and the potential for a fight that was about to kick off big time. Even if the Old Bill did come, we could do what the fuck we liked as they didn't know any of us. This was not like back home, where the police knew us by name and we couldn't get away with anything.

Quinny kicked open the front doors of the pub and the Dundee lads steamed right out into the street where the Wolves were standing. We were right in the thick of the action and loving every minute of it. The Stoke lads ran out right behind us and straight into the Wolves. They just scattered all over the place. We chased them down one street and then turned, to have it with the Wolves behind us. The Old Bill eventually came in loads of police vans. Unfortunately, one of the Dundee boys, Ronnie, got nicked. That was the only downer of the day so far, but it had been well worth coming down for. We were getting our first taste of football violence in England and we loved every minute of it!

With a massive police escort, the Stoke mob made their way to the match and I didn't think anything else was going to happen. As we got near to the stadium, we had to go under a subway to get to the ground. Now I knew where the old Wolves mob, the Subway Army, got their name from. The Stoke Naughty Forty got to the end of the tunnel and spotted the Wolves waiting at the other side. We just steamed right into them again, scattering their mob like before. But there were far too many police with us this time and the whole mob ended up being guided into the stadium.

The game finished with Stoke City winning the match 2–1. After the game, again under a massive police escort, we left the stadium and got put on the next train. Back in Stoke, some of the Dundee lads went into the city centre and hit a few of the nightclubs and tried to pull the local birds. It had been a long day, so the rest of us just went back to our hotel rooms and crashed out.

The next day, we were still buzzing from the events in Wolverhampton and how well we had got on with the Stoke lads. We decided there and then that we would definitely be coming back down to Stoke for another game. As we were getting ready to leave the hotel, we realised that we hadn't paid the hotel bill. We'd been told by the receptionist that we could settle up when we left, which was not the best idea on her part. Big Ian went to get the minibus and brought it around the side of the hotel, ready for our quick escape.

He passed the receptionist and she asked where he was going. He told her he was away to get the Sunday papers and would be back in a minute. Most of us were staying on the first floor, so we decided to jump out of the hotel window. The van was waiting up the street and we were all set to do a runner from the hotel. One by one, we jumped out of the window, pissing ourselves laughing as one of the lads landed flat on his face and ended up covered in mud.

AFTER THE MATCH, THE GAME BEGINS

While we were sneaking out, one of the Stoke lads that we had met the day before passed the hotel and saw us. What a sight it must have been. We ran into the minibus and made our escape. There was now only one more small matter to clear up before we went home and that was to try to get Ronnie released from the nick. We drove back to Wolverhampton and, after a while of driving around, we eventually found the police station where he was being held. The Old Bill were having none of it and told us that he was going to court the following Monday morning. We asked Ronnie if he needed anything and he told us he didn't have enough money for the train fare home, so we chipped in and gave it to him.

All in all, it had ended up being a great trip. The Dundee Utility would now look forward to many more trips down south, including Man City, Cardiff, Derby, Millwall and Nottingham Forest among others.

CHAPTER 45

RUMBLED

John's story, part fifteen

Around the same time that we were visiting Stoke on a regular basis, it began to hit home that we were not getting away with all that we thought we were.

One Saturday afternoon, I left the house to have a stroll into town. There was no one important playing in the city that day and, in fact, the scene was on its last legs. But we'd still meet in Jack Daniels on a Saturday for a few beers with the rest of the lads. With the pub being right across the road from the train station, there was always the off chance that someone might come into town, but if they didn't it was a great place to start the day anyway.

With my house only being a 10-minute walk from the city centre, it was a perfect stroll down on a hot sunny day. As I was walking down the Victoria Road, there was a man leaning against a wall. He looked in my direction and said as I passed, 'How you doing, John? What's happening today then?'

AFTER THE MATCH, THE GAME BEGINS

Totally baffled, I thought to myself, 'Who the fuck is this?' I looked across the road and saw an unmarked police car. It stood out a mile, with its double aerial a dead giveaway. There was another copper sitting in the car, also watching me.

All sorts of things were going through my head as to what they were after. I quickly tried to recall anything that had happened in the past few weeks. I thought it could have been anything, as Dundee was a bit mental at the time and some parts of the city centre had become no-go areas due to all the trouble on a Saturday night. Some of the local gangs wanted to have a pop at the casuals, so there was more chance at the time of a fight with them than there was at the football.

The CID tried to shake my hand and introduce himself. He told me that he wanted to talk to me about the football scene, to which I replied innocently, 'Why the fuck would you want to talk to me about that?'

Intrigued, I decided to stay and hear him out. He asked me what was the latest thing that was happening at the football. He told me that in return for any information he'd see me all right. I couldn't believe what I was hearing. I thought this only happened on The Bill *or fucking* Starsky and Hutch!

I told him in no uncertain terms that I couldn't help him, that he was off his head and, to put it quite bluntly, to get to fuck. I continued on my journey towards Jack Daniels as I couldn't wait to tell all the lads about my little encounter with the Old Bill. When I got there about 20 lads were already in the pub. I got a pint up and went about telling the boys about my chance encounter. All the lads were raging as I told them what had happened. None of them doubted what I had said. We all agreed that the bastards were probably trying to stir it up between us, hoping we weren't as close-knit as we knew we were and were trying to bring about our downfall by the old divide-and-rule trick.

From the start of the 1990s, the one thing our firm had going for it was that we were strong and solid and would never grass on each other. We were all loyal through and through. After a while, we put it to the backs of our minds, when, suddenly, the very man himself walked into the bar and got himself a drink. 'That's the cunt there!' I said to the lads. 'That's the fucking CID that pulled me up earlier.'

We couldn't believe the brass neck of the cunt. It was like he was playing mind games with us. As he stood at the bar, Marsie threw a nip glass at his feet, which was soon followed by a volley of abuse, at which he about-turned and took to his heels.

I was glad that he came into Jack Daniels, as the lads were now all aware of our new friend and that I wasn't winding them up. It wouldn't be the last time we saw our copper friend. We learned that he wasn't just any old CID – he was our Football Intelligence Officer. His sole job was to get to know us all by name and sight and to follow our every move.

Our trips to Stoke were getting more frequent, as the days out in Scotland were becoming less and less. The lure of pitting our wits against the best in England was far more appealing than running around in Dundee chasing shadows. The English First Division at the time was a hooligan's dream, with teams like Cardiff, Wolves and Leeds, to name but a few. But the one match that we all wanted to go to was the famous Millwall, which meant a trip down to South London.

The only Scottish lads we knew that had travelled to the Old Den in the past with a firm were the CCS of Hibs. They'd played Millwall there in a friendly in the late 1980s. Whoever pitted those two together must have needed their head looked at. At the time the two teams had the most notorious followings both sides of the border. By all accounts, Hibs gave a good account of themselves and the stories of mass brawls on the streets were splashed all over the papers.

There was history in the Stoke–Millwall fixture as well. The last time the two had played each other, a petrol bomb was thrown at a pub and reports were rumoured that the infamous London club were after revenge. Well, we wanted a piece of that action!

Any time we'd been to Stoke in the past, we never went down with any more than 15 lads. We didn't go with more than that as we didn't want them to think that we were trying to muscle in. We were welcome guests and wanted to keep it that way. But, on this occasion, Stoke wanted as many Dundee lads as possible to travel. This was the big one and they wanted to go to town. We decided that, instead of making our own way down as usual via car and train, we'd hire a 33-seat bus. If any more lads wanted to come, they'd have to catch the train. All in all, it looked like we'd have 50 lads making the trip.

With the Tayside police right on top of our firm, we had a nightmare trying to arrange any transport to away games. They'd go around all the bus companies, warning them about football casuals and giving them names to look out for in case we tried to book anything. In return, *we booked buses from out of town and gave false names.*

A few weeks passed and we couldn't wait for the day to come. We'd told the bus company that we were going to Alton Towers and were staying the weekend. We'd also arranged to meet up on the Friday night in Stoke with all the Fenton lads and some of Stoke City's main boys. The Naughty Forty, as always, were well organised and had our train tickets from Stoke to London booked. They even had match tickets sorted for us. Everything being well, all we had to do now was get our arses down to Stoke.

All the lads took the Friday off work and met up in the Stobie Bar in Dundee. As the day unfolded, the lads were turning up one by one, buzzing with excitement. After all the years of going to football, this had to be the ultimate test, the centre of all things for football hooligans. All that we needed for the trip south was bought beforehand and no one was unprepared.

We'd arranged for the coach to pick us up in a sports-complex car park off the main drag. It was a perfect leaving place. Just before it was time to go, one of the lads drove around some of the streets in his car, just to make sure there was no Old Bill about. The all-clear was given and we were ready to go on our way. As the lads settled down for the journey ahead, the bus driver started his engine and the usual cheer went up.

Then, at that moment, I looked out of my window and couldn't believe my eyes. Several police vans and people carriers loaded with Old Bill were flying into the car park and headed straight for the bus. We'd been rumbled before we had even started our journey. It seemed like the whole of the Tayside police were now in the car park and had surrounded the bus. It all happened that quickly that we never even had time to stand up before the Old Bill were on and running down the middle of the bus, shouting at us all not to move and to get our hands in the air.

A few of the lads managed to react quickly and dropped on to the floor things that they didn't want caught in their possession. The looks on all the lads' faces told their own story. All the hype of the trip to Millwall had gone in a flash. A police officer was stationed by each seat and was taking names and making an inventory of all the weapons and other things that had been dropped. I had a quick look down and I saw this little plastic bag. 'Fuck that,' I thought and booted it up the bus. There was no way I was getting done for something that wasn't mine. One thing was clear, though. The weekend was totally fucked. The bus started up and took us to the main police station.

One by one, we were taken off the bus and filmed. One cheeky cunt was lapping it up, telling us to smile for the camera. One of the younger Dundee lads had a Union Jack flag with 'Dundee Utility' written along the middle of it and the Old Bill made two lads hold the flag up while they filmed it. Complete wankers! The Old Bill were loving every minute of it.

As we got off the bus, we were told to identify our bags and what was in them. At the end, a couple of bags were unclaimed. I later learned that one of them contained a CS gas canister and some other naughty things. Whoever left it had had a lucky escape. They may have lost a few bob in designer clothes, but they'd also avoided getting a couple of years up their arse.

The Old Bill kept us in the cells until 11:00 pm before they let us out. They also impounded the bus and told the driver to take the rest of the weekend off. As soon as all *the lads were out, we went along to the nearest boozer to catch last orders. Pissed right off at the day's events, some of the lads were still talking about going down for the game in cars, but I decided to give it a swerve. When you get rumbled by the Old Bill the way that we had, it's time to call it a day.*

The next day, I heard around 15 Utility had made it down to Stoke and ended up having a good day out in London at the Den. It was even mentioned on the front page of the South London Press *that a bus full of known Dundee hooligans had been stopped in Scotland for trying to go to the Millwall–Stoke match to cause major disorder.*

It still makes me wonder how the Old Bill knew everything that we were doing. Did the football intelligence officers finally manage to get their hands on someone to give them information? We will probably never know the answer to that question, but one thing's for sure: if there had been an informer, I wouldn't like to be in their shoes if we ever find out.

The rest of the 1990s were to see the casual scene almost disappear, especially in Dundee. With most of lads either approaching 30, or past it, things began to change. With all-seater stadiums and CCTV driving the lads away, it was dead on its feet.

On the park, it was all change also. Two brothers, who were local businessmen, took over Dundee FC and set about trying to make the old club the biggest in the city once more. In May 2000, it was announced that old favourite Jocky Scott was no longer required as manager and that the Italian brothers Ivano and Dario Bonetti would take over the hot seat.

AFTER THE MATCH, THE GAME BEGINS

Over the next couple of seasons, Dens was the place to be. Season tickets sold at a rate not seen for 15 years. Stars such as Georgi Nemzadze, Juan Sara and Fabian Cabellero flooded into Dens as they pushed up the league. Then, unbelievably, in September of that year, Argentine superstar Claudio Caniggia signed for the dark blues. More followed, as Temuri Ketsbaia came, after a spell at Newcastle, among many others.

As United struggled to avoid relegation, the Dees finished the season in the top six for the first time in years. The tabloids also lauded the Dens Parkers for the great attacking football they played. It seemed that every other week another foreigner arrived at Dens, but this led to suspicion as to where the money for this came from. Soon, it all became clear. The club's new managers had run up about £20 million worth of debt. After spending more money than most managers could only dream of, without bringing any real success to the club, Bonetti and his management team were sacked. Old favourite Jim Duffy was left to try to pick up the pieces and work with 20-odd foreigners.

Next, the inevitable happened as the club plunged into administration and most of the players were paid off. Duffy incredibly led the depleted team to the Scottish Cup Final in 2004, to play Rangers. The game itself ended up the usual damp squib for a team from Dundee – 1–0 to Rangers. Off the park, all the old heads turned out for what also ended up as a non-event, as around 150 Dundee swaggered about Glasgow without any competition from the ICF.

As Rangers had already won the league and qualified for the Champions League, it meant Dundee went into the hat for the UEFA Cup for the first time for years. After a qualifying tie, they were paired with Italian team Perugia. The away leg in Italy was taken in by a good firm of lads, old and new, as they camped in the Italian city for a couple of days. On the park, they put up a good show, but narrowly went out at the first hurdle. Off the park, they had a bit of trouble with the local Ultras and were attacked in the square before the game. The rock-throwing locals didn't put up much of a fight, as the lads had them take to their heels as soon as the bombardment stopped.

Back to the end of the 2002/03 season, I met Kingy and a few of the old lads for a pint after the last game of the season. He told me that after reading Cass Pennant's *Congratulations, You've Met The ICF* book, the chapter about the reunion to Old Trafford had given him an idea.

It was planned for all the over-thirties to go to Aberdeen in the new season, for nothing more than a piss-up and a good laugh. If trouble came our way, so be it. The day before the trip, news travelled around town that our planned trip north had been all over the news and was even on Teletext. The majority of lads, including myself, got cold feet and decided to give it a miss. A half-empty bus became overcrowded as they were joined by John and a firm that came up from the train station. They were met in Aberdeen by one of the biggest-ever police operations for a game in Scotland outside the Old Firm. The game passed without incident, as the lads were taken to a pub and weren't allowed anywhere else as dozens of cops stood guard outside.

After the game, a lot of lads got the bug for it again. For

my part, I'd just become a father for the first time and I gave it a miss. But others were still up for it. The scene wasn't over yet, as John will show you in the next few chapters.

CHAPTER 46

MOTHERWELL

John's story, part sixteen

It was approaching the end of the season 2003/04 and Dundee were due to play Motherwell away at Fir Park. With the league positions being more or less decided, both teams had nothing to play for apart from pride. Myself and four others decided to travel to the game by car, with no real intentions for any trouble. It was mainly just to get away for the day and have a few beers.

In the 1980s and early 1990s, there was a little bit of history between Dundee Utility and Motherwell's Saturday Service (SS). However, there had been nothing to talk about for a good few seasons so we didn't expect any trouble. To our knowledge there was nothing organised and no Dundee were travelling for the match.

An hour and 20 minutes later, we arrived in Motherwell, just in time for kick-off. We parked the car outside the stadium and made our way into the ground. Fir Park is a total shit hole and it's the one stadium in

AFTER THE MATCH, THE GAME BEGINS

Scotland that I totally hate. There's just something about their ground that I don't like. There was a decent away support in the ground, about a couple of thousand Dundee fans. Not bad, considering Dundee only get 5,000 or 6,000 at home games.

The four of us decided to take our seats in the bottom corner of the stand, right next to the Motherwell end. There was another 10 Dundee who had also travelled through in cars for the match sitting behind us. The game started and I noticed another small mob of Dundee casuals coming into the ground. It was as if we had arranged to meet at the match, despite there being nothing planned.

Across in the Motherwell end, we could see group of lads who looked like the SS. They had certainly noticed our growing presence of about 25 lads. The Motherwell must have thought we were through as a mob for some aggro, but this couldn't have been further from the truth. All the Dundee lads were just there to watch the match of their own accord.

The game was a non-event and we didn't even pay attention to what happened on the pitch. A few of the lads suggested we leave the ground early and go round to the Motherwell end. Some of us thought there was no point as nothing would happen, but in the end we decided to go for a laugh anyway, seeing as we were there.

As we left the ground, we banged into another five Dundee, so that made 30 of us, all good lads. There were police outside the stadium but they didn't take any notice of us. As there had been no talk of any potential trouble the game had probably been classed as in the low-risk category.

MOTHERWELL

We all walked unhindered to the Motherwell end, the police oblivious. The 30 of us gathered and stood outside Motherwell's main gates. No one talked or spoke to each other. We just stood waiting for the game to finish and to see if there was any Motherwell SS wanting to have a go. The crowds then started to pour out of the stadium, but none of the Motherwell supporters crossed the road to where we were standing. There was also an eerie silence, which was unusual for a large crowd after a football match.

We spotted a couple of lads who looked like casuals staring over at us. One of the Dundee shouted over to them, 'Where's your Motherwell mob now?'

No reply. The Motherwell crowd filtered away and we got bored and decided to move on to the nearest boozer. The match had been finished for about an hour and, with no trouble expected now, one of the Dundee lads decided to nip to the shops. He left and then quickly ran back into the pub and said that he had been fighting with a couple of Motherwell lads just down the street. As there were only two of them, most Dundee stayed in the pub. A few Dundee lads left to see what the story was and to find out if there were any more Motherwell hanging about outside.

Five minutes passed, then suddenly the Dundee came rushing back into the pub to say there was a mob of Motherwell down the street and they wanted have a go. We all jumped up and left the pub. I couldn't believe my eyes. There were two Motherwell standing right across the road from us, shouting, 'Come on then, Dundee.' That was the cue we needed. Everyone charged across the road and chased them down the street. One of the Motherwell boys tried to jump a small garden wall but didn't make it.

AFTER THE MATCH, THE GAME BEGINS

He got caught by some of the lads and got booted to fuck. It was a bit of a liberty, but they shouldn't have been so cocky and stupid as to come with only two of them to the pub that we were in.

Then, to our surprise, we spotted about 20 Motherwell SS coming around the corner a bit further down the street. They started to run towards us. One of the Motherwell boys was on crutches and was waving them in the air. 'He must be off his head,' I thought to myself. Either that or he really trusted his mates not to run and leave him on his own. If they did, he would be fucked.

We charged into them. The boy with the crutches was a fucking nutter, whacking anybody who went near him. The Saturday Service were standing firm and the two mobs were in the middle of the road going toe-to-toe. The brawl continued for about five minutes, which is an eternity for a fight at the football.

Somebody then shouted that the Old Bill were coming, so the two mobs backed off from each other, but it was only one policeman walking along the road on his own. He stopped to see what was going on and immediately got on to his radio for back-up. Fuck it, we thought, it's only one copper, so we ran back into the Motherwell again.

This time, the SS backed off and the Motherwell lad with the crutches, who was at the front of their mob, threw them at us. Bad move! A couple of the Dundee lads just picked the crutches up and laid into him and his mates. By this time, the rest of the Motherwell lads were backing off around the corner into another street. You could hear the police sirens in the distance and this told us that it was about time to get the hell out of there before we all got nicked.

MOTHERWELL

We knew we had to move fast, so we ran back to the pub we'd been in. All the lads soon got the pints up again, talking about the events that had just happened and what a good fight it was. We should come to Motherwell more often! Give Motherwell their due, they stood their ground when they were outnumbered, but did eventually back off. Loads of respect to them – especially the boy on the crutches!

We got settled in the pub but it wasn't long before the local constabulary pulled up outside. The police entered the pub, told us to drink up and informed us that we weren't welcome in Motherwell any more. Some of us tried to finish our drinks, but the police just grabbed the glasses out of our hands. They told us to fuck off back to Dundee or we all would get lifted.

The police were seriously pissed off, so we headed back to our cars, happy with the day's events. It was a great fight – one that we did not expect – that lasted and none of us got arrested. That's what it was all about! For a battle between two mobs, however small, to unfold and occur the way it did was very rare in Scotland, especially in this day and age.

As the Dundee lads headed back in their cars, making our way out of town, we came to a roundabout and spotted some of the Motherwell lads on the other side, standing outside a pub on the corner of the street. I couldn't believe it. The boy with the crutches was still standing there. A couple of our cars drove right around the roundabout. When the Motherwell saw us, they started to retreat back into the pub, but we were just winding them up. We'd had enough excitement for one day, so we just gave them a little wave and made our way

AFTER THE MATCH, THE GAME BEGINS

back to Dundee, happy with the unexpected events of the day!

CHAPTER 47

FALKIRK

John's story, part seventeen

Early March 2003 and we decided to take in a cup game in Falkirk, with Dundee being the visitors. Our mob was getting it back together again and, with Falkirk having a small but game mob, we reckoned it would be a good challenge. The night before the game a few of us met in town to make plans for the day ahead and we decided to go by train.

When we arrived at the station early on the Saturday morning, to say we were disappointed at the turnout was the understatement of the year. A grand total of seven lads had turned up. After discussing whether or not to go, we decided to give it a bash, as we reckoned there would be other lads who'd make the trip by other means.

With a lot of Dundee fans being ex-casuals, we thought we could muster together some sort of mob, so we got on the train and made our way to Falkirk. The Dundee lads were drinking on the outskirts of town, so, when we got off the train, we got in taxis and met up with them. When we got there, they all had tickets for the game and none of them seemed to be interested in trouble. When they were ready to leave to go to the match, we jumped on their bus and decided to have a nose up at the ground. The lads who gave us a lift went straight into the ground and left us outside. Pissed off at them leaving us, we decided against going in with them and took our chances outside and went looking for a boozer to have a few pints.

With Falkirk's old ground being situated right in the centre of town and, with seven of us walking around, it wasn't looking like the brightest thing we'd ever agreed to do. We had a few close shaves, nearly walking into a pub full of their lads, for example. As soon as we walked away from that pub to ponder our next move, a police van pulled over and lined us up against the wall and asked why we weren't in the game.

We told them we were just through for a drink and weren't paying to watch that shite. As they did their usual warrant checks, I stood at the door of the van. I could see on the seat a book full of mug shots and I recognised a few faces in it straight away. It was mug shots of our mob. The checks eventually came up all right and we were left to carry on. We decided to find a boozer quickly before the Old Bill were on our case again – and, as we walked down the street, we bumped into Falkirk's top lad.

One of our lads, Dean, knew him and stopped to talk to him. He invited us for a drink as his guest. At first we weren't keen, thinking it was surely a set-up, but we eventually agreed to go as he seemed genuine. We found a pub down the street and tried to act calm, as we half-expected a mob of Falkirk to come in at any time and take a liberty with us. The Falkirk lad kept assuring us we would be OK and said he would get a few of the lads to come down and have a drink. Before we knew it, there were around 25 or 30 lads in the boozer, and big, fucking handy older lads at that. One of our lads was starting to get a bit pissed and lippy and was making the situation a bit dodgy, to put it mildly. He then disappeared for what seemed like ages. Thinking he'd gone to the bog, I left it for a bit. But the longer it went on, I began to worry what had happened to him.

Just as I was going to get up and look for him, the toilet door burst open and he came storming out, shouting, 'One of those cunts has just stuck the head on me. Come on, Dundee!'

We all stood up, not sure what the fuck was going on and feeling as though we'd been led into a trap. We managed to get out of the front door and on to the street, followed by the Falkirk lads. Just as it looked like our backs were going to be right up against it, the Old Bill that had been across the road stepped in and bundled us into the train station.

Some of the Falkirk lads were sound and one apologised to me for what had happened. When we were taken into the station, a couple of Dundee police spotters, who must have found our situation amusing, said smugly, 'Don't worry, lads, you'll get them back next time!'

'You better believe it,' I thought to myself. But when would we play them next?

18 July 2004. After years of trying to get planning permission for a new stadium, Falkirk finally got the go-ahead for their new home. And who did they choose to play against in the inaugural game? Celtic? Rangers?

AFTER THE MATCH, THE GAME BEGINS

Liverpool even? Nah, it would be Dundee! This was too good to be true. It was fucking payback time!

The game was to be played on a Sunday, which was even better, as Sundays are boring and what better way to brighten it up than a trip to a town with a score to settle? This one was planned properly. We knew Falkirk wouldn't match us for numbers, as by 2004 our firm was back up to 70–100 and we knew we'd only expect around 40 Falkirk.

We decided that, instead of alerting the Old Bill by travelling on the train, we'd make our way to Falkirk on minibuses. The meeting point was not going to be disclosed until the last minute, as we knew the earlier we planned things the better chance the Old Bill had of getting wind of it. It was agreed that a text message would be sent out that morning to every member of the firm, letting them know the meeting place.

We met on the morning of the match in the Powrie Bar, which is a little out-of-the-way pub behind the Fintry housing scheme, right on the outskirts of the city. With no CCTV around, it was the ideal place to leave from. Most of us decided on a quiet Saturday night, so that we were fresh for the Sunday. The rest of the lads had indulged in their usual Saturday night and turned up looking like shit. I got up around 8:30 am, as I could hardly sleep for excitement. Just as I was getting ready, I got the text message: 'Mobbing up in the Powrie! Dundee Utility! Let's smash these Falkirk cunts!' That got the pulse racing and I got changed double quick and jumped in a taxi to Fintry.

There were already a good few lads in the bar getting tanked up when I arrived, so I got myself a pint and settled down with them. We had hired three minibuses and it wasn't long before the pub started filling up with the boys that were going to go on them. A quick head count confirmed that we had 77 lads. Not bad for a Sunday friendly. When it was time to go, we all piled on to the buses and loaded them up with tins of beer for the journey ahead. The drive through was the usual carry on as the drink flowed. We only stopped once, at some small village to get more drink. Most of the lads who went into the shop were as usual helping themselves and came back on the bus with their pockets full.

Arriving in Falkirk, some of the lads were getting desperate and had started pissing in the empty beer cans. We were in the football traffic beside the new stadium when some bright cunt decided to throw one of the cans out of the window. It hit a copper on his bike and he was not a happy bunny and signalled the bus to follow him. Fuck! Everyone was going nuts at the lad who had chucked it out of the window. The copper flagged us into a lay-by but, by some work of God, just as he was coming over to us, he got a call on his radio and fucked off to an emergency. We couldn't believe our luck. Everyone gave out a cheer and we were on our way again!

We found the boozer we were meeting in and parked up. The rest of the lads began to arrive and we got settled in. The place was a bit of a dive, with a few pool tables up the back. The staff looked well chuffed though, seeing 80 thirsty lads coming in on a Sunday. We had a few drinks and Falkirk's main face decided to come round and have a look at our firm. As he walked into the pub, he was greeted by the Dundee lads who knew him. He seemed impressed by what he saw and told one of the lads *that he'd thought that Dundee only had a mob of young kids. This wasn't what he'd expected. He also said that Falkirk would only have around 40, but they'd give it a go anyway. He decided to sit and have a quick drink with us. One of the younger lads, who was a bit worse the wear for drink and trying to make an impression, started getting a bit nippy with the lad when he found out he was from Falkirk.*

One of the older lads told him to shut up and sit down, as the lad was on his own, which he did. The Falkirk lad finished his pint and shook hands with the lads before leaving. On his way out, he said he'd call when they were on their way. When he left the pub, some of the lads reckoned that they wouldn't make an appearance, as his face had dropped when he walked into the pub. As the day went on and the drinking started taking its toll, we got more and more impatient. Some of us went outside to see if they were on their way. We stood at the side doors, doubting whether or not they'd show, and one of the lads suggested that if they didn't come within the next five minutes we should get everybody out and go and look for them. The plan was they were to come from their pub over the way and that it would go off in the park between our two boozers. It would be perfect, if only they would hurry up. There were now around 30 of us standing outside, arguing whether or not to stay or go and look for them. Suddenly, a lad shouted that they were on their way. We turned to laugh at him, thinking he was at the wind-up, when 35 Falkirk came charging towards the front of the pub.

This was totally against the plan, as they were meant to

phone and we were meant to have it out the back. Yet another Falkirk mob were trying to pull a fly move. They were tooled up to the hilt, with sticks and bottles and lumps of concrete. That didn't stop the 30 of us from running straight into them, though we had to do a bit of ducking and diving while they threw everything at us that they could lay their hands on. The lads in the pub were still oblivious as to what was going on and were missing all the fun!

One Falkirk lad was waving a baseball bat about, which had the lads on their guard until he dropped it. One of the older lads, Stu, picked it up, and started battering fuck out of him with it. Most of the 30 lads from Dundee were youth, with Stu, Jim and Lee being the only older lads. It was some toe-to-toe, as no one gave an inch, especially our younger lads, who were giving as good as they got. Just as everyone was tiring – as it had seemed to go on for ages – the rest of the lads in the pub must have seen what was going on and emptied out on to the street.

One of the youth lads, Barry, came charging out with a pool cue and went right into them. Falkirk were now fucked and, with nothing to throw at us, were on the back foot. Most of them ran, but some of them were in the middle of the dual carriageway. They were challenging us but going backwards. The older Falkirk lads, who were too daft or too game for their own good, got terrible hidings. Two of them were laid spark out on the road as we continued the annihilation. We later heard that seven of them ended up in hospital. One of the young Dundee lads also had a really nasty gash on his head which was bleeding heavily.

They were now a shambles and were trying to escape by

any means possible. One of them was caught trying to run through someone's back garden and was followed by a few of the lads. He got a kicking in front of a bemused gardener, who stood rooted to the spot in amazement! We chased the remains of their mob up the road and it was all over. Credit must be given to them, though, as they stood as long as they could and went toe-to-toe with us a lot longer than most of the so-called 'bigger' clubs.

When we heard the familiar sound of the police sirens, we all ran back into the pub. On the way back in, there were two Falkirk lads lying in the car park, covered in blood and both out cold. One had his T-shirt pulled right over his head and his fat gut hanging out. He looked like a beached whale. One of the lads, who had been on the receiving end of the liberty the last time we'd been there, leaned over and said to him, 'Revenge is even sweeter than sweet.'

The police cars were now turning into the car park, but they couldn't get in for the bodies lying around. We all ran back into the pub and told the lad with the gash on his head to hide in the toilets and try to clean himself up, as the Old Bill would surely nick him. When the police came in, we all thought that we were fucked and expected to be nicked. But they seemed to panic and looked unsure at what to do – so they told us to go outside and wait in the car park.

They asked how we got there. One of the lads said to them, 'We're on minibuses, look I can get them to come in five minutes and we'll get to fuck out of your hair.'

It was a gamble that worked, as they just seemed to want us out of their town. As soon as the buses arrived, their inspector told us to get on them and get the fuck out of Falkirk. If only every police force could be the same!

FALKIRK

We were escorted out of Falkirk to make sure we had no stop-offs. We were buzzing like fuck all the way home. It had been one of the best ever battles we'd had – and not a soul had got nicked. When we arrived in Dundee, we stopped off at the Powrie Bar in Fintry and went right on the piss to celebrate. For months after we were all expecting the 6:00 am knock on the front door from the Old Bill. One of the Falkirk lads was eventually charged, but only ended up with a silly £150 fine.

The Falkirk Fear were respectful about what had happened, just as we were to them for standing and going ahead. They promised that they would bring a mob the next time they played us. They would have to wait a couple of years, though, until they were promoted to the Premier League. Things had changed in Dundee, because of the arrests at the 2005 cup final, which you'll read about later. This meant that we were worried if we would be able to pull any sort of mob.

We'd spoken to the Falkirk lads by phone and text message in the weeks leading up to game and arranged to meet them in a park on the outskirts of Dundee. The vibe going around Dundee was that this was our chance to come back and prove that the Old Bill hadn't totally fucked us for good! The plan was that Dundee would mob up in a pub in Mid Craigie and then they'd meet in another pub close by and we'd have it in a park away from the cameras. We were never going to underestimate Falkirk, though, and made sure all our best lads knew about this one. They'd put up a decent show the last time and had plenty of time to get organised.

The day of the game, I went to big Paul's house for a few cans and discussed whether or not they'd make an *appearance. Around 11:00 am, we made our way to the Midlands Tavern and got a drink in. By midday, our numbers had swelled to around the 70 mark, which was more than enough – especially with some of the lads that were there. The numbers were even boosted by a few older faces that hadn't been seen at the football for 10–15 years! Things were looking promising.*

One of the lads then said that Falkirk's top boy had been on the phone and said that he'd had second thoughts about coming to the arranged meeting place. He was told that the only way they could have it with us was to come to the arranged meeting place and that if they went to the town centre it would be crawling with cops and cameras. By the time of the arranged meet, we tried to contact them but they'd switched their phones off. Surprise, surprise! Here we were, sat away from the Old Bill and they walked through our town and got an escort. Fucking typical! Some of the lads thought we should go into town, but most just said, 'Fuck them.' They never came and it was jailbait in the town, especially with the high court cases hanging over some of the lads.

A few drinks later, some of the lads decided to go to the boozer in the town that we usually drank in. We found out they were drinking in a pub around the corner, at the top of Reform Street, and phoned the Midlands to tell them that they were close by. Within half an hour, we had a good 40 lads in there. Some of the lads reckoned it was jailbait, and decided against it, but some changed their minds and started to arrive in dribs and drabs. Falkirk called to say that they were going to come round to our pub, but that they had a police escort. I thought, 'What the fuck's going on?'

FALKIRK

As if the police were going to escort them to our pub!
But, then, a police car pulled up outside our pub, followed
by more coppers. We got up and made our way to the
door to see what was going on – and we couldn't believe
our eyes: they had escorted them right to the front door of
our pub! And then they stood and watched as Falkirk
attacked the door. Then, when we tried to steam the
doors, the Old Bill held us back. This was becoming
weird. It was like the cops had brought them round to the
pub and wanted us to go ahead with them, just so they
could start arresting cunts. I'm convinced it was a set-up,
but we couldn't help but try and oblige anyway!

Someone shouted, 'Let's get out the fire exit,' but when
we got to it the Old Bill were there, too. Falkirk let
themselves down. This had just been an easy way out for
them, to save a bit of face. They went down in our
estimation after this. They could have had it with us
earlier but they weren't up for it. The street was now full
of police cars and vans and they were moving the Falkirk
away from our pub.

We had to sit tight in the pub for a while, as they
wouldn't let us out. We could see the police lights start
flashing a couple of minutes later and we found out in the
following day's papers that they must have rubbed the
Dundee Old Bill the wrong way, as around a dozen of
them got nicked – and one had a flare gun on him!

CHAPTER 48

THE CCS

John's story, part eighteen

In the 2003/04 season, United were drawn at home against Hibs in the Scottish Cup third round. Seeing as we'd started getting the mob back together again, what better time to test the water than with a game against the CCS in the Scottish Cup?

Early that morning, I received a phone call from one of the lads, ranting and raving that the CCS were already in Dundee city centre and were shouting their mouths off. He told me that there was no Utility in sight.

Word spread throughout the lads and we started to firm up. A while later and it was also rumoured that Rangers ICF were in the city centre. Rangers were playing Arbroath that day, so they must have decided to stop off in Dundee for a few drinks on the way. Arbroath is only 16 miles from Dundee and a bit of a shit hole, so Dundee was a much better option for them as there were plenty of pubs for them to have a drink before the game.

AFTER THE MATCH, THE GAME BEGINS

The CCS were drinking in a bar called Sinatra's. One of the Dundee boys was in contact with Hibs and told them it was still early doors and that the Utility were still mobbing up. We would give them a phone later. However, we did inform Hibs that the Rangers had been spotted drinking down on Union Street by the train station. Something to keep them amused while we got our firm together! That was music to Hibs' ears. Rangers and Hibs hate each other and there has been a lot of history between the two mobs. Rangers were unaware that Hibs were on their way for what potentially looked like a good battle. Two mobs were roaming around Dundee, so to say that we were pissed off was an understatement!

If we'd arranged to go anywhere, we would make sure the opposition knew we were coming. On this occasion, Hibs and Rangers did not tell us that they were coming to Dundee. I suppose it takes the excitement out of not knowing when a mob gets off the train unexpectedly, but this wasn't the 1980s any more, when you just assumed that there'd be a mob getting off the train every week. By the mid-1990s, you had to have prior contact with other firms in order to make sure that they were going to come.

With the Tayside police being right on top of our mob at the time, we couldn't even walk down the street without getting pulled up. At certain games, it did not matter who you were with – relatives, kids, whatever – they still hassled you. That's what made it so frustrating. On this occasion, Hibs and Rangers were away to have a go in our home town, the police were nowhere – and the Utility weren't out yet.

What happened next was caught on camera and has since been watched on the Internet up and down the country countless times since. Hibs made their way through the city centre towards where the Rangers had stopped off. As the Hibs came into sight, the Rangers spotted them and then the two mobs ran straight into each other. A proper old-school toe-to-toe took place as innocent shoppers ran for cover.

I would have loved to have seen the look on the ICF faces. They probably thought it was Dundee they were running into. It should have been! To this day, I still can't believe that this was one of the best fights that had occurred in Dundee for a few seasons and the Utility were not even involved. Thanks for the invite!

Not to worry, news spread fast and the Dundee Utility now had a mob ready to face these cunts that had been swaggering about our town all day. The police were also in force and raging as much as we were. Once they gained control, Rangers were put on a train to Arbroath and the CCS were escorted to the match.

It was decided that we would wait until after the match and have a drink in Sinatra's, where the Hibs had been earlier. We anticipated that they would probably go back there, expecting to have a quiet drink before they caught the train back home to Edinburgh and with no Dundee in sight. How wrong they would be! By the time it got to 6:00 pm, one of the young Dundee lads came into the pub and told us the Hibs were only five minutes away and were heading straight for Sinatra's.

The lads were still pissed off with the events from earlier in the day, but there was still time to make amends and show the CCS whose town they were in. We got out on to the street and steamed right into them and backed them off, putting a couple of their lads on their arse. Almost immediately, we heard the sounds of sirens at the back of us. A few police vans screeched to a halt, their blue lights flashing, and loads of Old Bill jumped out, truncheons raised and began whacking everybody in their way. The Old Bill had been watching the Hibs mob coming down the road but were unaware the Dundee were in the pub they had to pass. It took the police totally by surprise. A lot of boys got lifted that day and big Jim received a broken jaw and the nick for his trouble, and also, several other small fights broke out in the town.

The CCS were eventually put back on a train bound for Edinburgh. That evening they said it was one of the best days out they'd had for years and that they would definitely be coming back to Dundee. Little did they know, but their earlier little encounter with Rangers had been captured on CCTV! The whole fucking lot! They would definitely be coming back to Dundee all right, but not for a football match. In the next couple of weeks, police raids across Edinburgh lifted about 20 Hibs that had been involved in the fight. I suppose because the two mobs had not been in their own home cities they didn't know where the CCTV cameras were and just went for it. It made us determined to pay the Hibs a visit as soon as possible – and to make sure they knew we were coming.

It was now time for revenge, to get the Hibs back for trying to take the piss in Dundee. Whoever played them first, either Dundee or Dundee United, it didn't matter. The whole crew was going! On the day in question, we got about 70 lads together for the visit to Edinburgh. But when we got to the train station we found a welcoming committee of Tayside police's finest waiting for us.

Myself and some other lads got on the train, but just as

we did a load more police arrived and told the boys that they weren't allowed on, even though they had tickets for the match. It was typical police bullshit. I think they just make the rules up as they go along. The lads that were turned away from the train station went off and regrouped on the outskirts of Dundee, determined to get to the game somehow. In the meantime, we were fuming at the police for not letting them travel. I was also fuming at what we were letting ourselves in for. Only 12 of us had made it on to the train and Hibs knew we were coming. Great!

As the train pulled into Waverley Station, there were plenty of police with dogs, and also a few undercover police. But we knew who they were and could easily spot their familiar faces from the amount of times we had been to Edinburgh. The 12 of us walked along the platform, attempting to mingle with all the other passengers and not be seen by the police as we made our way out of the station.

We had been to Edinburgh plenty of times before, so we knew quite a few bars to go to. Just as we were all getting settled, ready for our first pint of the day, I noticed two guys staring at us through the window of the pub. They were definitely not police, so we guessed they must have been Hibs lads who had followed us from the station. Even though we hadn't yet had a drink, we decided if it was the CCS who had spotted us and followed us to the pub then we would just have to go at them with everything we could get our hands on: chairs, tumblers, anything!

It was only a small pub, so we would have a good chance as long as they didn't get inside. If they did, we were fucked. The lads at the window eventually fucked off, so the 12 of us settled down to a pint. However, we remained on edge, awaiting the inevitable!

Half an hour passed and we started to forget about the two lads, thinking it must have been nothing, just us being paranoid. Another while passed, when I received a phone call from one of the Utility lads. He told me that he had just come off the phone to a Hibs casual that he knew and that he had been told that the CCS had mobbed up and were away to attack a pub down by the train station where some Dundee had been seen.

We decided to get the fuck out of there, as the Hibs had a habit of turning up on the fly. They didn't care if there were 12 of you or 50. We drank up and headed to Rose Street in the city centre, where there were plenty of other bars. By this time, a few other Dundee lads had made their way through to Edinburgh in cars, which was a relief and a blessing in disguise. There were now 20 of us and things were looking a little better.

Edinburgh is a great place to go for a drink and a night out, with plenty of hen and stag nights. There are also plenty of strip bars, in a part of the city called the Grass Market. It was decided that we would give the football a miss and venture up to some of the strip clubs and have a laugh.

Another few Dundee boys who had turned up at the pub informed us that the whole of the firm had been turned back at Dundee Station and was on its way to Edinburgh in taxis. They were now only half an hour away. I was impressed, to say the least. Dundee is not exactly close to Edinburgh, so getting taxis all the way there must have cost the lads a few quid. They must have really wanted it! This was total determination from the lads to overcome the *earlier events at the train station like that. It also meant that, when they got to the capital, they were going to make the most of it. They can stop people travelling by train or by bus, but how can they stop four or five guys hailing a taxi in the street and going to Edinburgh? It was a good move by the lads.*

Back in Edinburgh, there were now a few Hibs lads mouthing off outside the pub in Rose Street. There were five of us and about the same number of Hibs, with one particularly ugly bastard doing all the shouting. He looked a little like a boxer, with his squashed face. Either that or he'd had his nose smashed in loads for mouthing off. They wanted to have a go there and then. But with our mob coming through at any moment we weren't going to fuck it up for a few dickheads. I told them to fuck off and that we would give them a phone later.

All the Dundee lads were now making their way up to the pub, with the taxis pulling up one by one. Fucking great! Our mob had started to firm up nicely, with no police about. To top it off, the CCS thought there were only 20 of us. How wrong they would be! Half an hour later and there was about 80 to 90 Utility in Edinburgh. Loads of old faces had come out for some fun after hearing what the Hibs and Rangers had got away with in Dundee earlier in the season. We were now ready for them and the phone call was made.

As Hibs made their way up to the pub, one of our younger lads went outside to keep watch. In the meantime, we stood just inside the doors, quietly waiting for them to get as close to the pub as they could. After all, Hibs thought there was only 20 Dundee in there and they had tried to take a liberty with us earlier in the day. As soon as they arrived, the doors were kicked open and we let them fucking have it. A couple of Hibs stood their ground, but not many. The majority of the CCS were on their toes right away, probably due to the shock of seeing so many Dundee steaming out of the pub doors.

Me personally, I thought the CCS would have put up a better show than they did, considering all the effort the Dundee lads had put in to get themselves through to Edinburgh for a fight. There wasn't even any police about. There were a few other scuffles down side streets. One fight in particular, between 10 lads from each side, was pretty mental from what I heard. A few of the older lads and a few young lads led by Joe had it with the CCS. One of the Hibs lads jumped out of a van armed with a blade, which was a bit out of order. It's certainly not what Dundee are all about. We prefer to go about unarmed where possible.

When the Old Bill got there, they were fuming. They asked where our bus was and everyone began to piss themselves laughing. The police kept us in the pub for a while, then they took everybody's names and laid on a double-decker bus to take us to Waverley, where we were bundled on the next train home, free of charge. Just as well, after all the money that had been spent on taxis!

This chapter is dedicated to one of our most popular lads who recently, sadly passed away. To a friend of us all, who was instrumental in kick-starting it again after the millennium. Paul Hunter RIP.

CHAPTER 49

THE FINAL WHISTLE

For me, the 2005 Scottish Cup Final represents the day that Old Bill put an end to our Saturday-afternoon pastime for the third generation of Dundee lads.

On that day in May, over 40 lads from Dundee boarded a train for Glasgow to see Dundee United take on Celtic. Once in Glasgow, they were allowed to wander through the city-centre streets and up to the National Stadium without being stopped. What happened next I can't go into, as over 25 lads from Dundee and two guests from Airdrie were rounded up and arrested.

When the case came to court, the first two boys were given two years' imprisonment each. The next two, who are twins and good friends of mine from the same neck of the woods as me, were given 18 and 15 months each. This defies belief. The lad who was given 15 months got it for what was only his first offence. What made it even worse was that the local paper that same day printed a story about a repeat sex offender – who also happened to be an ex-policeman – who got just eight months for abusing two little girls!

You tell me where the fucking justice is in this.

The sentences were handed out without the slightest consideration for these lads' families or their futures. Sex offenders, heroin dealers or burglars are all given chance after chance to rehabilitate, with one scheme after another. Yet these lads were jailed simply for running up the street. It's a disgrace! It makes my blood boil!

Stranger still, even now, well over a year after the arrests, the rest of the lads keep getting their court date deferred and are left with the case hanging over them like a noose around their neck. Until they've all finally been sentenced, the truth of what happened that day cannot be told!

Another example of the police trying to hammer the final nail into the coffin came when the police threatened to arrest actor Danny Dyer and his film crew when he interviewed a few of the lads for a TV series called *The Real Football Factories*. After a brief visit to our two grounds, which he couldn't believe were so close together, Dyer met a few of the lads in Sheridan's pub in the city centre. After an interview with Big Steve and a few of the lads, an owner of one of the designer shops in the town phoned the lads and offered one of them, Paul, £200 if he brought along the actor to his shop. Everyone a winner!

What had been a good day for all involved – including the actor – was spoiled as usual by our friends the police. As in every city he'd visited up and down Britain, after interviewing some lads Dyer would go to a boozer to meet the firms. For his Dundee trip, he would have arrived at the pub to find around 80 of our lads sat there before Dundee's cup game with Airdrie, all looking their best and wanting to be TV stars for the day! But the whole thing was ruined when the actor and his film crew were threatened with arrest if they went anywhere near the ground, or the pub, with their cameras! A shaken and confused Danny Dyer thanked the lads for their hospitality and was soon on his way.

After these and other episodes, any intentions we had about returning to the fold were put to bed once and for all.

Funnily enough, in this mad world of ours, even though we've spent the best part of 25 years knocking hell out of one another, friendships have been made with lads from other firms up and down the country. The Internet and mobile phones have allowed the younger lads to organise their battles every Saturday, while older, retired lads like myself and co-author John can get together over a few beers and laugh about the old times. Through the Internet, I've met lads from Aberdeen and Motherwell, among others, with whom I've had a few top nights out and developed a few good friendships. Cheers to those lads. They know who they are!

I hope that after writing this book it has answered some of the questions about our Saturday-afternoon obsession and about why we run as one firm. We were never Dundee FC or Dundee United FC casuals, just casuals that represented the city of Dundee.

Even though I go to the football just as a fan now, I don't think the buzz will ever go away totally. Even now, every week when I leave to go to the match, it's the first thing I think about. If I'm not there, I'll ask the mates if there was any action. I still get a buzz thinking about getting up on Saturday morning, after speaking about it all week. In and out the shower, best gear on, grab a bite to eat, then off you pop. The buzz for me was always when the door shut behind me and I zipped up the coat and looked ahead up the street, almost ready to go to war!

It was the walk to the mate's house, or to the local or into the town, feeling a million dollars, not knowing what lay ahead, looking at yourself in car windows to see if you looked the part. That to me was the start of the buzz and I still get it to this day. I don't think it'll ever go away.

The incidents at the cup final, and the continual harassment from the Old Bill, mean the Dundee Utility as a football firm is almost at an end. So, for anyone who hasn't heard much of Dundee as a city, or the Utility as a firm, or doesn't rate us, here's something to ponder on. Why have the police gone to the lengths they have to arrest and convict almost all the main boys in our firm? Why have we received treatment similar to that dished out to better-known firms such as the ICF and the Headhunters in the 1980s?

Why were the lads in the cup final allowed on the train to Glasgow and left to swagger through the centre of Glasgow, especially in this day and age of cameras on every street corner and improved police intelligence and surveillance? Why was Danny Dyer and his film crew threatened by the Tayside police with arrest if they went anywhere near our firm? To me, it looks as though they wanted Dundee out of the equation!

The sentences handed out after the cup final have more or less put the tin lid on it for most of the active lads and any thoughts that boys like myself had of returning to the fold for the odd game have been put to bed. To risk everything I've got for a possible 18-month jail sentence, just for a bit of a punch-up in the street, doesn't bear thinking about.

With John getting married in 2005 and myself also settled down with my family, it looks like we're completely finished with our old Saturday pastime.

We say that after the match was when the game began, but it now looks as though the final whistle has just been blown!